RUSSIAN STUDIES OF CHINA

RUSSIAN STUDIES OF CHINA

Progress and Problems of Soviet Sinology

E. Stuart Kirby, B.Sc.Econ., Ph.D.

First published 1975 by
THE MACMILLAN PRESS LTD
London and Basingstoke
Associated companies in New York
Dublin Melbourne Johannesburg and Madras

SBN 333 18720 2

Printed in Great Britain by
THE BOWERING PRESS LTD
Plymouth

Contents

Introduction: Purpose and Method of this Book

The reader should first be clear as to the aim of this book and the manner in which the text may best be followed.

PURPOSE

Russia has been involved as a neighbour with China for almost three centuries. In that period, under varying but cumulating pressures, Russians have devoted much study, research and thought to all aspects of China. Their work, though extensive and of high quality, remains largely unknown in other countries. Even in Russia there are few publications giving a general appraisal or survey of Russian and Soviet sinology – which term is used broadly here to mean China studies in all their aspects. The first aim of this book is therefore to fill this gap in some part, to introduce the work and thought that have been devoted to China with reference especially to material on the academic, seriously political and cultural planes – in the Russian language. The main title, *Russian Studies of China*, defines this intention.

As shown by the sub-title 'Progress and Problems of Soviet Sinology', the principal focus is on the present situation of China studies in the USSR, the achievements and difficulties of Soviet practitioners in that field, with implications for their future interests and prospects in their profession. For scholars and men of affairs in all parts of the world it may be just as important to have a definition of the position and trends of Soviet sinology as to have clear notions of the state and currents of North American interpretations of China and the USSR : within the triangle of the superpowers we need, as current colloquialism has it, to know 'the state of play' in Soviet 'Pekinology' as well as we know 'the score' in 'Pekinology' and 'Kremlinology' in the United States. We are much less conversant with the first than with the second and the third. There is an analogy also with China studies in Japan, which, similarly, are very substantial and indicative but have until recently remained largely unknown to Western readers. It is thus to Soviet work and thought on China – under the rubric of sinology in its most general sense – that this book attends.

The subject is a complicated one, which can be fully introduced, but not finalised, in one volume. The situation from the Soviet point of view is one of severe trauma not yet healed, but of a new-found determination to make a fresh start – followed by a massive effort in that direction. When Communism triumphed in China in 1949 a new brotherhood was proclaimed and assumed, seeming to bring the World Revolution at last in sight. Ten years later, the two giant Communist countries became bitterly estranged and militantly hostile to each other. The end of the honeymoon was followed, with dramatic suddenness, by wranglings of divorce. Soviet sinology, which had hailed a wondrous new dawn, was dealt a parlous blow. Its practitioners, no less than the politicians and others, were reeling from the split for several years.

Their disarray, marked at the beginning of the 1960s, was, however, remedied towards the end of that decade, when surely with heart-searchings and agonising reappraisals far greater than have been allowed to appear on the surface, the Soviet effectives for China studies were remobilised and regrouped in a new and more extended order of battle. (In view of the militancy of the official Soviet intellectuality, in this field as in others, such warlike metaphors are entirely appropriate.)

A vast amount of work has thus been started in the Soviet Union in the last few years on all aspects of China studies, on a revised, reorganised and extended basis. This is one, perhaps not the least, of several significant changes and developments in the Soviet Union of which the rest of the world remains hardly aware. A large new activity with distinct new organisations and orienta-tions arose in the Soviet Union in the first years of the 1970s in this sphere of academic and general work. The present writer, having followed this meanwhile with distinct personal interest (from a long experience of both Far Eastern and Soviet studies), was able in a visit to the Soviet Union late in 1973 to complete the material for this present book, which is here updated to 1975.

METHOD OF TREATMENT

The following pages contain a general survey of the work in Russia on problems of China, with a comparatively cursory treatment of the whole period of Tsarist Russia, brief reference also to work in the earlier Soviet period, moving to a focus on the present situation and its implications for the future. There is one Soviet document that is convenient to the purpose. A key point in the *ralliement* of the forces of Soviet sinology came at the end of 1971. In November of that year an All-Union (pan-USSR) conference of sinologists was held, to review the situation generally in the disciplines concerned and set out the perspectives for their future work and duties. This was under the auspices of the Academy of Sciences of the USSR, in particular of its new Far Eastern Institute (*Institut Dal'nevo Vostoka*, or 'IDV'), supplementing the Academy's well-known, long-standing and more general Oriental Institute (*Institut Vostokovedeniya* – 'IVAN') which deals in orientalism more broadly. (Of these more will of course be said below.) The report of this key conference was published almost two years later, in 1973, by the IDV; but not widely published, remaining indeed an 'in-group' document, since only 1000 copies were printed.

The title of this basic *referat* is *Problems of Soviet Sinology: A Collection of Papers [dokladov] Delivered at the All-USSR Scientific Conference of Sinologists [kitayevedov] held in November 1971*. It will be convenient to use this report particularly as the general frame of references (though there are hundreds of other bibliographical entries to be cited below). It will therefore be frequently quoted – under the abbreviation 'PSS' (1973), which the reader may please note and bear in mind. In the following pages the assessment and conclusions drawn out in PSS are followed in some detail, in the sequence and priority of subjects adduced by the Soviet authorities themselves, with a survey of the efforts that have ensued to implement the 'directives', which amount to a 'new turn' and a wider approach by Soviet experts towards their task of understanding China.

PRACTICAL POINTS

Various technicalities are involved, most of which are explained in the text as they arise. A few need clarification here. A minor aspect is the transliteration of names and expressions; as far as those in Russian are concerned, general usage has simply been followed, but Chinese is rendered differently into the Cyrillic, so both Russian and English equivalents have been used. A greater problem – where the translator can most easily (as the Italians say) become a traducer – is that terms, concepts and their implications differ in the various languages. For example, one may speak in English of 'handicrafts' and 'cottage industries', while ostensibly equivalent Russian terms *(remeslo, kustar)* may have somewhat different connotations or associations. This and other instances are discussed in the text below, which proceeds broadly in the spirit of *solvitur ambulando*.

A wider problem, in extension of the last-mentioned, is the politicalisation of the subject-matter. The basis proclaimed by both Russia and China today is that of Marxism-Leninism. Within that body of doctrine there is intrinsically a welter of debate on the hermeneutics and heuristics, a sustained *Methodenstreit*: the methodology, matters of interpretation, research and exposition, as such, are all widely and hotly in debate. In the great schism between Russia and China, Marxism-Leninism, Maoism and all other approaches are ubiquitously, tirelessly, meticulously and dialectically argued on all sides, in a manner as bitter and polemical as that of the great theological disputes that Europe knew in the past. What then, in this setting, are the true limits of sinology? It is defined here in the broadest way, to comprise linguistics, international relations, political science, economics, sociology, literature and the arts, etc., in so far as all these relate to China.

The Russians and Chinese, even more than other disputants within the many mansions of Marxism from China to Peru, from Belgrade to Moscow, from the New Left to the Old, under a thousand and one headings, carry sinology promptly and volubly over into the realm of current political diatribe – from fundamental and philosophical study to denunciation, vituperation and denigration on the lowest planes of polemic. All kinds of red rags, it may be said, are waved over every kind of bull. A common reaction in the free-thinking world is therefore to question whether Soviet sinology is worth the trouble of studying, seeing that it is so swamped with political vilification, so orchestrated with rhetorical abuse.

This reaction must of course be resisted, considering the world importance of the confrontation of these two very great powers, the vital necessity of understanding their possible relations and possible incompatibilities; considering also that Russia, directly involved in Asia (Islamic as well as Sinic Asia), has contributed much to sinology. There are and have been many Russian and Soviet savants and experts. The scientific level of the country is high; it has produced and is still producing notable contributions in all fields, including 'sinology' proper. Under all the invective, useful knowledge and insights are to be found in these vast and resource-rich countries that adjoin each other. In the Soviet Union there are many good workers, in this field as in others, more or less accepting, more or less subservient to the political superstructure, who must be contacted and encouraged in the basic and productive work that they are nevertheless doing and wish further to do.

To appraise the contribution of each Soviet writer or to enter very far into general characterisations of trends, in a country that is still very far from being an 'open' society, would be beyond the scope of a single work. It is therefore a general survey that occupies the first part of this book – divided into chapters by subjects – followed by a bibliography of essential current references, which involves other small technical points that the reader should note at the outset, as follows. All the works cited are in Russian, except where specifically indicated otherwise, and are referred to by the numbers (in square brackets) by which they may be found in the bibliography.

With reference to the bibliography, there is another comment which it is essential to make. Almost all Soviet academic publications (like other activities in the USSR) are collective. Books, papers, research reports, etc., are prepared and published nearly always by some group of persons, or by an institution – rarely in the name of an individual. There is always a strong element of collaboration or joint ascription. Sometimes there is a single or 'responsible' editor; more usually a plurality of editors (sometimes with a 'chief editor'). Frequently the editors are also part-contributors of the contents, in which the specific share of each may or may not be designated. However, works are often cited by the name of one of the contributors, whether or not he or she is listed among the editors.

This aspect must be mentioned here simply because it affects the organisation of the bibliography or list of references; in English, a 'Smith, (1971)' may suffice, whereas in Russian the work may be cited under the name of some other editor, or any one of several participants, or by the name of the institution or State publishing-house that issued it. The numbering and cross-references in the bibliography herewith should, however, suffice to furnish all the necessary connections. All the items cited may be found in, for instance, the catalogues of the Lenin Library in Moscow (similarly in the Library of Congress and other centres). Useful publications to which all in this field of study are indebted are *Soviet Works on China: A Bibliography of Non-Periodical Literature, 1946–55*, by Peter Berton and others (University of Southern California, 1959) and *Russian Works on China, 1918–1960, in American Libraries*, by Tung-li Yuan (Yale University, 1971).

Finally, topics may be located with the aid of the comprehensive index at the end of the book. It is hoped that the whole may furnish a useful introduction or a first workbook for those who wish to pursue research in this important subject.

1 Marching Orders: Moscow 1971–1973

In the first years of the 1970s a new approach to China studies was laid down in the Soviet Union. Like everything else in that country, the new move would be planfully devised and directed. It would involve a new attitude to this type of work, on a more comprehensive, integrated and purposeful basis than had hitherto prevailed. The recently established Far Eastern Institute (IDV) of the Academy of Sciences of the USSR called the first national conference of sinologists on this new basis. They met from 29 November to 1 December 1971, to discuss 'Problems of Soviet Sinology'. The documentation at this meeting, under that title, was 'signed for press' in April 1973 and published later that year. This book is referred to in the following pages as PSS.

BASIC DIRECTIVES

PSS opens with a short statement (pp. 3–6) by P. N. Fedoseyev of what was required of Soviet sinologists. He stressed first the great importance attached by the Soviet Government and Party to Chinese studies. This keynote was to be much developed subsequently. Work in this field now certainly has wide and deep backing from higher authority of all kinds in the Soviet Union – provided, of course, it follows the political and attitudinal line prescribed by the authorities and remains under their ultimate (if not direct) control. Experienced academics and administrators may discount this emphasis to some extent, bearing in mind that this was a gathering of the particular profession concerned, motivated to assert the importance for the national policy of its own work. Expertise-groups in the Soviet Union are, no less than those in other countries, inclined to seek to build their own institutional empires and grind their own axes where policy is being hewn.

Nevertheless, it is clear that a fresh and substantial development of China studies in the USSR has the support of the highest authorities, whose blessing was conveyed at this gathering and through other channels.

The first and most basic directive declared to the Soviet sinologists at this conference was that they should clearly justify the rectitude of the Soviet stance and Soviet conduct, in principle and by the record of practical action, in the past and at the present time, and prove the sincerity and correctness of Soviet intentions for the future. They should analyse the past and present misdeeds, the erroneous concepts and policies of the Chinese authorities, and point the abysses towards which the Maoists' mistakes of theory and practice would increasingly lead China and its people in future – all of which should be done on a sound basis of Marxism-Leninism.

The speaker's second concern, in counterpoint to this stress on the righteousness of the Soviet position, was to assert the basic weakness of Maoism. 'Maoism', he said, 'operates on a very unstable social basis, as the events of the past few years have shown ever more clearly.' This is one basic element in the Soviet attitude : the Russians sharply contrast the erratic and chaotic courses followed in the Chinese People's Republic (CPR) with the stability and solidity of the social, economic and political development of the USSR, in both internal and foreign policy. The Soviet Union is a secure and advanced society, orderly and systematic at a high technical level; whereas China lurches from purge to purge, as Mao depends on what is essentially 'adventurism'.

Maoism, Fedoseyev specified, 'plays with the immature rebellious *hungweip'ing'*, i.e. China's contemporary 'Red Guards'. It is semantically interesting that the Russians use the Chinese word for these youthful stalwarts. It would rile them to use in this context the term 'Red Guards' in Russian, which has different connotations in the history of the Soviet Revolution. Where the Soviets do use the Russian words for 'Great Leap', 'Cultural Revolution' and some other key moves in the CPR, they put these in quotation-marks, or with the qualification 'so-called', to make clear that they brand them as alien or spurious from a true Marxist-Leninist point of view.

'At the same time', the conference-opener continued, Maoism 'preserves the national bourgeoise. Depending on the army, Mao seeks to divert to his side the petty-bourgeois strata of the peasantry and the backward elements among the workers. Veering between the most varied social strata and . . . heterogeneous elements, [that] is what is socially the most vulnerable in Maoism. In foreign relations, too, it veers between extreme left and extreme right.'

The directive was drawn that the Communist Party of the Soviet Union (CPSU) calls on Soviet sinologists to expose Maoism in all its aspects, particularly its chauvinism. This is a noble purpose, in the interests of all – including the Chinese people themselves. 'In the last few years', therefore, 'a series of decisions has been taken to concentrate and strengthen studies in the USSR on contemporary China and other Far Eastern countries. The IDV has been founded, its tasks defined; among which is that of co-ordinating in our country scientific researches on China, in the domains of economics, history, politics and ideology.'

The word 'scientific' in Russian (*nauchny*) tends to imply more broadly the sense of 'academic' than does the English equivalent : it shares the root of *uchit'*, to teach, *uchyony*, a learned person. As for the IDV, it is thus clearly the academic centre of the ideological counter-attack on Maoism. It has a strong political colouring. If a personal observation may be intruded here, the present writer was surprised to find (late in 1973) that this was the only Institute of the USSR Academy of Sciences security-guarded (in a mild way, just so far as visitors' reception and messenger services were concerned) by uniformed policemen. The premises give the impression of serving especially as an information-sifting and brief-preparing agency for the higher offices concerned with Far Eastern policy. Its competence does not include the *Soviet* Far East, i.e. the parts of the Soviet Union beyond Lake Baikal; it deals with the *zarubezhnye* (foreign) East Asian countries.

Its premises were (at the end of 1973) modest enough, in a square on Krzizhanovski near Profsoyuznaya streets in Moscow, though nearby a large new modern building was under construction which the IDV is to share with the Institute for the study of the 'countries with socialist economies'. The present writer's impression is that activities within the IDV may be broadly analogous to those in the Foreign Office Research Department in London; or, in the China-watching context particularly, he was certainly reminded of the research activities in the US Consulate-General in Hong Kong in the first half of the 1960s.

To revert to Fedoseyev's 'keynote' remarks : 'In the last few years Soviet scholars in sinology have widely spread their study of the current problems of contemporary China. Works of scholars of the IDV, IVAN' (the Oriental Institute of the Academy of Sciences, which continues to exist, as a broader and more old-style centre for Asian studies in general) 'and other Institutes of the Academy of Sciences are making a definite contribution to the understanding [of these matters and] . . . the unmasking of the anti-Marxist conceptions in Maoism.' The 24th CPSU Session (1969) stressed a programme to develop the social sciences in general, within which 'the Soviet scholars of sinology face great tasks : broadening and deepening their investigations' to give 'a basis for fundamental critique of the great-power policy of the Maoists, and at the same time seek' – which will demand consider-able dialectical agility – 'ways of normalising Soviet–Chinese relations', especially relations with the Chinese people.

This requires of the Soviet professionals 'co-ordination . . . not only on the organisational side . . . but above all concerted collec-tive efforts', including 'integrated' studies. Admittedly 'the cadres of Soviet sinologists are still relatively small in number and not always rationally used'; so 'co-ordination' is a prime necessity. The new journal of the IDV, *Problems of the Far East* (quarterly since 1972, with a print of some 13,000 copies), will play a key part in this, the spokesman continued. In it 'the central place must be taken by the problems of contemporary China – on which it is clearly to be the expounder of the Party line. 'This journal may touch upon [*sic: zatragivat'*] the problems' (in the monotonous repetitive Soviet prose, it is always 'problems') 'of Japan, Australia, New Zealand, South-East Asia; but questions of contemporary China, and also its history, culture and language, must take a leading position.'

The opening address concludes with an exhortation to the Soviet colleagues to enhance the effectiveness of their work, to remember that it is for the sake of the Chinese people too, and finally prescribes that their labours 'must render practical help to our party and to the State organs in the elaboration of concrete measures in our policy towards China.

Thus rang, in very definite tones, the Kremlin call, supported by explicit messages from Mr Brezhnev himself. The Director of the IDV, Dr M. I. Sladkovski, followed with a substantial exposition of the 'position and tasks of Soviet sinology' (pp. 6–21). The first section of his address reviewed the history of Russian and Soviet studies of China, after which Professor Sladkovski spelled out in more detail the duties of the comrades. 'China', he said, 'will undoubtedly play a great role in the world', so 'the study of it demands a new, more all-round, deeper approach. . . .' It 'must be a complex [Sovietese for integrated] science, studying all aspects, the internal material and spiritual life of the Chinese people as well as its intercourse with the world outside'. [*Sic:* this utterance is perhaps a little odd from a Marxist point of view, positing the 'superstructure' as 'internal' ?]

However, the Director stated, Soviet sinology 'must assume the leading position in worldwide sinology', no less. The fight is on two fronts, against two agile devils, Maoism and Western sinology. He sees these as playing leapfrog, or Chinese checkers. 'The anti-socialist sinology often masquerades in an arch-leftist toga [*sic:* some confusion here between patricians and *sans-culottes*] and from these positions [*sic*] supports the anti-socialist extremist slogans of the Maoists.' Yet the devil is multipersonal, not just a Jekyll and Hyde : 'The bourgeois and the revisionist literature now exaggerates the anti-scientific theory that Maoism expresses specific Chinese traditions : [that] it arose naturally [*zakonomerno:* cf. German *regelmässig*] out of the social structure of China, whereas Marxism was always something artificial, foisted on China from outside.'

K. Wittfogel is instanced as an extreme-right imperialist who uses Mao's perversions to attack socialism in the USSR and elsewhere. But the hosts of Midian lurk on the New Left also : 'The "latest" theories of R. Garaudy, on the other hand, propagate ideas of the multiplicity of models of socialism, with China approximating to neither the Western nor the Soviet model, but fit only for Maoism. This is an insult to the Chinese people, practically denying it any right to socialism.'

The Soviet sinologists were then instructed to prove that in the 1950s, when it was collaborating with the USSR, China made spectacular progress, possessing at that time not only the material basis but also the social superstructure for the transition to socialism; then suddenly turned away, as helmsman Mao steered his 'special' course into 'adventurist' experiments like the Hundred Flowers Blooming, the Great Leap and the Cultural Revolution.

The Soviet sinologists are to refute the contentions of 'some people' that 'traditional Chinese society was not feudal, but some kind of "peasant-bureaucratic" society' which still falls naturally into the latter mould. 'We fight Maoism because it revives the reactionary traditions of China, suppresses the revolutionary ones.' Thus the fight against Maoism is primarily on its 'incompatibility with [the Communist movement. It is] one of the forms of national communism and social chauvinism.'

Such terms are possibly meaningful to the Soviet audience, but somewhat puzzling to others. Some may ask, for instance, 'What is national communism?' Did Stalin's 'socialism within one nation' approximate to that description? Or does the very nationalistic exaltation of 'Soviet patriotism' in the USSR today? And what is social chauvinism? Certainly not simply a contrast to 'anti-social chauvinism'; so possibly something like the 'social fascism' for which, older readers will remember, the Communists in the 1930s attacked the Social Democrats, giving a clearer field to Hitler? The obfuscation of terminologies creates no less difficulty than the rewriting of history.

THE FIRST PHASE

On the factual plane, the IDV had already sponsored ten conferences by the end of 1971. In the light of the foregoing remarks one of the most interesting activities was, however, a whole series by the other centre, the Oriental Institute (IVAN), on 'Traditions, the State and Society in China'. There had also been conferences mounted by the Institute of the International Workers' Movement. In conclusion, the Director of the IDV presented the action-list headings as 'problems of ideology, of the history of social thought', 'problems of the economy of China', 'the national[ities] problem of China', 'the problem of the foreign relations of the CPR' and problems of culture, linguistics and science'. These were only the headings, to be itemised subsequently. Clearly, Soviet sinologists have a heavy load of work and responsibility with so many problems in so many fields – in which they must fully and frankly re-educate China and the world, while at the same time enhancing friendly relations all round.

Specifications for a new approach must necessarily be based on evaluation of what has been done hitherto : Dr Sladkovski's pre-

scriptions listed above, were founded on a brief review by him
(PSS, pp. 6 ff) of the whole previous development of Russian and
Soviet sinology, to which it is useful to turn in the next chapter,
as it further defines the main lines of the official standpoint in the
early 1970s.

2 History of Russian and Soviet Sinology

ORIGINS

Sino–Russian relations began with contacts on a long frontier in the sixteenth century, deepened and widened in the eighteenth and nineteenth centuries. China was, from the beginning of this intercourse, ruled by the Manchus, who wished to isolate China. The initiative therefore came from Russia, on both the material and the spiritual planes.

Interpreters were the first practical need. At the beginning, people from Bukhara were used in that role, notably Seitkula Ablin, in the first official Russian mission led by Baikov in 1656. Subsequently an organised linguistic effort began, after the establishment of the Russian clerical mission in 1719. The first Russian sinological scholar of note, according to Dr Sladkovski, was N. Ya. Bichurin (the priest Iakinf, 1777–1853), who published descriptive works on the Mongols and their area, also a Chinese grammar, between the last years of the 1820s and the first of the 1840s [57–63].

THE CLASSICAL PHASE

N. G. Senin later in PSS (p. 152) specifies as 'the most eminent Russian sinologists of the eighteenth century' Ilarion Rossokhin (1717–61) and Alexei Leont'iev (1716–86), who 'first translated into the Russian language a whole series of Confucian books, such as the *Analects* and the *Great Learning*. Rossokhin's translations of philosophical texts were not published during his lifetime, but Leont'iev's renderings, which were in a high-flown style, were published by the Imperial Academy of Science.' However, Bichurin in the early nineteenth century may truly be called the broader founder of Russian sinology, because of his many original and circumstantial works. He very ably translated a number of Chinese classics, including the *Three Character Classic* (in 1832) and the *Four Books* with Chu Hsi's commentaries. At the Academy of Sciences' Library in Leningrad there is a rich store of his manuscripts still claiming further attention.

The second generation was that of P. I. Kafarov (the reverend Palladii, 1811–78), who published between the 1860s and 1880s historical works in the same field [203–5] and left the first Chinese–Russian dictionary [206]. It was in a third generation that Russian sinology assumed a leading place in world scholarship. This may be dated from about the time of Kafarov's dictionary of 1888. Comparison suggests itself with Herbert Giles's great Chinese–English dictionary. The way was notably prepared by V. P. Vasil'iev (1818–1900). At the age of 22 Vasil'iev joined the Russian clerical mission in Peking, but moved to an academic career, being appointed to the first chair in this field in Russia (at Kazan) at the age of 33, and four years later to another at St Petersburg. The courses, it may be noted, were given in German and French in those days.

Vasil'iev was a broad scholar, well abreast of his times, interested in the history of religion, with all its implications. He produced in 1857–69 a study of *Buddhism: Its Dogmas, History and Literature*, in 1857 a work on the *History and Antiquity of Eastern Central Asia*, in 1873 his *magnum opus* on the three great religions of China [521]; but wrote also an 'experimental' Chinese–Russian dictionary in 1867, over the years 1866–84 an *Analysis of Chinese Hieroglyphs*, and in 1880 an *Outline History of Chinese Literature*. There were some contemporaries who receive less notice in Soviet work – notably, for example, K. A. Skachkov (1821–83; see the useful appreciation by J. Gershevich in *Asian Affairs*, London, vol. 60, part 1, Feb. 1973).

PRE-REVOLUTIONARY MATURITY

Next in time and ranking is S. M. Georgievski, whose works (concentrated in the last years of the 1880s) included studies of the practical aspects of antiquity [142] and its interpretation [143], also an advocacy of the need for more and better Chinese studies in Russia [144]. Georgievski and N. Monastyrev (both pupils of V. P. Vasil'iev) collaborated in a study of Confucianism, *The*

Principles of Chinese Life, published in 1888. This 'classic' period of the subject in Russia was especially enriched also by the contributions of that nation's travellers and explorers in Central and East Asia. N. M. Przhevalski (1839–88) was a major contributor [393–8] well known also in the West, where much of his work was published. The longer-lived G. N. Potanin (1835–1920) produced several works between 1863 and 1901. Many of these earlier works are now of course scarce; it is significant that many of them have been republished in the Soviet Union since the Second World War [e.g. 386, 377]. In Potanin's case there is a very good survey of his whole career by two modern Soviet writers [387]. The third great name in this group is that of M. V. Pevtsov (1843–1902), who had extensive knowledge of Tibet and Chinese Turkestan.

Most of these works were substantially academic in tone or attitude, with the touches of (say) Aurel Stein or Huc or Sven Hedin rather than the 'huntin', shootin' and fishin'' travelogues that tended to proliferate in English in the same Imperial period. Characteristically, the Soviet spokesman is torn between patriotic pride in that academic excellence 'which put Russian studies of China in the front ranks of world sinology' and severe deprecation of the bourgeois basis of works which, 'not possessing a scientific materialist method of investigation, unable to rise to the level of objective historical generalisation . . . were limited predominantly to the description of facts and gave disproportionate space to the study of religion'. At the beginning of the present century, P. S. Popov produced translations of Mencius (1904) and the Analects (1910) – heavily influenced, as Popov acknowledged, by the work of the great British sinologist Legge. In 1912 A. I. Ivanov produced the first translation into Russian of Han Fei-tse, though it was a partial rendering [193]. His *Grammar* was still influential in the 1940s [194].

THE MODERN PERIOD

By the end of the nineteenth century, comparatively large sinological centres were forming in Moscow, St Petersburg and Vladivostok, the main locations for the work of the next period, which extended until the consolidation of Soviet power in the 1920s. The leading scholars, in that extensive and formative time, were the following. V. M. Alexeyev, born in 1881, graduated in the Oriental Faculty at St Petersburg in 1902. He was Professor at Leningrad from 1918, *persona grata* to the new regime. He became a Corresponding Member of the Academy of Sciences in 1923 and a full member in 1929. He produced a number of works on Chinese literature and the understanding of other Chinese arts. His interest in the folklore [15] and his production of a more modern dictionary (in 1948) may be especially noted here; but the range and quality of his works are impressive [12-28].

At the other end of the country, major activity in Oriental studies developed at Vladivostok. Naturally enough; until the Revolution, or more specifically the end of the Civil War (with final Japanese withdrawal only in 1922), Vladivostok seemed to be destined to be as much a gateway to the East as Petrograd was to the West. Accordingly, the interests pursued at Vladivostok were rather pan-Asian and utilitarian. One of the prominent scholars there was A. V. Grebenshchikov, an expert on the Manchu language and literature [166–7], another N. V. Kyuner, who spread his mind widely over the geography and history of Japan and China [267–71] with an eye also to the ethnography or northern Asia [272].

From the mid-1920s, the extrovert glory of Vladivostok faded; it became part of the autarkically inclined Soviet Union. Developed later as a fishing and naval base, it is nowadays completely closed to all foreigners and to most Soviet citizens, contacts with the outside world, limited to the sphere of trade, being channelled through the new port of Nakhodka. (For the background to this, see the present writer's *The Soviet Far East,* Macmillan, 1971.) One other leading scholar at Vladivostok, A. V. Rudakov (born 1871), produced treatises on the Manchu and Chinese languages in the first decade of this century [416–17], and his influence continued at Vladivostok until the end of the 1920s, when his *Practical Chinese Dictionary* [418] was published.

Most recently, Vladivostok has in contrast come back into prominence, not only in the visit there (or, more exactly, to a conference site in its vicinity) of US President Ford at the end of 1974, but in the very promising redevelopment of a major centre of Oriental studies there, headed by the very prominent Dr Kapitsa.

The earlier centres in European Russia flourished, however, without any such change in fortune. There, A. I. Ivanov's work, beginning as early as 1860, had come to the fore in the period of the First World War [190–3] and his grammar of modern colloquial Chinese was influential through the 1930s [194]. One of the greatest and most respected names in Soviet sinology has to be mentioned next in sequence – that of N. I. Konrad (born 1891), who began in the 1920s with work on Japan, in both the general political and the literary context [235–6], continuing through the 1930s with a study of the Japanese language [237]. In the 1950s, however, Konrad devoted his attention to China, with a special interest in the celebrated treatises on war of the ancient machiavellianists Sun Tse and Wu Tse [238–9], but also producing broad studies of Chinese literature [240] and a wide range of commentary extending into the 1960s [241].

THE SOVIET REORIENTATION

As demonstrated already in Konrad's work, 'a new direction arose' – as Dr Sladkovski put it in his review at the conference in 1971 – 'in Soviet sinology, born of the socialist policy of the Soviet State in its relations with the countries of the East and of the revolutionary practice of the Soviet people in extending international help to the Chinese people in its struggle . . . .' In other words, the full politicalisation of the subject was begun, from the time when Lenin saw the main line of attack on capitalism to lie through its soft under-belly, the colonial territories, especially those in turbulent and awakening Asia.

A certain A. S. Khodorov gained immortality because his monograph on *World Imperialism and China* was favourably reviewed by Lenin himself; but the work may perhaps be 'unsound' in the light of subsequent hindsight, as copies are hardly to be found in the Soviet Union today. A more scholarly stamp is borne by the work in the 1930s of A. A. Petrov [373–4], hailed as the first Marxist philosopher in the field of sinology, and by that of K. A. Kharnski, credited with the first attempt at the periodisation of Chinese history on Marxian lines in correlation with the history of other parts of the world [217].

The welter was, however, of works of a more or less frankly *agitprop* (Agitation and Propaganda Department) character. Hundreds of these could be cited, but the outstanding names in this connection are probably the following. M. P. Pavlovich (pen-name of M. L. Vel'tman, 1871–1927) is one of the most interesting personalities. At the time of the 1905 revolution he wrote abroad about Russia's war with Japan [361], at the end of the First World War about the course and effects of the war in Asia [362]. He had always had a keen interest in railways (if not a mania), and at that time Germany's scheme for a Baghdad railway was one of his cherished topics. In the 1920s he produced a number of studies in what might be called Communist geopolitics [363–5]. V. D. Vilenski-Sibiryakov, V. N. Kuchumov, G. N. Voitinski and Pavel Mif (all cited by Dr Sladkovski) seem to have no lasting claims to academic remembrance.

These strictures do not apply to V. S. Kolokolov, part-author of a useful general book on China in the mid-1920s [224] and some readings [225], who was able to proceed in the 1930s with a concise dictionary and a grammar, finally being responsible, at the end of the 1950s, for the first full scientific and technical dictionary of Chinese in Russian [228]; nor to L. I. Mad'yar (Magyar), who produced, at the beginning of the 1930s, useful monographs on the economy and agriculture of China [295–6]. It is noteworthy that there was still little solid work on the economic aspects; the Marxists should have made this the foundation, but lost themselves in all-pervading vituperation, backbiting and betrayal.

Such was the atmosphere of the deadly period of Stalin's dictatorship. It was a time of universal distrust, fear, denunciation; public and private treachery, humiliation, execution or disappearance were the order of every day, more particularly of every night. Millions went to death, torture or broken lives, instantly by shooting or lingeringly through the concentration camps, which in extent if not in 'efficiency' greatly exceeded those of Hitler's Germany. No profession or sphere of life was exempt from that Terror, least of all one so 'politicalised' as the new Soviet sinology. Casualties in that *métier* were accordingly heavy. The attempt will not be made here to estimate the overall effects or identify individual instances – which would be as difficult as trying to calculate the impact, in any field of learning, of other times of horror in human history.

The terms used here are of course the present writer's. Soviet citizens refer to these matters as briefly as possible, and so discreetly as to prove that mastery of understatement is not a British

monopoly. Stalinism is called, rather demurely, 'the cult of personality'. By such meiosis, Attila's 'cult' might go down in history
as equestrianism, Hitler's as genetics. Thus the Director of the
IDV in his summary of the past achievements of Soviet sinology
(PSS, p. 8) has only a pregnant dwarf of a sentence on the Stalin
period : 'at the end of the 1930s the cadres of Soviet sinology, in
the conditions of the "cult of personality", suffered heavy losses,
which could not but affect this branch of Soviet learning.' The
name of Stalin himself is printed only once in the whole of the
PSS report.

COMMUNIST CHINA : HONEYMOON AND DIVORCE

Hence 'a new impetus in Soviet sinology began only after the
Second World War'; indeed, the movement was not large until
Stalin had been dead for a few years and the new course had
become clear enough for it to be safe to embark again on the paths
of Asian studies. Nevertheless, fresh recruits were coming forward,
though still cautiously at first. Obviously a prodigious transformation occurred in China in 1949, when suddenly the most populous
country in the world, a very large adjoining territory, went over
to Communism. This development may have been as much a
surprise to the Soviet Union as to anyone else; neither the authorities nor the academics there seem previously to have had any
exultant confidence in the prospects of the Maoists succeeding.
After the victory, however, the structure for canalising the new
wave of interest in the Soviet Union did still exist – the institutes,
the courses, the libraries, etc. Also some of the personnel; despite
heavy losses, a number of sinologues (presumably the more astute
politically) had survived.

    Among the latter were such (to take only one leading example
from those already mentioned) as Kolokolov. Another 'bridger'
between the foregoing period and the new stage was M. I.
Oshanin, who produced in 1952 an excellent Chinese–Russian
dictionary, and was able greatly to revise and enlarge it in a
further edition in 1959 [356]. If Kafarov's dictionary was (as
opined above) comparable with Giles's, Oshanin's may be compared with (say) Matthews's. Other major works of the period
were the following. A modern history of China [536] by G. V.
Yefimov appeared opportunely in 1949 and was smartly revised

two years later. V. A. Maslennikov produced a book on *China* shortly after the war [309] and twelve years later manifested the revived and improved Soviet interest in substantial studies on the economic side with his well-known book on *The Economic Structure of the CPR* [310]. G. V. Astaf'iev, who dealt in 1949–50 with US imperialism in China [33–5] and continued his interest in foreign policy aspects and economic factors, is of authoritative standing; in 1973 he was Chief Editor of PSS and a main contributor to it [36–7], fourteen years earlier he had collaborated with A. S. Perevertailo, V. I. Glunin, K. V. Kukushkin and V. N. Nikiforov in a 'landmark' book on recent Chinese history [371].

Literary and linguistic studies also figured prominently. N. T. Fedorenko, an expert on Chinese literature (contributor of the section thereon in PSS), Corresponding Member of the Academy of Sciences, also has an eye to political events, instanced by his timely editorship in 1966 of an Academy of Sciences study of the Cultural Revolution [121–2]. Old-timer A. A. Petrov, author in 1936 of a monograph on Wang Pi's tract on the *Book of Changes*, the first work in Russian on that period, had contributed the section on philosophy in the notable symposium on China which appeared in 1940 [373–4]; his influence was again felt after the Second World War. The name of S. L. Tikhvinski came on the honours board at the end of the 1950s with his study of the reformer K'ang Yu-wei and his period, the end of the nineteenth century [495]. In the 1960s he produced interesting works on the history of China and neighbouring areas, studies of Sun Yat-sen's foreign policy (with much reference to West European materials), and the first Russian translation of the (earlier part of the) memoirs of Henry P'u-yi, puppet Emperor of 'Manchukuo' [491–501].

The 'honeymoon' period in Sino–Soviet relations hardly lasted through the 1950s; by the end of that decade the breach was deep, practically complete and overt. This was a shock, as much to sinologists in the USSR as to their political rulers. All reeled from the blow and took several years to recover their stance and their equanimity. Indeed, full recovery dates from the beginning of the 1970s, with the reorganisation proclaimed in the PSS which is the subject of these pages. Inevitably, as the impact was felt, as China moved into successively deeper political turbulences and the Soviet Union moved into successively sharper denunciation and riposte, a new wave of politicalisation swept over Soviet sinology. This may perhaps be illustrated in the work of M. S. Kapitsa. Of the new generation of Soviet scholars, he lodged his doctoral thesis some time after 1949. In 1958 he published a book on *Soviet–Chinese Relations* [209], firmly stating the Moscow viewpoint; but reassessment in the USSR had hardly begun at that time. There was a gap for re-thinking, in the Soviet Union generally in this field, in the earlier 1960s. In 1965 Kapitsa participated in a study of Soviet relations with Mongolia [210] – the good relations with the MPR are offered as a model, sometimes in sorrow, sometimes in anger, to the CPR. By the late 1960s Kapitsa (used here as just one example) was more sharply on the attack against Maoism as such, its actual policies within China, with books defining Maoism as ultra-leftism and contrasting its good work in the 1950s with its reprehensible record in the 1960s [211–12]. Recently he was placed in charge of a new 'academic city' at Vladivostok, to develop as a centre of Far Eastern studies.

L. D. Pozdneyeva came forward at the end of the 1950s with her book on the great modern populist-revolutionary writer of China, Lu Hsun [388], but her subsequent work has been on philosophy and literature, with a translation of Chuang Tse [389], some material on his *Lieh Tse*, an interesting study of the atheism, materialism and dialects of the early Taoists [390] which provided the first translation into Russian of the thoughts of the immediate successors of Lao Tse, in 1970 a survey of Chinese literature [391] and in 1973 the article in PSS on the 'idealisation of Confucianism'. Many important Chinese works of all periods were translated and commented upon, ranging from the selected works of Sun Yat-sen in 1964 and a symposium for his centennial five years later [486–7], back to the ancient economic classic *Kuan Tse* (translated and commented on by V. M. Shtein and others at the end of the 1950s in a book [450] which included also valuable references to Mencius and others).

Such were the principal works; there were many others, as Dr Sladkovski noted. He had, however, to complain that despite the overall advance there were many deficiencies. 'The main flaw in our abundant historical, political and other literature', he stated, 'is that it did not evaluate critically the experience of the Chinese revolution and, often following the official Chinese historiography, facilitated the popularisation of Mao Tse-tung's cult of personality, did not objectively clarify historical events, ignored particular facts that illustrate the contradictory processes at work in the CPR.' 'How', he asked, 'did that happen?' His answer (PSS, pp. 9–11) deserves full quotation, as follows :

> With the coming of the CPC to power and the establishment of close relations with the USSR, the CPC virtually renounced many of Mao Tse-tung's bourgeois-nationalist concepts and recast its general line for the transitional period, basing itself mainly on the Leninist theory of socialist revolution; and Mao himself agreed to the editing of his previously published works. In the *Selected Works of Mao* published in four volumes in the Soviet Union in 1951–53 by Soviet and Chinese Communist scholars (a commission of the Central Committee of the CPC for that purpose), essential corrections were introduced. For example, on p. 502 of the fourth volume of the Russian edition, concerning the structure of the New Democracy, the phrase was added 'which is under the leadership of the working class' and the following phrase in the Chinese text omitted : 'The New Democratic State of the union of some democratic classes differs in principle from the socialist State of the dictatorship of the proletariat.' (See Mao Tse-Tung, *Selected Works,* in Chinese, Harbin, 1948, p. 316.)

Such a correction altered the essence of the Maoist doctrine of 'New Democracy' in the edited [Russian] version. Mao, who had denied the leading role of the working class and the dictatorship of the proletariat, appeared to the Soviet reader as a follower of Marxism-Leninism. In a series of documents of the CC of the CPC, especially in the resolutions of the first session of its 8th Congress, Marxism-Leninism was proclaimed to be the world-view of the Chinese Communists, the cult of personality was condemned and the conditions were established for fully overcoming the bourgois-nationalist attitudes in the ranks of the CPC. Thus, in those years, when the CPC was directing the development of China along the socialist path and striving to consolidate Marxist-Leninist teaching as the stable foundation, keeping silent about the weak points in the Chinese reality, including even the anti-Marxist essence of the 'thoughts of Mao', was to some extent politically justified.

A different situation arose after 1958, when the Maoists liquidated the general line which the CPC had adopted in the first years after the formation of the CPR in 1949, and the 'thoughts of Mao' were proclaimed to be the basis of China's new ideology. Mao, concentrating power in his own hands, began to steer the development of China towards turning the country into a militarist State, into a 'united military camp'. Without putting forward one single concrete programme of ways of developing China, Mao continues right up to the present day to make use of Marxist terminology, to declare his adherence to Marxism-Leninism, though the objectives for which Mao utilises his theory and practice remain sufficiently clear and unchanged – Great-Han chauvinism, restoration of the former greatness of the ancient Han, T'ang and Ming dynasties.

Mao obliterates the whole modern history of China and tries to justify a falsified representation of the paths of development of the Chinese revolution, to vulgarise the culture of socialist realism, to slander the unselfish aid given by the Soviet people and blacken our friendly relationship with the people of China. Mao Tse-tung considers the chief obstacle to the attainment of his chauvinist aims, and the chief enemy, to be the Soviet Union; hence anti-Sovietism is the main component of Mao's conduct. In the light of the circumstances taking shape in China, new tasks of a more responsible nature than those of all the preceding periods confront the Soviet sinologists.

They have to unravel all these distortions, expose all these errors, detect and check – preferably in advance this time, instead of condoning as they did in the early days of the CPR – all the wrong-thinking and evil-doing.

The PSS conference papers, discussing the directives for that formidable task, are sectionalised broadly in a sequence of subjects : history, ideology, politics, economics, culture and linguistics, concluding with some side glances at the progress of sinology in the West and in Japan. In the following chapters the main subject-headings are similarly considered in turn.

3 Recent History of China

History is the first field of study to be examined, and the survey begins with the contemporary history of China. This may seem strange, the usual practice being to follow the whole development forward from the beginnings – not least in the case of China, a culture so deeply and so long shaped in an all-pervasive development that can only be fully explained in the perspective of its great antiquity. Nevertheless the Soviet procedure is generally to begin with the 'most recent' history and work back to the foundations. This is because the 'remit' given to the Soviet sinologues is first to identify the present errors of the Chinese leadership, second to explain the derivation and origins of those errors, third to reconstruct the true circumstances in the preceding period and point the 'correct' inferences that should have been drawn from them (in contradistinction to the false deductions or inductions pursued by the Maoists); only fourth, when all this has been clarified, will the way be clear for a 'positive' recasting and rewriting of Chinese history as a whole. This is not an absolute scale of priorities; research may certainly adduce material for the later phases of this sequence, while the earlier ones are still in process. For example, a collective work is going on under the IDV to produce an authoritative *New History of China* as soon as possible; but the political directives are firmly in the order given above. It is likely that the *New History* project will itself concentrate primarily on the current heresies in Peking.

Since the manpower in Soviet sinology is relatively 'scanty and weak' (as Director Sladkovski himself stated), it must be concentrated on the immediate political task, rather than on more remote academic objectives. The priority of current politics was clearly expressed by Mr Brezhnev himself, at the 24th Party Congress and the International Communist Meeting in Moscow in 1969. S. L. Tikhvinski and L. P. Delyusin open the next section of PSS

(p. 21) with a call for 'struggle' against both the 'leftist, pseudo-revolutionary, subjective, also nationalistic Great-Han' ideas of the Maoists and the imperial-colonist views of China (which the Maoists in effect subserve) as a 'peculiar' or 'exceptional' nation; to both, Soviet scholars should demonstrate the worldwide validity of the Marxist analysis.

ROLE OF THE CHINESE PROLETARIAT

Coming to specifics, Tikhvinski and Delyusin note with satisfaction that many scholars in the Soviet Union are moving into the field of modern history, who were formerly working on other periods. They give priority to the history and role of the working class of China, asserting immediately that the Maoists minimise the role of the proletariat, as do the Western bourgeois analysts, though both make much of the Fourth of May Movement. 'There is no work in China on the role of the working class in the fight against the Japanese occupation and the overthrow of the Kuomintang (KMT). The Maoists have directly falsified the history of the Chinese working-class movement, forged [sic] the book by Teng Chung-hsia, distorted the role of Liu Shao-ch'i, Li Li-san and other leaders of the trade union movement in both the earlier and later stages of the revolutionary movement.' The book referred to must be Teng's *Short History of the Chinese Labour Movement*, which he wrote in Moscow in 1928–30.

'It is well known', Tikhvinski and Delyusin continue, 'that after the formation of the CPR many Party workers came out sharply against measures for improving the lot of the workers; on the grounds, forsooth, that the working class not only did not take an active part in the civil war, did not strike, sabotage and raise diversions in the KMT's rear. In the leadership of the CPC at that time the view was expressed that the needs of the workers should be met by distributing among them the capitalists' property, including lathes and machines – just as the land had been distributed to the peasants. Several researchers, though stressing the decisive role of the proletariat in the revolution, at the same time acknowledge its weakness in numbers, its low political level, the extremely low proportion of workers in the CPC.' All this must be disproved, the 'vanguard' role of the proletariat demonstrated.

It will indeed be valuable if the history and record of the industrial working class in China can be fully documented; but many who were in China in those days will attest that such strictures on the revolutionary-mindedness of that class are not unfounded. In fact the skilled workers, particularly, were a comparatively favoured class under the KMT: the factory legislation in Nationalist China was comparatively (stressing, throughout, *comparatively*) enlightened and well enforced, while the factory workers actually enjoyed rising wages (even in real terms) during the war period, in both the KMT- and Japanese-occupied areas, owing to the munitions boom. They suffered less from the inflation than did the middle and agrarian classes. If this is true, the Soviet investigators may find the detailed evidence disconcerting to the Marxist dogma that the proletarians, in any but a Communist state, must always be the most exploited class, the least likely to enjoy 'rising expectations', the most underprivileged socially and politically (yet by some dialectical magic to develop, in such a down-trodden state, qualities of leadership so high as to make them the harbingers of a better state of society).

'To solve this contradiction', the PSS congress was told, 'they [the Maoists] advance the postulate that the role of the proletariat was fulfilled, in the Chinese revolution, by the army.' In the light of the situation both then and now, it must be commented that this 'postulate' rings very true. Tikhvinski and Delyusin at this point insert briefly the suggestion of their own explanation of the 'contradiction'. It was perhaps the Soviet proletariat, i.e. the Soviet Union as a workers' state, that came in to fulfil the required 'role': this question is closely connected with that of 'demonstrating the revolutionising influence of the Soviet Union on China'. 'Especially poorly studied', complain the authors being cited, 'is the military action of the working class in Manchuria and other Japanese-occupied areas.' Admittedly, however, this was 'after the destruction of the Japanese militarists by the Soviet army', which 'compensated for the relative weakness of the working class of China and . . . protected it from the importation of counter-revolution'. So it was the army; but particularly the Soviet Russian army. It is noted that the difference in the conditions of the proletariat in governmental, foreign and national-bourgeois enterprises in China is one of the many aspects not yet studied, all of which demand a 'many-sided' approach.

The Maoists are, however, to blame; under their system the

workers have at best an 'illusory' participation in decision-making. All Mao's 'thoughts' are directed towards reducing the significance of the prolelariat in the formation of the new society. The Maoists 'have in recent years attacked in every way the United Front policy of both 1937–45 and 1945–46. The literature of those times, calling for strengthening of the anti-imperialist and anti-Japanese front, is shamefully defamed . . . the Maoists at that time sought to disrupt that correct policy, now they seek by "ante-dating" to rehabilitate their record.'

'It is very interesting', Tikhvinski and Delyusin continue, 'to study the links between the Maoists and the ruling American circles in the 1930s and 1940s. Recent documentation in the USA on the affair of the journal *Amerasia* and the admissions of the former State Department collaborator A. Whiting show that there existed active secret contacts between Mao and his circle and the USA long before the present "ping-pong diplomacy" began.' This is perhaps too childish to deserve comment, psychologically revealing though it is; one wonders, however, how much the cause of sinology would be advanced if the Chinese were to retort '*tu quoque*', beginning perhaps with Lenin's sending Leonid Krasin to London in 1921 to make 'active secret contacts' aiming at diplomatic recognition, trade and coexistence.

NATIONALISM AND PROGRESS

Sun Yat-sen is suggested as a special subject of study exemplifying the connection between the battle for national liberation and the drive for social regeneration, which he pursued together; but Sun, holding European liberal ideas, rejected the concept of class-struggle. The consequences for the KMT, especially the right-wing victory in that party from 1927, must be studied in relation to other parts of the background, the prevalence of militarism or warlordism.

A long list of other key subjects for study follows, which can only be summarised here. The socio-economic nature of the People's Revolution and its power-system : Mao is double-faced and contradictory on this. Studies of the actual working would reveal much, with special object-lessons from Manchuria, where the Soviet experience was more deeply imbibed by the Chinese. The peasantry : class-analysis is required, in relation to the 'declassed *lumpenproletariat* which engendered Maoism' (another example of the kind of insult which is unforgiveable among Marxists). The interesting comment follows that it must be noted that there were in China 'isolated political-economic regions within which processes developed involving enormous masses of peasants' under very different conditions in various parts of China. Problems of relations between central and provincial authorities are still very diverse in different parts of the CPR and in various respects. The course of the 'Cultural Revolution' was strikingly different in different localities. (What then becomes of the 'universal' validity of the overall Marxist approach?)

The landlord class : its internal stratification and its relations with other classes or strata. This relates to a study of Chinese political groups, wider than the 'black and white' (or red and white) dichotomy of KMT and CPC, to include the Democratic League, the Young China Party and others, possibly going far back into the history of secret societies and the like. Analysis of the bourgeoisie should extend also to the overseas Chinese, with comparative studies of the bourgeoisies of other parts of the Third World. The view that mainland China is itself part of the Third (or underdeveloped) World must, however, be corrected; China is (even if blunderingly) on another course, that of the socialist camp, from which it is not to be 'torn away'. The work of the Soviet specialists, advisers and other helpers in China in the early 1950s must be fully recorded and its lessons pointed. In what manner, how objectively and consequentially did the CPC take account of the real interests of the various sectors of the population – workers, peasants, national-bourgeois, intelligentsia, students? These had only a brief period of expression, during the time of the 'hundred flowers blooming'. A dozen similar questions follow, on the Constitution of 1954, the 'Great Leap', the 'Cultural Revolution', educational and cultural policy and other subjects.

Maoist errors in all these fields give ammunition to the bourgeois claims that socialism is not the way ahead for the countries of the Third World. 'We cannot accept the Maoist version that . . . up to 1966 there was a struggle in China between the socialist and capitalist paths of development, and that Mao represented the former, Liu Shao-ch'i the latter', which (like all the other splits and upheavals, before and since) gives the same kind of ammunition to the same kind of people. The attack must be carried into the bourgeoisie's own rear, by showing how foreign capital and foreign aggression disrupted and ruined China in the past, increasingly supporting the internal reactionary forces, intensifying the exploitation and demoralisation of the Chinese masses.

SOVIET AID

The spokesmen recommend that the past record of Russians in China be positively contrasted with that of the Westerners and the Japanese. Primarily, of course, the performance of Soviet Russians; but it must be noted that since the middle part of Stalin's period of absolute power (even before the Second World War, which he called the Great Patriotic War), criticism of the conduct and purposes of Tsarist Russia, especially in foreign policy, has been muted. Not infrequently, the Tsarist Russian past is glorified – as part of the living heritage of the contemporary Soviet patriotism. Characteristic is the depiction of Russian relations with China as not only longer, more regular and more intrinsic than those of any other nation, but as more 'positive' and constructive.

Nevertheless, the main stress is on Soviet aid to China. 'Historiography in the CPR . . . dealing with 1937–45 . . . unfoundedly ascribes to the Eighth [Route] Army and the New Fourth Army [of China] a number of powerful and successful military operations, while ignoring a number of important military operations planned by the Soviet military advisers with the Chinese High Command and saying nothing about the decisive part played by Soviet military aid and about the participation of Soviet military specialists and volunteer airmen in the defence of Nanking, Wuhan, Chungking, Changsha, Lanchow, Sian and other Chinese cities. To bring all this out, much more should be done in the writing, gathering and publishing of memoirs and reminiscences of Soviet participants – over and above the distinct vogue for materials of those kinds in recent years in the Soviet Union, which has seen the publication of such items as documents about Marshal Blyukher [318] and memoirs of Cherepanov, Vishnyakova-Akimova [523], Konchits, Blagodatov [64], Kalyagin [207], Kazanin [215] and others.

Of these, the most notable are the following. Marshal V. K. Blyukher (Galen) (1889–1938) was a hero of the Revolution and Civil War, Commander-in-Chief in the Far Eastern Republic in

1921–22, the main military adviser to the Canton Government in 1924–27, commander of the Special Far Eastern (Soviet) Army in 1936, thereafter disappearing in Stalin's purge of thousands of officers of all ranks, which greatly facilitated the German invasion. He was posthumously rehabilitated in 1956 and literary or artistic memorials of him are still being produced. A. V. Blagodatov was another high-ranking military man sent to Hankow in 1938–39, as was A. I. Cherepanov. A. Ya. Kalygin commanded the first party of Soviet volunteer aviators who arrived in Nanking at the end of 1937. M. I. Kazanin's work relates to a much earlier period; he was secretary to the first official (but inconclusive) Soviet mission to China in 1920 (in the name of the Far Eastern Republic, but on Lenin's instance) led by I. L. Yurin. All such activities relate not only to the internal affairs of China but also to that country's foreign relations; they will therefore be further considered in Chapter 4 below.

CONFRONTING THE CHINESE PUZZLE

This catalogue could be extended at great length. The Chinese historical experience is immensely long, the materials, documents and commentaries on it extremely numerous – and still largely unutilised. Systematic and conscientious work on all this evidence – archaeological, antiquarian and politico-polemical – continues in the CPR itself, constantly adding to the vast store. In the present chapter the focus is on the recent history of China – on which, incidentally (or rather substantially), the Soviet terminology is a little confusing. The Russians speak of the 'newest' history of China or other countries (*noveishaya istoria*), meaning the most recent, even 'contemporary' historical period; then for the next layer of the past they use the term 'new' history (*novaya istoria*), i.e. broadly what we could call modern history; though they would generally extend the latter term no further back than the maturity and decline of capitalism.

Regarding the more distant past, their third category is 'medieval' (*srednevekovy*) – which in China's case they apply to a very long period, something like the third to the mid-nineteenth centuries of what they call, to avoid a Christian reference, 'our era'; while their fourth category, 'antiquity' (*drevnost'*), means very early history, or protohistory. The present chapter deals with recent history in the Western sense of the term, i.e. in Soviet terms with the 'newest' and some part of the 'new'; though the latter (later eighteenth and early twentieth-century aspects) comes more explicitly into the subsequent chapters, which are by subjects or fields of interest.

The foregoing may suffice to draw some conclusions. First, what a prodigious task is being set the Soviet practitioners! Labours of Hercules : kill the Nemean (or Chinese) lion and the hydra of capitalism, catch the (deviationist) Erymanthian boar and the (neutralist) Cerynean hind, clean out the Augean stables of non-Communist thought, deal also with the Amazons, the Cretan bull, Cerberus, the horses of Diomed (whatever personifications these may fit today) and gain possession of the girdle of Hippolyte and the apples of the Hesperides (the crown jewels of Marxism and the fruits of knowledge). Do all this in a Marxist interdisciplinary sense, showing the dialectical interpenetration of all these matters with each other.

However, the 'remit' (as the current jargon has it) proves not to be so hopelessly wide as the metaphor of these twelve labours suggests; for, in the second place, it is made abundantly clear by those in authority that 'the purpose of the exercise' is, 'when the chips are down' (and, in the Great Game as the Soviets see it, things are always *en jeu*), to justify Soviet viewpoints and Soviet behaviour, past, present and future.

The third field of reaction is, how much has actually been done or is under way, in all this? The Soviet bibliography so far, in the modern history sector, is only moderately extensive, and mostly not specialistic in an expert sense. Contrastingly, in every one of the subjects mentioned above, the Western literature is much more abundant, if not prolific, and in much greater depth. The description 'Western' is almost habitual in Europe and America; in fact there are also plentiful and abundant sinological (and other) studies in Japanese, little known in the Occident (see the present writer's earlier work, *Introduction to the Economic History of China*, 1953, which gave some exploratory indication of the extent and quality of Japanese work).

Tikhvinski and Delyusin in PSS (p. 34) note this very briefly : 'The history of China is now being studied in the West and in Asia on a broad front, many publications on China are appearing which contain an abundance of factual matter; it is necessary to take systematic account of all these materials, documents and sources, to introduce them into everyday use in our scientific information and research.' Yet in PSS itself, apart from the very slender section specifically on Western sinology (fourteen pages out of a 343-page volume), there is only one single reference to a Western work. Professor C. P. Fitzgerald is selected for this signal honour [134]. There are a dozen pages on Japan, even more lacking, however, in content (see Chapter 11 below). Hong Kong, the apple of the China-watchers' eye, India and other places are significantly not even mentioned.

The final question is, how effective or convincing will this great and new wide start in Soviet sinology – thus launched with considerable fanfare – prove to be? As the bibliography below may illustrate, the majority of serious Russian-language scholars do not appear to have been drawn holus-bolus or irresistibly into this prospect of working to justify political strategies, in terms especially of current events, but prefer to study a more remote past, or the more 'cultural' aspects. Academics, in Russia as elsewhere, are not unskilful in the art of sidestepping.

This chapter has been concerned with the internal history of China, matters intrinsic to the developments within China. Clearly, however, it is the relations between China, Russia and the neighbouring countries that constitute the primary field of Soviet interest, which is the area adjacent to and overlapping that of recent history. China's international relations are therefore the subject of the next chapter in this book.

4 China's International Relations

A RUSSOCENTRIC VIEW

The PSS papers in this field centre exclusively on the Russo–Chinese conflict. They astonish the Western reader by making no significant reference to China's actual or possible connections with Japan, South-East or South Asia, not to speak of more distant regions. No mention was made of the Vietnam conflict, then at its climax, or any of the many other current and potential tensions involving China (other than the Sino-Soviet fracas). China's role in the United Nations is not mentioned. The foreign reader of the PSS material would conclude that in the Soviet view, even among the highly educated sinologists, the hinge of China is the Amur and Ussuri frontier; that the Soviet approach to China is completely self-centred, obsessed with its own involvement to the point of seeing no others'.

This seems an egotistic, egocentric stance for the self-proclaimed headquarters of the World Revolution, the monopolists of true internationalism. It would seem flagrantly nationalistic, even tainted with chauvinism (to use the terms flung at the head of the 'ruling group in Peking'). It certainly ignores the injunctions constantly given by the authorities to the Soviet sinologists to study China comprehensively, seeing all aspects together. It raises many questions concerning the national psychology of the Soviet Union, or its 'ruling circles'.

Is the USSR simply obsessed with the China issue? It must be wracked by some neurosis about its Far Eastern position; a schizophrenic anxiety, perhaps, contrasting the low state of population and development in Siberia (in some respects) with the terrifying nuclear and other power the USSR might be tempted to unleash against a recalcitrant China? A guilt complex, possibly, on the political plane – realising that the past Soviet record cannot be waved aside by some passing allusion to Stalin's 'cult of personality' (without even naming the person), and perceiving that Maoism is at present more attractive to poor peasant peoples than Soviet Russianism?

The following account will show the extent to which Soviet interest and Soviet sensitivity centre on the long Siberian frontier. All this smoke – and the heavy concentration under it of Soviet military power in the Far East, larger now than its concentration against Europe – can but indicate where the fire is. This is a very real and major crux in geopolitics. Moreover it is considered – by both China and the USSR – as a long-term and intrinsic issue, not one that will fade away with evolving circumstances. One more reflection seems especially relevant in this connection. It is striking that no single Soviet commentator mentions the fact that Chairman Mao must soon die, and speculates that his successor(s) may change the situation; Soviet expositions invariably assume a continuation of the present basic relationship.

A STRUGGLE FOR WORLD POWER

However, the PSS discussion came at a particular moment. The exclusive attention drawn at that meeting to Russo–Chinese relations may soon be modified, China's relations with all the other countries may duly be considered by Soviet researchers and commentators in the next period. One major work in that direction by the IDV, an interesting survey of all *International Relations in the Far East*, appeared (in two volumes of 518 pages) in 1973. Apart from this it is true there is no very significant academic work at present in the Soviet Union on China's relations with other countries. Such will, however, undoubtedly be forthcoming in future. The great emphasis in the PSS discussions of 1971–73, through which the 'fresh start' in Soviet sinology was organised, was to bring home (with all the heavy-handedness characteristic of the *apparat* when it is proclaiming a new course involving major efforts) the political and patriotic urgency of this matter. With these remarks – which are necessary because the reader may wonder whether this chapter is not falsely titled, if it deals almost entirely with Sino–Soviet relations in particular – the perspectives in the following account may appear more clearly.

G. V. Astaf'iev and A. G. Yakovlev introduced the topic of

China's foreign relations in PSS 1973 with the statement that China 'emerged on the international arena as an independent sovereign state in 1949'. Thus the Moscow line ignores the previous recognition of China as one of the Allies and Great Powers during the war and in 1945–49, including at least *de facto* recognition and support as such by Stalin; ignoring also that Mao's stand in 1949 was one of 'leaning to one side, the side of the Soviet Union', on which latter Mao was very dependent indeed. While the Soviet Union was the only one of the Allies to have occupation forces in the area which was at that time 'China proper', namely Manchuria : Taiwan was then a Japanese colony still in process of being handed over to China, Hong Kong's status as a British colony was not on the agenda, the concessions and extraterritorial rights elsewhere had previously been ceded. All this had been with the concurrence of Stalin. History is rewritten not only by changing the text, but by omitting some of the circumstances.

In the same opening sentence (PSS, p. 47) Astaf'iev and Yakovlev say that not only China's emergence but also 'particularly the subsequent transition of the leadership of the Chinese People's Republic to nationalistic standpoints' impose a large and important duty on Soviet scholars, who should study especially China's foreign policy and relations. 'The nationalistic, great-power chauvinistic nature of [that] foreign policy is the sharpest and most dangerous feature of Mao's "special course"; it not only involves the fate of socialism in China but operates, by the force of the enormous territory, resources and population of China, on the situation in the socialist system and in the whole world and has an ideological influence on the unstable petty-bourgeois elements in the world revolutionary movement.'

The 'anti-Soviet' Maoist course prevails in a country adjacent to the USSR; directly significant, therefore, to both the 'progressive' and the 'reactionary' forces in the world. The struggle between the 'socialist-internationalist' and 'petty-bourgeois-nationalist' forces has 'shifted from within China on to the wide international arena' as a burning question in a world divided into two antagonist systems. (Are there only two systems? And are these *absolutely* 'antagonistic'? Present Soviet policy rather stresses 'co-existence', with reference also to a 'third' or neutralist 'world'. The reader has simply to bear with some learned men who cling to the old dichotomistic formulae on which they have so long fed; and with their naïveté, e.g. when they are surprised that a nation they represent as having just attained for the first time independence and sovereignty adopts a 'nationalistic' standpoint.)

The threat is great, according to these two spokesmen for Soviet sinology : 'The strategic aim of the Maoist leadership is to establish hegemony, the domination of China, first in East Asia, then in the whole "third world" and finally in the entire world.' To this aim, they focus 'an ever-growing war-potential and all the advantages of a socialised economy led by a unitary centre'. History shows that all such 'feeble impulses' towards world hegemony are doomed to disaster (this is a 'feeble' impulse, because it is not founded on Marxism-Leninism). On the way to its downfall, however, it will do great harm to the Chinese people; Mao's economic experiments, the Great Leap and the people's communes, have already held back the economic development of China for ten or fifteen years.

The 'drive for nuclear-rocket armament' and the 'militarisation of the economy' have meant heavy privations. They obstruct economic development; the rest of the economy is condemned to remain on a small-scale basis, the system of Chinese poverty. 'Most significant for us is that the great-power aspirations of China are directed in the first place against the socialist countries of the world, against the Soviet Union; and this is the core not only of the current but of the long-term policy of China. This is conditioned by certain circumstances', namely the idea of Sinocentricity; Maoism re-emphasises the concept that China is the centre of the world, albeit in a new 'revolutionary' version. This, assert Astaf'iev and Yakovlev, is done with the actual connivance of 'the imperialist countries, world imperialism. These can in no way be the opponents of Peking in its fight for hegemony vis-à-vis the international revolutionary forces. On the contrary, they can only be its helpers in this fight, true helpers at that, completely sincere ones. This is confirmed by the present process of *rapprochement* with the imperialist countries, in particular with the USA.'

This diatribe is most interesting, especially since all the Soviet sinologues must be aware that exactly the same things are being said by Chinese spokesmen about the USSR; and since the Soviet public, especially the intelligentsia, are somewhat indifferent to clarion calls of this kind, after nearly sixty years of reiteration.

Moreover they are aware that this hardly represents the official stance of the Soviet Government today at the 'summit' level. Astaf'iev and Yakovlev at this point themselves quote L. I. Brezhnev at the International Conference of Communist and Workers' Parties at Moscow in 1969, not as brandishing accusations of collaboration with the imperialists but as stressing the national danger to Russia: the Maoists' 'struggle for hegemony in the Communist movement, against the Marxist-Leninist parties', he said, 'is inseparably linked with the great-power aspirations of the present Peking leadership, *with its claims on the territory of other countries*' (emphasis inserted here).

It is indeed a major 'problem' of Soviet sinology – and of Soviet life in general – that a solid 'middle layer' of the Party *apparat* is still trundling some 1930-style catchwords, while above them a higher leadership deals in more sophisticated and up-to-date terms, below them a younger but increasingly competent and broadly informed new generation of professionals is sceptical of the sayings and doings of the *apparatchiki*. This does not, of course, exclude the possibility of some division of functions: of ministerial headmen being diplomatic, while leaving it to the lower echelons to keep up the *agitprop*.

WORKING REQUIREMENTS

After this fanfare, the PSS conference settled down to something more like a sober assessment of the state of Soviet studies in this field (with occasional reminders of the accusatory 'line' that has been summarised above). In the present writer's experience, this is essentially typical of Soviet academic and scientific etiquette nowadays: the proceedings tend to open with a heavily 'political' statement, then switch (to the relief of some at least of those present) to more substantive discussion of the subjects on the agenda. In extreme cases, this ritual can be simplified to the initial utterance of one Old Testament text (Marx) and one New Testament reference (Lenin), after which the speaker says: 'Now, to come to the subject of our lecture. . . .' If this tendency continues, it will not be long before the rite will be reduced to that of grace at an Oxford college; the master murmurs two words of benediction, there is a scrape of chairs and the meal, the conversation, begin.

The lecture in PSS 1973 stressed the need to trace first the concrete historical conditions at each stage in the evolution of the CPR, and second the influences of preceding epochs on each current period, with reference to the complex matter of 'tradition', which plays such a strong part in China, 'both superstructurally and basically', under four headings, as follows :

1. The traditional diplomacy of Imperial China. This had great-power aims and methods. 'Soviet scholars dealing with medieval and modern Chinese history have not made a definite contribution' on this theme, with the exception of Yefimov's book on the end of the nineteenth century [537], some outline histories [496] and articles that deal with the Western powers rather than with China's response to them. The China section of IVAN in Moscow (Duman, Vyatkin, Perelomov, Vasil'iev, Gurevich, Melikhov, Khokhlov) and the Leningrad branch of IVAN made some contributions touching on this subject; but it must be treated more 'deeply', especially the traditional diplomatic methods which have been taken over by the Maoists, including the way in which bourgeois nationalist concepts were infused into a classical ideology. A key period for this was the last quarter of the nineteenth century when a rising Chinese bourgeoisie pressed on the eunuch Empire of the Manchus new methods of 'regenerating' China as a modern power.

2. 1912–27. In that period China was the victim of the most direct and comprehensive imperialist oppression and exploitation. The forms of China's dependence on the powers, in foreign policy, must be studied, the counter-influence of the October (Soviet) Revolution adduced, also the Fourth of May movement, the 'revolution' of 1924–27. This period, too, has received only 'episodic' treatment in the Soviet academic literature (PSS, p. 51). Special comparative studies must be made of the foreign policies of Peking and of the warlords, 'especially Chang Tso-lin, Wu Pei-fu, Sun Ch'uan-fang and Feng Yu-hsiang', also the first steps in international relations of Sun Yat-sen in Canton.

3. The period of Kuomintang rule, 'when, under a screen of anti-imperialist phraseology, Nanking was in fact dependent on American imperialism' and 'made all sorts of arrangements in the interests of the bourgeoisie, needs deeper study than has yet been given it in our works', the latter including the books by Sladkovski and Nikiforov [458–9, 340]. The 'anti-people, anti-

Soviet, anti-national pointedness of the KMT foreign policy, verging on capitulation to Japan, contrasts sharply with the gradual activisation of foreign policy by the CPC, in which the Comintern (especially its 6th Congress) played an enormous part in actions aimed at resisting Japan'. Though (it is immediately added) 'at the same time, already in that period, nationalist tendencies were manifested [within the CPC] directed to artificial adventuristic stimulation of the Chinese revolution by provoking Japan to make war on the USSR.' To go more deeply into this is one of the tasks of the large *New History of China* being compiled in Moscow. 'It must be noted that chauvinist elements were widely manifested in the policy of the Chiang Kai-shek Government, despite its dependence on the imperialists' because 'China was at that time becoming a bourgeois state . . . forming a nationalist ideology'. This was expressed in China's great-power conduct towards neighbouring Asian countries, territorial 'pretensions' against them (especially against the USSR), in the patronage of the overseas Chinese bourgeoisie, in 'cultural anti-Sovietism' and in an anti-imperialism that was simply 'demagogic', merely verbal.

4. The foreign policy of the Maoist Government could have been a correct socialistic one, but Mao himself 'came out in direct opposition' to such a line, though the CPC was inclined to it; the clash of the two tendencies within the CPC, Marxism-Leninism and Maoism, actually emerged 'much earlier in this field, foreign policy, than in any other. National impulses were, we know, manifested in the revolutionary movement in Asia as early as 1946. In 1947–48 the Chinese way to revolution began strongly to foist itself [*sic*] on the liberation movement in Malaya and the Philippines. In 1948–49 there was a discussion, led by the CPC, about the choice of orientation – towards the USSR or towards the USA. In 1949–51 the Chinese experience and the Chinese path to revolution were strongly propagandised to, and thrust upon, countries of Asia and the Pacific. A temporary weakening of the great-power nationalist pretensions occurred during the Korean war and in the period of the Five-Year Plan, when the Chinese leadership needed the help of the socialist camp, particularly of the Soviet Union.'

After that war, however, Chinese nationalism revived : it was in action not only at the Geneva conferences and in Bandung 'but also in provoking conflicts in the Taiwan Strait and on the frontiers with India'. This basic stance was made clear in the CPC's 9th Session in 1959; it was 'expandingly' applied during 1960–63 in 'a strategic aim that was and remains the same – gaining world hegemony', though the tactical steps towards this are 'masked as objectives in themselves', on pretentious theoretical grounds. 'At the beginning of the 1970s' the Maoist 'strategic plan changed. Its main characteristic [is now] struggle against the socialist forces of the world in one bloc together with imperialism.' The groundwork of this development has been studied only to a limited extent in the USSR, noted Astaf'iev and Yakovlev. Soviet scholars dealt only with those aspects 'which came within the framework of socialist principles'; they must deal on the Maoist territory, the domain of nationalistic great-power behaviour. 'The struggle between the internationalist [Soviet] and the Great Han [Chinese] tendencies in Chinese foreign policy has not been traced either in the open [published] or the closed [unpublished] works of the [Soviet] academic centres', the spokesmen complained.

Some work had, however, been done in the preceding years, when considerable archival material on China was released by the Soviet Government for the use of the academic centres. Studies in the latter 'are only just gathering strength, but have taken on definite organisational shape', though the output is 'not impressive', 'especially in comparison with the mass of literature on the foreign policy of China that is published abroad'. There was a 'small collective work' in 1971 by the IDV [180], which also produced in 1973 the larger book on *International Relations in the Far East* mentioned above. Kapitsa's work in this period [211–12] took the present critical line – more certainly than his earlier 'smiling' account in 1958 [209]. Other notable works followed: an IDV symposium on *The Leninist Policy of the USSR in its Relations with China* (1968) (covering the last half-century), another more specifically on Mao's views [305], and works by Sergeichuk [440], Alexandrov [11] and Sladkovski [458–9]. 'That really isn't much' was the lugubrious conclusion of Astaf'iev and Yakovlev, though they admit that there were significant references in writings on other subjects and that other publications were in preparation.

'The activities of the Maoist State . . . engender serious difficulties for the whole anti-imperialist front.' China's true position in the world must be assessed. The more immediate and the longer-term aims of the Maoists must be precisely identified. (It seems to be assumed, as noted above, that Maoism is for ever; though this contradicts the interpretation that it represents some personalistic, 'adventuristic' abberation inconsistent with some basic 'class forces', which latter should certainly overthrow Mao's system after his death if not before it. The non-Soviet reader is again prompted to make comparisons with Stalin and his system – on which there is certainly a 'lack of deep and systematic study' in the Soviet Union.)

On China, however, every study must be made of possibilities of 'neutralising' in every way the nefarious consequences of Maoism. It is stressed that the latter is a conservative political philosophy, deeply rooted in very old Chinese traditions; while conditions are changing in Asia and the world, in ways to which Maoism cannot easily adapt. Notably, there is 'the growing power and expansionism of Japan, the strengthening of its role in Pacific Ocean and Asian affairs', which could be pivotal in the 'development of Sino–Soviet and Sino–American relations'. China's relations with other regions in the world, its place and likely behaviour in the United Nations, its 'splitting' role in world Communism and the national liberation movements, must all be subjects of study; this is not just an academic obligation, it is a 'quite definite political duty', as laid down by the 24th Session of the CPSU. The 'positive' aspect is to make quite clear how much 'the USSR and the other socialist countries' contributed in the 1950s 'in aid which compensated for the weakness of the internal base in the CPR, to forward and hasten China's economic development'.

These veins are probed at some length; it would seem repetitious to pursue them here in full, but some of the further directives must be noted. The Maoists' involvement with the United States is especially stressed; their 'mutual understandings' began even during the war [440]; the confluence must be studied of the evolution of a 'China policy' in America and an 'America policy' in China, also the reciprocal 'wooings' of China with Western Europe, Canada, Australia and the Third World; while the military, economic and political motivations in Peking's policy must be distinguished. Finally, 'struggle' must be waged against the 'extensive falsification' of all these matters by 'bourgeois sinology, which supports the Maoist position and its anti-Soviet line'.

On the other hand, some Western exponents may be redeemable : 'It is necessary to develop links with foreign sinologists who are trying objectively to assess the role of Maoist policy in international relations, to seek ways of influencing them, giving them support in one way or another.' And, it seems, above all 'to extend co-operation with the Marxist-Leninist forces in sinology in the West and in the "third world" to give them real help', including 'publication of the results of their work'. Many Western sinologues are presumably willing, like Lenin, to have dealings even 'with the devil's grandmother' if it is useful to do so – their criterion of usefulness being a free and uncensored exchange of facts and interpretations. The challenge is really to the Soviet Union and to China to prove their greatness and self-confidence by opening doors to a free traffic both ways. Many Soviet sinologists would welcome this; as Khrushchev might have said, who is afraid of whom?

Needless to say, the profession in the USSR was not presented, through the PSS conference, with any such train of thought. It received instead another list of tasks. It was bidden to make up the following deficiencies : 'the shortcomings in our work that lower its quality and therefore its effectiveness', 'insufficient knowledge of the antecedents of present Chinese foreign policy', 'weak analysis', 'almost complete absence of criticism of bourgeois theories of international relations'. Much has recently been published of documents and archives, but in that respect also 'there are still difficulties', especially a shortage of trained personnel. All these matters must be organised on a nationwide (pan-Soviet) scale.

EXPLAINING THE RUSSO–CHINESE CONFLICT

The political line having been thus heavily laid down, the Soviet sinologists discussed especially the field of Sino–Russian relations. V. S. Myasnikov, reviewing the earlier periods (PSS, pp. 64 ff.), found the work of Soviet historians 'chronologically and thematically uneven'. The first period of Russian relations, the mid-seventeenth century, the Russian occupation of the lands on the

Amur river at that time, has been the main focus of interest. It is presented as a reaction to 'Manchu expansionism', a defensive Russian policy conducted somewhat legalistically by Tsarist efforts to establish normal and equitable diplomatic relations, resulting 'successfully' [*sic*] in the Treaty of Nerchinsk (1689).

The Nerchinsk accord certainly deserves special interest as it was China's first treaty with a European power. The view presented above is, however, curious; in fact the Manchus, far from being 'expansionist', wanted to preserve their homeland Manchuria, discouraged Chinese settlement there, kept no garrisons north of the Amur and limited their control to occasional visits of inspectors. The whole trouble was that they left this borderland 'empty', an attraction to the expanding and acquisitive Russians. In the seventeenth century the latter were, however, interested primarily in trade. In the Kyakhta agreement of 1727 – not mentioned in PSS – they bound themselves to the caravan trade through that outpost. By the mid-nineteenth century the circumstances totally changed and territorial acquisitions east of Nerchinsk were strongly desired by the Russians. Myasnikov rightly adds that other agreements, 'the Aigun, Peking, etc.' treaties, should be equally closely studied. (For a useful summary of a Western view of the basic position, see H. MacAleavy, *The Modern History of China*, 1968, pp. 38–41.)

Soviet work on Sino–Russian relations falls into three separate periods, as Myasnikov notes. In the 1920s and 1930s the setting was one of 'struggle against the courtier- and bourgeois historiography of Tsarism', for overthrowing old views and developing entirely new critical approaches. (Joy was it, no doubt, in that dawn to be alive.) 'As a rule', says Myasnikov three war-weary generations later, 'new sources were not utilised in these [works].' Well-known works of that time and sort are V. P. Savvin's account (Moscow and Leningrad, 1925–30) of *Russian and USSR Relations with China*, Bakhrushin on the Amur Cossacks [41], K. V. Vasil'iev's *Guests of Bogdo Khan* (Leningrad, 1927), relevant sections of general works (including those of the great M. N. Pokrovski and other historians such as K. A. Kharnski) and some provocative or stimulating articles [31]. Characteristic of all these, in Myasnikov's view, was 'the pointing of all and any evidence to show the aggressive intentions of Tsarism, directed towards injuring the interests of China'. There was, however, the beginning of some effort to trace also an 'aggressor' or 'invasionist' behaviour on the part of the Manchus [266].

A distinct lull ensued over the period of the more indubitable occupation of Manchuria by the Japanese, when there were 'only some works' on current questions such as the Chinese Eastern Railway. It was not until the end of the 1940s – when liberating Soviet forces had replaced the Japanese – that a second wave of Soviet studies began, which lasted through the 1950s. 'This was a time', comments Myasnikov, 'when, under influences connected with the growth of patriotic tendencies among Soviet historians in the period of the Great War for the Fatherland, a great change took place in attitudes to the past of our Native Land, a serious reconsideration began of former evaluations of the main features of the history of Russo–Chinese relations.' (When a similar reconsideration is undertaken in Peking, it is of course branded in Moscow as 'nationalistic Great-Han chauvinism'.) Myasnikov adds at once that 'another characteristic trait of the works of this [second] period is a certain idealisation of Russo-Chinese relations in the seventeenth and eighteenth centuries and of the significance of the Nerchinsk treaty in the history of Russia'.

At the same time, a great deal of archival and documentary material became newly available which 'enabled the historians to liberate themselves from the mistaken concept that the Manchus had the priority in the acquisition or development of Amuria in the seventeenth century'. (The Russian word rendered here as 'acquisition or development' is interesting : it is *osvoyenie*, etymologically 'making into one's own'.) The new material and the new policy also prompted reconsideration of the record of the great Russian explorers or conquistadors (Nevel'skoi, Poyarkov, Khabarov and others [530–1, 337, 332, 537]; see also the works of L. A. Derbov and G. Ya. Rabich). Narochnitski considered the Aigun treaty the greatest success : 'In spite of the reactionary policies of [both] Tsarism and the Ch'ing Government it cemented Russo–Chinese relations. Russia never made war on China and never brought opium to China.' Another Soviet writer has gone further in stressing the purity of Russian relations with China, noting that there was 'another poison', which the Russians were also guiltless of imposing on China, namely private enterprise, their relations having been generally governmental [333, vol. i, p. 792].

A third period ensued on the breach with Maoism at the end of the 1950s 'The CPR's affirmation that the present frontiers of China are "unjust", discussion by Chinese historians about the formation of China's territory and the role of the Mongol and Manchu conquests, also the publication of a map on which large areas . . . including the Soviet Union [*sic*] were shown as "torn away" from China' focused attention on the frontier problem. The Maoist ideas had to be exposed as 'bourgeois-nationalistic in essence', also the efforts of 'the imperialist propaganda, which picked up and "embellished" this aspect of the "thoughts" of Mao'. Most characteristic for the early part of this period, the Soviet sinologists were officially informed, was continued 'overestimation' of the Nerchinsk treaty as a great gain for the Russian State. In fact it was a retreat from regions Russians had already 'made their own', a restriction to the Gobi trade-route and the placing of a small mission in Peking, accepted 'under the pressure of overwhelming forces of Manchu troops'.

Instances of works of the period in question are Kabanov's book [202] and Yakovleva's article [531]; in the latter the author 'substantially corrects' her previous view that the Nerchinsk treaty was a good thing. V. A. Alexandrov's contribution [11] is praised; but the clearest rebuttal of 'the unfounded demands of the Peking leadership' came in V. M. Khvostov's article [222] which was the first to denounce Peking's reliance on the Nerchinsk treaty and his academic compatriots' previous acceptance of it, on the grounds that it was from Russia's point of view an 'unequal' treaty signed under 'duress'.

Khvostov asserts further that in the subsequent Aigun and Peking treaties 'Russia only recovered a part of what had been seized by China by the Nerchinsk treaty.' The view that these later treaties were 'equitable' was accepted by the Soviet Academy of Sciences. Khvostov referred to the subsequent Russian annexation of the Maritime regions as justified : 'This too, of course, cannot be called usurpation' as the Maritime area was not delimited in accordance with the Nerchinsk treaty'. This seems a bald assertion, since the Russians were held by the Nerchinsk treaty to the line of the Stanovoi mountains (though the Mongolian sector further west remained 'undemarcated'); however, a massive Soviet official documentation followed in 1969–71 which endorsed all the main lines of Khvostov's thesis [423].

THE FRONTIER CLASH

The early Russian settlement of the Siberian Far East, sub-sequently the real political and economic factors in the second half of the nineteenth century, established (from the Soviet point of view) frontiers that are exactly appropriate and equitable. Equally 'correct' was the outcome in 'Central and Middle' Asia (the Russians tend to distinguish these as their own holdings and the surrounding areas, respectively) where 'this process occurred on lands first inhabited by nomadic or semi-nomadic peoples which had no stable form of State, also on the territories of independent feudal States'. The dealings were 'not between Russia and China but between Russia and the Manchu Ch'ing Empire, which had destroyed the Chinese State and included China within its own [Manchu] State as one of its component parts'.

A Marxist-Leninist examination 'makes it possible to correct mistakes made in Soviet literature on this subject published in 1920–40, when the historians mostly assessed the actions of Russia during the almost 300-year period of Russo–Chinese relations from the point of view of the actions of imperialist Russia in the Far East at the end of the nineteenth and beginning of the twentieth centuries. On its part the Ch'ing Empire saw itself, in the whole course of that period, solely from the point of view of its character in the second half of the nineteenth and the beginning of the twentieth centuries, i.e. the time when it was becoming the prey of the Western powers. This view left out of sight the [preceding] nearly two centuries of aggressive wars of conquest by the Manchu emperors, which were most significant for the recent history of China and the neighbouring countries.'

Myasnikov claims (PSS, p. 70) that 'it is now no secret that a series of Chinese and Western constructs about [these] frontiers are based on versions of the Nerchinsk treaty falsified by the Manchus themselves. . . . The Peking theoreticians fully share the Kuomintang and Western-bourgeois conceptions' on these matters so 'the Maoists have embarked on active ideological co-operation with imperialist scholarship and imperialist propaganda, as is evident from their both sharing the thesis of a continuity in Tsarist and Soviet policy towards China'. The Maoists are, however, worse than the bourgeoisie; their attacks invoke the name of

Lenin himself, saying that the Founder's 'proletarian policy was never implemented'.

The Chinese quote the epoch-making note of 27 September 1920 from the People's Commissariat for Foreign Affairs of the Russian Federation to the Chinese Foreign Ministry, which said : 'The Government of Russia, repudiating all previous Tsarist treaties concluded with China, returning to the Chinese people all that was taken from it and appropriated by the Tsarist Government and the Russian bourgeoisie, proposes to the Government of China to enter into official negotiations for the establishment of friendly relations.' This text is included in an official Soviet collection of documents [475, p. 51].

This presumptuous citation by the Chinese provokes Myasnikov to a lengthy explanation (PSS, pp. 71–7) of the context of the note and of Lenin's full views in this field. The note of 1920, he explains, was a 'derivative' document following up an 'Appeal by the Soviet of People's Commissars to the Chinese People and the Governments of South and North China'. This more basic document specifically enumerated the treaties on which negotiations could begin, with a view to annulling them. 'Neither in this document nor in any other was there any question of "returning" to China territories of the former Tsarist Russia. There was not and there could not be', thunders Myasnikov. He proceeds to quote Lenin's positive statements on the question in general. Lenin defined 'annexation' as involving '1. Compulsion (compulsory unification). 2. Imposition of a foreign yoke and – sometimes – destruction of the *status quo* . . . the destruction of a self-determined nation, establishment of State frontiers against the will of the population . . . of a people with an identity and a will to exist on its own.' At the April 1917 conference of the Bolsheviks he listed Schleswig-Holstein, Alsace, Courland, Finland, Poland, the Ukraine' etc.' as instances of annexation by the Marxist definition.

The first enactment of the Soviet Government, the 'Decree on Peace', defined annexation as 'seizure of alien lands . . . by a large or strong State against a small or weak one', but spells out conditions and variants at some length. Lenin is quoted further as noting that the frontiers attained in the second half of the nineteenth century were the 'optimal' ones which might be broadly acceptable at the inception of a new socialist era, in the sense that they represented a kind of final equilibrium in the period in which capitalism completed its historical mission of forming a world economy. On this, Lenin quoted Engels's article on 'The Rhine and the Po'. (All this, it must be commented, must be considered a very Europocentric view; but such was the view of Marx and Engels, who did not think the Oriental despotisms worth much consideration in current politics.)

Lenin perceived that roles might be reversed over historical time; a weak State undergoing annexations or amputations at the hands of a strong one might in due course of time and development become stronger than the annexor. Accordingly the Soviet Union, on its formation, granted the right to any of its component units to secede and become independent; over more than half a century, none of them have elected to do so. On the contrary, other (weaker) States have joined the Soviet Union. (Thus the spokesman of Soviet sinology, quoting the collected works of Lenin, vol. 30, pp. 18, 20–1, 350–1; vol. 31, pp. 261, 373, 390, 392, 439; vol. 32, p. 115; and vol. 35, pp. 14, 121. His interlocutors must surely be aware that someone was holding a gun; that, in the vocabulary of a recent film, joiners like the Baltic States were being made an offer they could not refuse, while the foundation members of the USSR had a standing offer which they could not accept. China, and even some weaker States in South-East Europe, have, however, been able to refuse.)

In this wider excursion into Lenin's thoughts, the spokesman thus began somewhat to dissipate his argument, which remains specifically that the Amur and Ussuri lands were not inhabited by a distinct population desiring or capable of desiring to be autonomous, that Chinese control of them was only formally, perfunctorily and listlessly exercised, on the tenuous basis of ancient usages of the occasional collection of 'tribute', which was a merely ritual formality, that the few inhabitants were primitive nomads who were neither able to develop the area nor interested in so doing.

The Chinese people were not even involved in this question, which lay between Russia and the alien oppressors of China in the past, the Mongols and the Manchus. The Soviet Union has therefore 'no territorial obligations to China'. If these 'facts' – the whole picture, not artificially selected portions of it – were accepted in Peking it would, say the Soviet spokesmen, be possible to attain what it constantly asserted to be the Soviet desire : 'normal' relations between China and the USSR.

CHINESE INGRATITUDE

In the following section of PSS (pp. 77–83) R. A. Mirovitskaya reviews the most recent work. She blames 'the anti-Communist Western historiography' for inciting the Maoists by joining in the process of selecting aspects unfavourable to the USSR and continually representing the latter as the aggressor; the Maoists get some of their intellectual armaments from the West. She repeats the call to counter-attack on all fronts. A good start has been made in stressing the extent and value of Soviet aid to China [71], not only to the CPR but to the Chinese Republic before it.

The Western and Chinese public is probably unaware of the extent of the latter. The following summarises recent Soviet claims. October 1937 : 750 trucks allocated to open supply route to China. From then to February 1938, 5600 loads carried by these; over 4000 Soviet workers engaged in this. November 1937 : first dispatch of aeroplanes to China : 62 medium bombers, 155 fighters, 8 trainers, 450 volunteer Soviet pilots and maintenance staff. August 1938 : (allocated) 100 I-15 planes, 2000 machine-guns with 20 million rounds, 100 37-mm guns with 90,000 shells, 160,000 shells for 76-mm guns and 50,000 for 115-mm howitzers, 300 trucks, with spare parts. November 1938 : 6 heavy bombers, 146 medium ones, 331 fighters and 8 trainers. From 1938 : numerous military and advisory missions.

These particulars are from *International Relations in the Far East*, published by the IDV in 1973, vol. II, pp. 130–5. They are not exhaustive and are given here only in illustration. Western, Japanese, Chinese and other views give, of course, different interpretations of the Soviet aid. A Western expert, curiously named R. A. Kilmarx, in his *History of Soviet Air Power* (1962) pp. 148ff., notes that 'the Soviet air units kept to themselves . . . according to their own tactical plans and political interests, although on occasion they engaged in joint operations with the Chinese. Not even high Chinese Government officials could intervene . . . the Russians kept trying to obtain more authority over the Chinese . . . but were rebuffed . . . as in Spain, the USSR supplied . . . only enough air power to further its own interests and never enough to defeat the enemy. . . . The largest air-battles fought between the Soviet and the Japanese forces occurred in 1938 and 1939, but these were only along the Soviet border.'

Many documents have recently been published. The Moscow Foreign Ministry's series [318] reached seventeen volumes, with over four hundred items, by 1971. Useful personal commentaries on the participants were published; these have already been noted in Chapter 3 above.

In sum the Soviet discussion of China's international relations shows, so far, the taking-up of an attitude rather than the development of extensive studies; the enlargement of a political issue, generating more heat than light. The attitude appears, however, to be deeply rooted in psychological and situational factors, which are not transitional but inherent, endogenous rather than exogenous. The Sino–Soviet quarrel will continue in bitterness and strength for some time yet. There will necessarily be notable Soviet studies of other aspects of China's international dealings, however, even if the main focus remains on the borders with Siberia. Last, but not least, it may be stressed that the Soviet explanation of Chinese behaviour is largely, at present at least, in terms of China's own past rather than of China's new or present-day relations with other countries : the policy of Maoist China, not least in foreign affairs, is seen by the Russians as a continuation of the traditional culture and policy of China. The next chapter therefore deals with the Soviet depiction and interpretation of the long and formative 'medieval' period in China's history.

5 Medieval China

L. V. Simonovskaya, in her posthumously published paper (PSS, pp. 99–108), introduces the subject of China in the middle ages as being until recently 'almost unstudied and unilluminated in the [Russian] literature. The brilliant galaxy of the Russian sinologists of last century left us only a few fragmentary works on the history prior to the Manchu conquest.' Such eminent scholars as V. M. Alexeyev and N. V. Kyuner followed the artistic and literary aspects. Between 1920 and 1950 Soviet scholars had to turn to the past, in their search for explanations of the genesis and nature of modern Chinese society; but even they dealt only with a few problems that they considered important. At least they laid some foundations for the 'periodisation' of this very long epoch, notably Grinevich [170] and Duman [111].

In the 1960s much more began to be done, both in general and in specific studies; but there was still a tendency not to see 'the general rules of the human species' at work in China, to exaggerate the 'traditionalism' of that country and make of it a special case. 'Voices were raised proclaiming that "there was almost no development in China (or it was so insignificant in scale that it cannot be argued in the pages of academic publications)" ', notes an official symposium in 1970 (*State and Society in China*, 1st ed., p. 29). 'Objections were raised against the five-stages schema of social evolution'; so wrote Ilyushechkin at the same date. Some even affirmed that 'there was no real difference whatever in the level of development of productive forces of the ancient and the medieval class societies' of China [183]. Simonovskaya adds that 'there are attempts to consider the society as multifarious [literally, 'many-usaged'] and not forming classes; as a society where slave-owning and feudalism arose simultaneously and coexisted for thousands of years. The idea of a cyclical dynamic was adopted and regenerated out of the works of bygone centuries.' This hangs on the discussion about the 'so-called Asiatic mode of production' [519]. All this prevented 'real thematic research, although our young sinologists did achieve much'.

Simonovskaya attacked these heretical tendencies, noting that a large amount of writings and translations in the last few years had begun to work towards a more correct handling. The first step is a better understanding of agrarian social relations [488]. Soviet medievalists exposed the 'myth of the equal-field system' (well-field system) adopted from ancient edicts by bourgeois writers, as being in practice an administrative device to 'attach the primary producers to the soil'. They showed the conflict between the State's efforts to solve the land problem and the local magnates' desire to affirm the private form of feudal property; also the primitive communities' struggle for independence. Thus the young Tyurin had recently identified a dual process of attachment to the soil and taxation, in terms that imply serfdom and conscription [512]. 'Though there was a large body of State-tax payers, the so-called "good people", the whole system predetermined the possibility of the rise of forms of exploitation, to the extent that the development of Chinese society was retarded.'

The study of agrarian relations in the eighth to twelfth centuries shows that landed feudal property could take varying forms [274, 465–8], but extensive landowning increased overall. Nomads, especially the Mongols, often wrought much destruction [112, 74]. The earlier Ming rulers were forced to vacillate and make concessions to the people; they declared their concern for the people and for agriculture, made allotments of State land to peasants, while at the same time tightening the net of taxes and levies, as Svistunova makes clear in her book.

In the sixteenth and seventeenth centuries there was a great struggle between the large feudal and the small private landholders, with a 'mass ruination' of the peasants on the allotments, who were in part payers of dues to the landlords. The stratification became significant at the end of the fourteenth and beginning of the fifteenth centuries. Late Ming sources make constantly diminishing reference to the capture of runaways, yet constantly increasing reference to dispossession of land and eviction of peasant owners or holders. The Manchu dominion brought a great extension of slave labour and enserfment. There are several recent works and translations on the class-struggle in this context, especially on peasant risings in the seventh to twelfth centuries [314, 465, 468, 74, 383–4].

SUBJECTIVE AND OBJECTIVE FACTORS

It is admitted that the peasant struggle was 'many-sided'. There is interest, for instance, in the question 'why did some of the movements take a religious character, others not?' This is taken to indicate the greater 'regressiveness' of some periods compared with others. 'Our [Soviet] historians disprove the negative evaluation of the peasant movements, but are far from idealising them' – as do the Maoists, who glorify everything that is peasant, setting up the peasantry as an especially revolutionary class with 'an elevated historical mission', capable of independent leadership. This claim is explicitly made in Peking (see Hou Pai-lu in *Lishih Yenchu*, 1962, no. 4); Smolin is accused of having 'repeated' it in 1971 in his doctoral thesis at Leningrad [468], to the extent that he attributed an independent class-consciousness to the peasants in view of the fact that they made one rebellion after another, through many centuries. (Which seems, however, fair enough, given this stubborn record and the non-existence, until about the twenty-fourth century of China's existence, of any proletariat.)

Questions of handicrafts and trade are the next subject-field. These are complex, and the tradition lingers of making unwarranted analogies with European history. Stuzhina recently distinguished herself with a good identification of the levels of technique in various activities, of specialisation and differentiation in some handicraft industries, in both the public enterprises and the private shops which were arising in the sixteenth to eighteenth centuries; showing the great development of manual processes, which did not, however, lead to the elaboration of machinery or a clear system of payment by wages. She considers also the various types of direct and intermediary trade, the evolution of a nation-wide market. 'But the hypertrophied activity of merchant capital, often connected with the bureaucratic apparatus, had a negative effect on the progressive elements in the economy and the society.' In less hypertrophic language, the city workshops were torn between their functions of defending their members' interests on the one hand and serving the official structure on the other.

Stuzhina indicates the further development of this dilemma in the nineteenth and twentieth centuries.

The urban economics of earlier periods have been little studied by Soviet sinologists; exceptions are Yermachenko's study of the organisation of trade in the seventh and eighth centuries [539] and Stuzhina's paper at the international congress in 1964 [482]. There were risings of townsmen as well as peasant rebellions, but these are little noticed by Soviet historians. Such conflicts may impinge on the field of 'politics and ideology' rather than economics, but they were acute. Lapina's work disproves the traditional view that there were no political struggles in China in the middle ages, particularly the 'feudal and bourgeois' treatment of 'every conflict, even the movements over many years for reform, as a clash of unprincipled groupings, of people pursuing merely mercenary aims'. Lapina, though her book [274] deals specifically with the eleventh century, uses Wang An-shih's programme to illustrate the presence of advanced political concepts which were used by other movements in later centuries – and opposed or stifled by narrow-minded Confucians and others.

It is interesting that the foreign policy of the Chinese dynasties was often in 'conflict' with their home policy, in the view of some Soviet writers, with reference to the Tartar–Mongol area on the one hand [498–9] and South-East Asia on the other [67]. Western writers are accused of representing China as having always sought 'self-isolation' and evolved without being influenced by other countries. This accusation is of course a travesty of the general Western view of an alternation of centripetal and centrifugal periods of assimilation, but it may have been useful in setting some Marxist scholars to work on the nature, composition, profitability and direction of China's foreign trade. Western specialists are represented as considering that medieval China had an adverse balance of trade; Martynov's article [307] is therefore concerned to show 'that China imported valuable materials' (as well as giraffes and other fanciful curiosities) 'and exported local products'.

There is much greater emphasis, however, on conquest than on trade. Through all the centuries China was the 'centre of the universe, the most civilised country, the other peoples of the world were treated as ordained by the "grace" of Heaven to submit'. Chinese diplomacy was 'cunning and unceremonious' in 'using barbarians to subjugate barbarians', resorting to all means – intervention, stirring up troubles among neighbours, economic pressure, making vassals of sovereign States. This has been widely examined by Soviet researchers – with a gap for the seventh century. Most recently the work of I. N. Mashkina and G. V. Melikhov has been praised.

The conclusions are of course applied in criticism of the Maoists. 'In the CPR the feudal tradition has been revived in attempts to exaggerate the territorial holdings in past centuries of the Son of Heaven' (*Podnebesnoi*; cf. the Chinese T'ien Hsia, 'All that is under Heaven'). The present-day Chinese include in China, as having been substantively parts of the country in the middle ages, non-Chinese peoples and lands which were subjugated by the Manchus only in the eighteenth century. Simonovskaya notes that this error has been repeated in a recent Soviet textbook for higher educational institutions (*History of Foreign Countries in Asia in the Middle Ages*, 1970, pp. 72–6, 234–44), though Svistunova and Myasnikov (in *China and her Neighbours*, in the same year) disproved the Chinese territorial pretensions.

The Soviet writers believe that Chinese depredations or exactions in the lands they occupied or dominated wrought 'massive destruction of the production forces' of the peoples and tribes of those areas. 'Marxist historians consider the invasions and the foreign yoke to be the second cause of the retarded development' of China (the first being the internal bias of the social system towards intensified exploitation). Yet the Maoists glorify all of this shameful record; even Jenghis Khan has been hailed by the Maoists as a 'progressive phenomenon'. (Some older readers may, by the way, recall a Soviet film of the 1930s called *Storm over Asia* which certainly enlisted the ghost of Jenghis Khan on the side of the modern World Revolution.)

General studies in the Soviet Union have, however, done much to restore a correct perspective ([526, 449]; see also articles collected in *Historical Science in the CPR*, 1971). Simonovskaya's conclusion was that

the works of Soviet medievalists on China have destroyed the myth of the age-old stagnation of Chinese society. They showed that, unlike the ancient times when a scanty world-population endured primitive conditions or the rule of slaveowners, the unevenly developing society of medieval China saw changes that were, for that time, significant. During the rise of feudalism, there were invented and widely developed the water-wheel, special means of transport (which did not exist in antiquity), making possible the extension of the cultivated area. In the middle ages the peasants devised trans-furrow sowing and the vernalisation of seeds, began to cultivate sugar-cane on a significant scale, and to use silkworms. In the later middle ages a revolution occurred, by which this land of silk and hemp began to dress, summer and winter, in cotton cloth. In the feudal epoch, printing, porcelain and gunpower were invented, the magnetic compass was used for navigation.

But the back-breaking pressure of the feudal society closed the ways to further progress, the existence of which (albeit in feeble forms) cannot be denied. The feudal epoch has long passed, but survivals of medieval social features remain, venerable prejudices have not been eradicated. In the China of today, elements of the past are evident. The instruments and methods fashioned in the old medieval Empire are being used in ill-will. All this strengthens the need for Marxist historians to study the feudal relationships, as a current and important task.

THEORIES AND REALITIES

Following the usual pattern of a basic statement followed by amplificatory contributions, the 'keynote' paper by L. V. Simonovskaya was followed by an informatory essay by G. Ya. Smolin (one of those incidentally criticised by Simonovskaya in the foregoing). He emphasised the close connection these studies, at first glance theoretical and remote, really have with present-day practicalities. (The rising Soviet generation does broadly prefer to head for the technical or applied professions – engineering, etc. – partly on such grounds of 'practicality', including the material rewards, partly to avoid the 'politicalisation' inherent in work in the USSR in the social sciences.) Soviet studies in this sphere have had 'the stamp of actuality', from the earliest [170], published in 1935) to the latest (e.g. [274], appearing in 1970, and a symposium in 1971 on *Secret Societies* in Old China). The question is now still more 'actual', because the Maoists and the bourgeois are using all the medieval survivals in present-day China 'for their own definite purposes', apparently in a worldwide conspiracy, which the Soviet Marxists must expose and defeat.

Smolin considered that the first steps were taken, in the field of civil history and in the vein of 'historico-philological' work, in the mid-1950s, when there had been notable interest in the ancient history, but it was perceived that medieval history was the 'missing link'. Research is still not specialised in terms of medievalism as such, various aspects are taken in combination; but Soviet works are beginning to appear 'on the world market' in foreign periodicals, etc. Courses and seminars in the USSR, general and specialised, are beginning to give medieval China its due place in the curriculum. The Soviet publications of the last fifteen years had, however, been of a 'general outline' character. Most readers have relied on the relevant articles in the *Greater* and *Lesser Soviet Encyclopaedias* or other overall references (notably 'Peoples of East Asia'); but in the last few years there has been progress, with the appearance of monographs on the agrarian structure, towns, handicraft and trade, the class-struggle, 'contradictions' within the ruling class, foreign relations and wars. Smolin then presented a lengthy bibliography, which, it is interesting to note, begins especially with the period of the tenth to thirteenth centuries. This section may be summarised as follows.

Agrarian relations and the lower classes : Smolin.

Towns, crafts and commerce : Stuzhina.

Political, ideological and reform questions : Lapina.

Military history : S. A. Shkolyar.

Literature and arts : Serebryakov, T. A. Postrelova, K. F. Samosyuk.

Economic and general, of the Sung period : A. I. Ivanov, K. K. Flug, V. M. Shtein.

Nationalities : on the Tanguts and their Hsia State, E. I. Kychanov, who continued the work of N. A. Nevski; on the Jurchen, M. V. Vorob'yev and I. V. Ivochkina; on the Kitan, L. I. Duman, V. S. Starikov and V. S. Taskin.

Smolin takes primarily this period of the tenth to thirteenth centuries, he says, because it is drawing much attention in sinological work in other countries : he specifies 'Japan, France, the USA, East Germany, Hungary and others', in that order. Some countries have special centres for 'Sung studies, etc.' This is 'not accidental', as the period is a key one. Smolin opined that a comprehensive and definitive symposium ought to be held on this period, interrelating especially the economic and the cultural aspects, to make a real 'organisational beginning', as 'meanwhile the co-operation of the Leningrad and Moscow sinologues is semi-elementary and patchwork'.

On the two next periods, a lesser 'beginning' had been made, according to Smolin : the Mongol [326–8, 74] and the Ming [488, 482–3, 67]. For other periods, for example the Sui and T'ang (seventh to ninth centuries), Soviet work is 'extremely weak, not to say non-existent'; though this is a 'vital' period, and one that is given 'immeasurably greater attention both in the West and in Japan'. This shows the danger of dealing with selected periods, in isolation.

The early middle ages are especially deserving of attention. On this there have been only a pre-war article by I. I. Belyakevich on 'The Three Kingdoms and the Western Ch'in' (third century and early fourth) – not traced by the present writer – some work by Duman [112], articles on the Toba Wei, Tyurin's materials on the exploitation of the peasants in the third to eighth centuries, and the like. In sum, 'no forward step has been taken in the 1960s in resolving the complicated questions of the genesis of feudalism in China . . . [though] such questions are focal' for Soviet historians. Agrarian changes in the early centuries of the feudal epoch, the rise and consolidation of various forms of feudal property in land, forms of rent, the evolution of rural and urban communities, State and legal institutions, together with numerous other aspects, have all to be comprised in a consolidated study.

It would be necessary to draw also on Soviet experts' knowledge of Byzantium, of Russian antiquity and other areas, as well as of other Asian countries. The Chinese variant of feudalism must be studied in the light of comparisons with the West and other regions. (The reader will be well aware that most Western historians do not believe that there was ever a feudal system, in this sense of the term, in China; Japan is the only country in Asia, in the view of most people, that passed through a phase thus defined.) 'It is known', said Smolin, however, 'that among scholars who are specialists in studies of the West there is now a clear understanding that questions of the genesis of feudalism cannot

be resolved by considering facts from the history of Europe alone, without using material from other continents. A desire for comparative historical research . . . can be traced in the documents of the international congress of historians held in 1970 in the Soviet Union.'
In the Soviet Union the issue hung to some extent on the debates about the 'Asiatic mode of production'. 'Symptomatic' was the article in 1965 by A. Ya. Shevelenko, a specialist on Frankish Gaul, entitled 'A Comparison of the Ways in which Feudalism Originated in France and in Indonesia', but 'Shevelenko, or any other among his Occidentalist colleagues, could hardly find at the present day sufficient *points d'appui* in our sinological literature for identifying the similarities or dissimilarities in the origins of feudalism in China and in any of its European variants'. Not to speak of other Oriental countries. 'The whole Orient also presents heterogeneous specific forms of such processes in various States and regions.' Nevertheless, it would be useful to try immediately to make some comparative studies. (The Western literature is not mentioned in this connection. It is far from deficient in comparisons; one thinks for example of the work of Wolfram Eberhard.)

SHORTCOMINGS OF SOVIET HISTORIOGRAPHY

Smolin commented that in recent years Soviet scholars had reached agreement as to the dating of the beginning of the feudal era, the 'watershed' separating it from 'antiquity'; the once burning disputes on this have recently subsided. 'But this calm is . . . illusory.' The question can only be clarified by further and deeper investigation. What does seem to be agreed is that the delimitation between 'the first and second stages – the earlier medieval and the developed feudalism – is the eighth century'.
It is warmly debated, however, whether the threshold of the 'late middle ages' lies in the sixteenth or the eighteenth century; and 'in just the same way, [Soviet] sinological historians have still not confirmed the opinion that the upper limit, the completion of the medieval, dividing it from modern times is located at the turn of the eighteenth and nineteenth centuries'. Clearly the basis of periodisation by dynasties has been rejected in principle, yet had often to be retained in practice because it is traditionally im-

planted, the basic materials and references are in the succession of reigns and, last but not least, the cyclical nature of the historical processes in China is distinctly correlated with the succession of dynasties. The concept of successive cycles of rise, maturity, decline and fall is basic to Marxist historicism. For China, it is exhibited in a series of twenty-four dynasties, each in turn following such a life-cycle or Gomperts curve. Marxism must, however, postulate as the fundamental and underlying 'cyclicality' the complex and 'dialectical' rise and decline of economic systems.

Considerable ingenuity – sometimes mixed with Procrustean ruthlessness – is devoted to tracing the correlation or interplay of the socio-economic fluctuations with the politico-dynastic alternations. Smolin considers 'it is entirely correct' to take the dynastic chronology 'not merely as a datum of historiographic tradition, but as giving internal landmarks' connecting general basic processes with particular events. 'It is true that none of our [Soviet] colleagues in the study of literature, of the history of socio-economic thought, of philosophy and art have fully renounced the absolution of the dynastic principle, sometimes basing themselves in part, without any reservations, as they have always done before, on this criterion. Meanwhile specific works have [however] shown that . . . in [the study of] the history of the spiritual culture' it is sometimes 'productive' to depart from the dynastic demarcations.

A central theme is class-struggle and 'people's liberation' movements; much effort is directed to identifying 'the strong and weak sides' of such movements. Those which have long interested historians are such as the peasant wars in the first half of the seventeenth century led by Li Tzu-ch'eng (L. V. Simonovskaya was the accredited expert on this) and the so-called 'Red Troops movement' ('Red Turbans') of the mid-fourteenth century (L. A. Borovkova). (The complex history of these matters cannot be gone into here, the present purpose being simply to present the self-assessment of the Soviet academic authorities; for a most useful commentary, see J. P. Harrison, *The Communists and Chinese Peasant Rebellions*, 1970.)

Yet Smolin noted that in this sphere also there were 'many blank spots'. The peasant war of the seventeenth century is being studied, but still at the level of finding source-materials (V. G. Doronin). Leningrad University had just initiated a main work on the revolt led by Huang Ch'ao in 874–901 [*sic*]. Studies are also noted of the earlier rebellions of the 'Yellow Turbans' and of Tou Chien-te's activities in the years 610–24. Strife began much earlier and went on much longer in China than in Europe. Soviet scholars are instructed to consider smaller-scale happenings as well as the above-mentioned major revolts that were strong enough to overthrow a dynasty. The national minorities of China deserve greater attention; there is only an 'incomplete picture, engendering many contradictions and errors' in the Soviet work in that field.

On the whole, concluded Smolin (PSS, p. 115), Soviet work on medieval China was proceeding 'more slowly than was desired and desirable', with reference especially to certain specific problems identified by the work of Svistunova, Nepomnin [334], Delyusin [104] and others. A historian of India [32] had shown the way to effective use of comparative studies, as had various works of general history and university texts [311, 314]. Work was still developing on original materials (e.g. those from the Tun huang caves kept at Leningrad University). Leningrad University produced a 'recapitulory' collection of articles in 1969 under the title *Historiography of the Countries of the Orient* which focused on the social and economic history of feudalism, and a wider collection, on Africa as well as Asia (2 vols, 1972, to be continued).

The staffing at Moscow and Leningrad is, however, 'modest'. More labour-power is required in this field : a project was being 'pushed', hopefully as a means of obtaining more backing, to write a major collective work on China on the lines of the *History of India in the Middle Ages* which appeared in 1968. The situation-report is thus broadly the same for medieval studies as for other branches of sinology : much done, much more to be done, many definitional and chronic problems, last but not least the pressing need to expose and frustrate the distortions and heresies of Maoism, which is in unholy alliance with Western and bourgeois thought.

6 Ancient China

While the spotlight is on the present-day problems of China, it is clear that every aspect of the country's life and thought is still dominated by concepts and institutions peculiar to that country, which come from the very beginnings of its unique civilisation.

DEEP ROOTS OF HAN CHAUVINISM

L. S. Perelomov (PSS, pp. 83–99) summarises the Soviet work on Ancient China. That immensely long period, from Peking Man (400,000–500,000 B.C.) to the fall of the Han Empire (first half of the ninth century A.D.), certainly made the mould in which China was lastingly formed. It is 'not accidental' that China studies in the West start with prehistory and are closely based on the classical origins of Chinese civilisation [55]. Soviet sinology, however, has only 'in recent years' acknowledged the 'actuality' of this distant past: frankly, as a result of 'the white-hot irreconcilable ideological struggle we are waging with the Maoists'. The latter have revived the chauvinism of the Han 'on the basis of two Leviathans: the great number of people in China and the great length of the country's history'.

Thus the first all-China congress of historians held in the CPR, in March 1959, laid down the principles that China is unique and has a special mission in the world. Chou Yang, then Deputy Director of the CPC's Propaganda Department, stressed that nowhere else was there such a long continuous development. Kuo Mo-jo, President of the Chinese Academy of Sciences, underlined this with the claim that 'in the history of the world China alone had followed so long a path from primitive communism to socialism. We are happy that we are Chinese.'

These utterances were in closed session, but the press proclaimed the same sentiments. Examples of the statements that angered the Russian Communists are that the cultures of the feudal epoch in other countries 'are not in any way to be compared' with the brilliant three-thousand-year-long history of China (*Lishih Yenchu*, 1960, no. 5) and that 'China was the first country in the world to attain a feudal society, eight or nine hundred years earlier than the States of Europe, sixteen or seventeen hundred years if we include the Western Chou as feudalism' (*Kuangming Daily*, 10 April 1961). Chinese feudalism, the last-quoted passage continues, was 'the splendid model, with which European feudalism is not to be compared'. The Soviets are shocked that feudalism should be described as splendid, and consider comparative studies an essential part of Marxist technique. However, they are somewhat literal-minded in bandying quotations verbatim, not allowing sufficiently for the more figurative Chinese way of speaking and writing.

Perelomov notes that the work of the Soviet historians greatly increased in 1961–71, in face of the great increase in Maoist 'falsifications'; especially 'after the notorious "Great Proletarian Cultural Revolution", all serious research disappeared' in China. 'A succession of the Fatherland's [the Soviet Union's] sinologues' – listed in order of seniority as 'Academicians V. M. Alexeyev and N. I. Konrad, Corresponding Member of the Academy N. T. Fedorenko, Yu. K. Shutski, A. A. Shtukin, A. A. Petrov, V. M. Shtein, L. V. Simonovskaya and L. I. Duman – coped with the task, under five headings.

The first was the genesis of Chinese civilisation. This is 'one of the most complex and least studied problems, on which monographic treatments are still lacking in Soviet sinology'. However, two 'firm concepts' emerged, one from L. S. Vasil'iev, one from M. V. Kryukov. 'A long-standing dispute in worldwide sinology concerns the indigenousness of Chinese culture : can the history of China start directly with Peking Man or should one, considering the great influence in the most ancient times of components from the West, begin with the inception of the Yangshao culture, i.e. 4000–3000 B.C. ? The racial diagnosis of the remains of the late-Palaeolithic people who inhabited North China, also the ethnic attributes of the bearers of the culture who directly preceded Yangshao, are matters still in dispute.'

'Vasil'iev, following F. Weidenreich, considers that the Shang-tintun people (50,000–25,000 BC), who had Negro-Australoid and even Europoid characteristics, could not have been the direct predecessors of the Chinese.' Vasil'iev himself stated that 'only the bearers of the late-Palaeolithic culture of Yangshao, whose anthropological type may be called "proto-Chinese", can be considered indubitable ancestors of the Chinese, as the proto-Chinese. . . . Despite excavations on a gigantic scale – just in the last 12–14 years about 2000–3000 Neolithic sites have been opened – even so, the Chinese archaeologists have not been able to discover relics of a culture that could be considered as preparatory to the appearance of the Yangshao' (*Peoples of Asia and Africa*, 1964, no. 2).

He postulates major migrations in which a highly developed agricultural people brought decorated ceramics from Iran through Central Asia to the territory that is now China, in the fourth and third millennia BC. They mixed with the local pre-agricultural mongoloid tribes, then passed through the Kansu corridor to reach the fertile Hoangho basin, where they settled. 'A definite ethnic type, from that amalgamation, influenced the formation of the Yangshao culture.'

Kryukov, on the other hand, believes the Yangshao culture to have originated on the spot. Considering Weidenreich's descriptions of the Shangtintun skulls, Kryukov noted that Weidenreich had not properly classified these objects : he compared them with contemporary specimens, moreover with a partial range of the latter, of Mongoloid types taken from a limited geographical purview (Eskimos and Melanesians). Kryukov held that they represented a period in the development of the Mongoloids when many of the characteristics of that great race had not yet been formed. The Shangtintun skulls have some 'Pacific' (south-eastern) Mongoloid characteristics, which later spread among the populations of China, Korea and Japan : namely high crania (130–150 mm), alveolar prognathism and a tendency to platyrrhinism (or, in plain English, they had long heads, protruding jaws and broad noses).

The painted pottery appeared independently, he considers, in Europe and Asia in the foothill and steppe strips of an agriculture based on the hoe. The relative time-sequence, in his view, disproves the theory of a Western origin; in the area where the Mach'iao (the nearest culture to the West) and Yangshao relics are found together, the former are the overlay, the upper layers.

The movement was not eastwards but westwards. Moreover the

skulls in question are similar to those of present-day Northern Chinese. The divergence of views between these two schools of thought has not, however, been 'antagonistic'. Kryukov, while holding firmly that the pure nucleus was thus formed within China, agrees that subsequently (but still in early antiquity) the Chinese people were strongly influenced by the 'economic and cultural achievements of the peoples of Central Asia'. It was 'a process of mutual influence and mutual enrichment'.

ASIATIC MODES OF PRODUCTION

Perelomov's second heading is 'the formation of the appurtenances of Chinese society', i.e. the socio-economic relations within it, which are deemed to account for its retarded development. Soviet work on this topic is extensive and varied. Up to the end of the 1930s there were three 'conceptions'. L. I. Mad'yar, M. D. Kokin and G. K. Papayan held to 'the Asiatic mode of production' in the Marxian formula. The concept of M. P. Zhakov and E. S. Iolk is termed a 'feudal' one, that of G. A. Safarov and A. G. Prigozhin a 'feudal-slaveowning' one. A useful review of these was published in 1970 by V. N. Nikiforov [342].

In the 1940s and 1950s it was the last-named definition, 'feudal-slaveowning', that 'came out victorious' in the Soviet Union. The orginal author of this conception was V. V. Struve, who drew it from Near Eastern, not Chinese, evidence. L. I. Duman, L. V. Simonovskaya, N. I. Konrad and T. V. Stepugina adhered to this concept as definitive for China up to the third century A.D. In the 1950s and 1960s 'concrete investigations were made of the role and the specific nature of slavery in Ancient China at various stages in its development'. A massive *World History* was published (in Chinese as well as Russian) in ten volumes in 1955 [529] in which Duman and Stepugina contributed the sections on China. The former believed that the Yin–Shang State in its rise, from the fourteenth to the eleventh centuries B.C., retained vestiges of 'racial-tribal warrior democracy', but the further development of the State organisation led to the rise of traits of despotism : the kings acquired all the power. The basic classes in the Yin were slaveowners, slaves and free 'members of the community' (*Obshchinniki*).

The slaveowners included the temporal aristocracy, the priestly nobility and the aristocracies of subjugated tribes. Duman opined that the basic producers of agricultural wealth were the free members of the community, though slavery played an ever-increasing part. He has the same interpretation regarding the Western Chou. T. V. Stepugina, in her analysis of the social evolution in the fifth century B.C. to the third century A.D., stressed the situation of the free cultivators who, as a result of the development of commodity and monetary relations and the growth of large landed properties, were ruined and became slaves or 'hireling tenants'. In the Ch'in and Han periods the slaves worked mainly in the sphere of handicrafts, though slave labour was increasingly applied in agriculture too; with reference especially to the second and first centuries B.C., such a development could not have occurred if the basis was feudal. Feudalism developed in connection with the rise of a 'natural' economy (in the Marxian term, i.e. payments in kind), the appearance of dependent or partly dependent farmers of the *bin ke* and *pu tsui* types, the spread of *métayage* and 'rent-bondage'. All this happened during the second and third centuries A.D.

The publication of the *World History* made Soviet sinologues realise the need to look in close detail at processes, to take 'deep cuts for microscopic examination'. Not all of Duman's work has been published, notes Perelomov. Duman's examination of numerous inscriptions on bones and tortoise-shells led him to five main conclusions :

1. Slaves were mainly prisoners of war taken (as part of the live-stock) from various conquered tribes. Chou sources indicate that criminals were also enslaved; and the Yin kings (*wang*) and nobles received slaves as gifts from dependent tribes.
2. This class was numerous and employed in various occupations : as hunters or herdsmen, in some part as warriors or craftsmen.
3. Thus they were not merely domestic servants, they were so much the basis of the Yin economy that, even though agriculture was based on local communities of freemen, this may be classified as a slaveowning society.
4. Though limited from above by the conditions of Oriental despotism and from below by those of agrarian communalism, which kept it in an early stage of development,

this slave system advanced considerably above the level of 'primitive domestic slavery'.

5. Besides the princes' State slaves there were certainly private persons' slaves, but the latter were also under the princes' power. There is no evidence of the purchase, sale or pledging of slaves, or of their being paid wages by the representatives of the nobles [110].

In 1961 L. S. Vasil'iev produced what is now proclaimed to be the first correct evaluation of the evolution of 'the basic social cell, the *obshchina*' in the Chinese setting, i.e. the community, or communal unit [517]. This is another instance of special semantic differences in the Russian terminology. The root of the word, *obshch*-, suggests 'general' or 'public' (ownership or participation); it might indeed closely parallel the contemporary Chinese word for a commune, *kung she*. Vasil'iev found the primitive communal unit to have evolved from a consanguinity grouping to a rural neighbourhood one with family landholdings. He considers the formation of classes to have come later than Duman postulates, namely in about the ninth century B.C., as he finds kinship communities prevailed in the Yin period and territorial ones were lacking.

He acknowledges the existence of two opposing classes in the Chou period – peasant communards and a class of possessors of land and slaves consisting of patrimonial nobles and officials – but leaves the matter somewhat open. 'If', he wrote [517], 'we take the basic relations to be those between the community and its exploiters, the conclusion is that this was early feudalism. But if we consider this society only from the point of view of its tendency to develop slavery, by comparisons with other relevant Oriental societies we may conclude that it was an early slaveholding, patriarchal, slaveowning society. There may be some truth in each of these definitions.'

In 1962 Perelomov's monograph on *The Empire of Ch'in: The First Centralised State in China* [369] examined the agrarian relations, the forms of property and the various modes of exploitation, particularly to reject his previously held notion that the prehistoric communes were feudal. There were communities as collectives of landowners who were free persons; they included both free workers and slaveowners, as members of the communities. A considerable part of the produce came from the free members, but as the slaveowning economy grew, more slaves were used in all spheres of production – agriculture, industry (chiefly iron mining and smelting) and trade. A slave-trade then developed in the Ch'in Empire, and the free citizens were under increasing pressure, especially in the civil wars of 209–202 B.C. when the effectives consisted of both slaves and freemen fighting against the system that exploited them, especially against enslavement by the State. The largest and most effective rebel armies consisted mainly of State slaves. The Soviet writers note that the Chinese historians 'always consider this to have been the first peasant rising'.

In 1966 Academician Konrad contributed a short article, in a collection which he himself edited called *The Orient and the Occident*, on the nature of productive relations in Ancient China. Making wide comparisons across the two hemispheres, he found three eras or stages of slavery :

1. A formative period (eleventh to eighth centuries B.C.), in the Chou a combination of semi-patriarchal and semi-slave-owning States of various sizes.
2. Consolidation and development of the slave system (eighth to third centuries B.C).
3. Its climax and decline (second century B.C. to third century A.D.).

Konrad asserted that 'not slavery as such, but the social structure in which slave labour is the means of production, defines the economic basis of communal living in that period'.

These leads were not sufficiently followed up, it is now asserted – with some benefit of hindsight. 'Concrete studies should have been made of the evolution in the lower strata of social organisation : kindreds, communities and families in the earliest stage, the Yin and the Chou. Those who postulate the early development of class relationships in China affirm that there were small individual families and agrarian communes as early as the Yin period; those who think classes developed later assert the associations were on a wider kinship basis.' In 1967 Kryukov [262] found in the Spring and Autumn period the 'skeleton' of the Yin–Chou society – 'not a patriarchal but a patronymic system . . . an exogamous group of hierarchically subordinated families, connected by descent from a common ancestor'.

Kryukov recognises differences of wealth and social position in the Yin–Chou, but does not deem it to have been a class society, 'only a transitional stage' towards one. A class society would show some historical succession of methods of production in some 'antagonism' to each other. Yu. V. Kachanovski discussed these questions further in his *Slaveowning, Feudalism or Asiatic Mode of Production?* (1971) on the broader basis of Marxist theory. 'It is extremely significant,' notes Perelomov (PSS, p. 93), 'that none of the Soviet antiquarians dealing with China were entirely in support of the [concept of the] Asiatic mode of production. Vasil'iev adhered only partly to it', though 'many . . . both among ourselves and abroad turned to the ancient history of China in search of a concrete embodiment of the Asiatic mode of production'. 'Otherwise', he comments, they 'would have had to deny the fact that private landownership was widespread, i.e. to deny our real achievements in the 1960s, which would not have been easy to do.'

Meanwhile Vasil'iev came forward with more exact formulations of his views. He posited a 'secondary pre-capitalist formation' with two components, a slaveowning and a feudal. The considerable fuss which had suddenly arisen about the Asiatic mode of production induced two authoritative contributors, basically specialists in recent history, to come out with works in this field. 'V. N. Nikiforov', as Perelomov expresses it, 'adopted the slaveowning conception, unselfishly defending it from the attacks of the time; while we found in V. P. Ilyushechkin an active opponent of [that] concept. Thus, in Soviet sinology today there are somewhat differing conceptions: "the slaveowning one" (Konrad, Simonovskaya, Duman, Stepugina, Perelomov and Nikiforov), the concept of the "late ripening of class relationships" in Ancient China (Yin–Chou) with a tendency to develop towards feudalism (Kryukov) and the "slaveowning (cum) feudal" view of Vasil'iev and Ilyushechkin.' It is to be noted that 'even among the proponents of one or the other concept there are sometimes differences of opinion concerning the degree of development in one period or another, especially regarding the Yin–Western Chou epoch. Is the state of study of this problem at any higher level now than it was in the 1930s, and what are the future prospects?'

In answer, the following points may be made. Information and understanding of the social structure in Ancient China were en-

larged by a considerable amount of new material. Professed
Marxists could, however, not draw much comfort from the broad
failure to achieve any close confirmation of basic propositions
such as the Asiatic mode of production in particular or the class-
struggle as the determinant 'dynamic' of human evolution in
general. In Perelomov's judgement the discussions 'showed un-
certainty regarding a whole row of problems of the general theory
of pre-capitalist forms. In our [Soviet] historical science there are
diverse theoretical definitions of the laws governing slave and
feudal formations. The complexity deepens when slaveowning
and feudalism are found to have much in common.'

POWER AND IDEOLOGY

Of more interest to non-Marxist observers are the evidence and
interpretation of the nature of political power in Ancient China.
The Soviet scholars approach this from such points of view as
identifying what was 'the supreme property in land', its ultimate
ownership, which is 'one of the cardinal questions strictly related
to the configuration' of the original Chinese society; but confess
that 'this question too has not been decisively settled'. L. S.
Vasil'iev, like the proponents of 'the Asiatic mode of production',
bases his argument firmly on the concept of (the ruler's) 'supreme
landownership'; while his opponents, I. M. D'yakonov and L. S.
Perelomov, hold that no ancient State or Emperor, in China or
elsewhere, had the whole territory as its, or his, property. As early
as the 1940s the eminent Soviet jurist Academician A. V. Vene-
diktov had criticised V. V. Struve and others for not distinguish-
ing clearly between 'supreme ownership by the State of the land'
and 'State supremacy over the whole territory of the State'. The
believers in 'supreme landownership' do not consider that payment of taxes to the State by the people of the communities is
evidence that the latter were dependent feudally or as serfs.

These discussions, too, reached no finality. The PSS report in
1973 calls for another pan-Soviet academic conference to discuss
problems of pre-capitalist societies in general and establish some
common understanding on them. Perelomov states, on this, that
'the situation would be much easier and simpler if the advocates
of the various tendencies would follow the "gentlemanly rules of
the game" [*sic*]. The supporters of the slaveowning interpretation

often observed that their opponents treated [the matter] one-sidedly, enlarging on the features of the lands of "classical" slavery, Rome and Greece; which are an exception, an optimal variant, the limit to which the tendency leads' [519, p. 32]. For slave-owning to develop, there must be a combination of private land-owners eroding the free community and enslaving its freemen. Then the society is not slaveowning in its nature, it is fundamentally communal, though increasingly eroded by slavery.

Vasil'iev, dealing with the so-called second and third stages of Chinese history (the third century B.C. to the second A.D. and the third to sixth centuries A.D. respectively), detected no difference in principle in the situation of the immediate producer, in the forms of property in land. The same features continued through the third period and the slave system of production developed further, yet all the Soviet historians call the third stage 'feudal' [519, p. 114]. It was indeed feudal, but it differed quantitatively from the preceding second stage because the free commune of private land-owners was replaced by the commune of partly dependent peasants who had little or no land.

Vasil'iev also considers that the scale of private landownership should not be exaggerated. He is accused by Perelomov of ignoring (in [518] pp. 455–515) the 'mass enslavement of the members of the communities' (PSS, p. 95) by the Shang Yang reform which was the first great piece of legislation extending the scale of both State and private ownership of slaves. For the 'slaveowning' school, Kryukov acknowledges the importance of that event, but Vasil'iev does not mention it. This is adduced as another example of the need for closer intellectual co-operation based on much more comprehensive research into all the main tendencies, of which the evolution of landed property is an important one, from the point of view of Soviet sinology, especially for the Han epoch when qualitatively new forms of private exploitation arose in agriculture.

Having thus dealt with the origins of Chinese civilisation and the society in which it was first embodied, the PSS conference prescribed as the next heading the classical-political thought of Ancient China. These ancestral doctrines were indeed formative, continuing to dominate the Chinese thinking until the twentieth century. They took shape in the sixth to the third centuries B.C., the Golden Age of Chinese philosophy. Until the 1960s this was hardly a fashionable field of study in the Soviet Union. There was only one notable work in all those years – Radul'-Zatulovski's which was published in 1947 [399] – and in fact that book dealt mainly with Confucianism in Japan, though it was a masterly study of the cult as such.

In no sphere, however, have recent political vicissitudes induced a swifter and more urgent change of attitude than in this one. Perelomov opined at the PSS conference that there had been 'some underestimation' of the importance of the part played by ideology in the formation of China : 'We have paid too much attention to morphology, to the fivefold schema of development, when the life and political events in the CPR were demanding from us an answer to the questions : what is Confucianism? what part has it played in the history of China? how strongly has Confucianism influenced the formation of Maoist doctrine? or the ethno- and socio-psychology of the Chinese?'

Only in very recent years has this neglect begun to be remedied. A general account of the several schools was provided in 1966 by F. S. Bykov, whose book [87] – drawing widely on recent Western, Japanese and Chinese works [87] – traced the origin and development of the classical thought. L. S. Vasil'iev added to his laurels in 1970 with a more analytical treatise [520] going especially into the fundamentals of Confucianism, Legalism, Taoism and Buddhism; this, too, drew freely on recent non-Russian studies. By the later 1960s Soviet scientists, technicians and scholars were able to draw more explicitly than their predecessors on foreign work and thought.

There are three other contributors worthy of special mention. M. L. Titarenko, similarly of recent emergence, deals especially with Mo Tse and his posterity. He adduces a concept of 'contractual' derivation of power – a social contract – in Mo Tse, and discusses the social basis of the latter's opposition to Confucianism [502–3]. V. F. Feoktistov, even more of a newcomer, takes a more generally current political line but illuminates it with reference to classical Chinese philosophy [125–7]. He interprets Hsün Tse as 'justifying class-differentiation in Chinese society'. This is a 'correct' view, according to the Soviet authorities in 1972. Hsün Tse 'led Confucianism into just such a political blind-alley as did Mencius'. L. S. Perelomov has interested himself very prominently in this direction. His recent works [368–70] stress the basic political and economic theories of the Legalists and their influence on the formation of the Chinese State in the Ch'in and Han periods. The next, fourth, heading in the PSS action-list concerning Ancient China is the foreign relations of the first Chinese State. Here again, Perelomov as spokesman admits 'that until the 1960s we knew too little about the internal structure of the first Chinese empires'; though 'indeed it was precisely in the Ch'in and Han that many institutions took shape (social mobility, the censorship, the mutual guarantee [system], ranking, State monopolies, etc.) which stabilised the bureaucratic mechanism of power'. Perelomov had studied these particularly in 1962 [369], but more was required. The Oriental Institute of the Academy of Sciences (IVAN) held annual conferences on 'Society and State in China' from 1968 onwards at which 'numerous interesting contributions were made on the role of the bureaucracy, its place in society, the processes of legislation, on secrecy' and the evolution of doctrines concerning foreign policy.

This last subject is the cue for recalling the Soviet readership's attention to the *bête jaune* of current politics : 'The events of the last few years forced us to concern ourselves especially with the analysis of the foreign-policy doctrines of Imperial China and its relations with the neighbouring peoples. IVAN published in 1970 a symposium on *China and Her Neighbours (in Ancient Times and the Middle Ages)*', by the Moscow and Leningrad sinologists S. L. Tikhvinski, L. I. Duman, L. S. Perelomov, I. N. Machkina, P. Sh. Dzharylgasimova, A. A. Bokshchanin, N. P. Svistunova, A. S. Martynov and G. V. Melikov, who were praised for 'exposing the sources of the great-power tradition in Chinese diplomacy, showing that many of the so-called "territories subject to China" were only nominally so; this applies to ancient Vietnam and ancient Korea, and even in the period of actual vassalage the Chinese influence embraced only the centres – in the localities there functioned a national administration'.

PRACTICAL DIFFICULTIES

The fifth and final heading in this section assesses the work of translation. In that respect the Russian heritage is noteworthy : in the earlier Soviet period, the principal translators of Chinese classical works were Yu. K. Shutski, A. A. Shtukin, N. I. Konrad and Yan Khin-shun (Yang Hsing-shun). In the 1960s Pozdneyeva produced her Chuang Tse [389] and Perelomov his Legalist classic [370]. In 1970 Krol' produced a study of Ssu-ma Ch'ien [256] with extensive direct citations; in 1972 Taskin and Vyatkin furnished the actual text of the *Historical Record* [478].

Once again, it is stressed that it is not a matter of mere antiquarian interest : 'It is evidently desirable to continue this work, to promote deeper understanding of the State institutions and political theories which are now rising again in the CPR : above all Confucianism, Legalism and those traditional appurtenances of Chinese statehood that have enabled the consolidation of an authoritarian bureaucratic regime.'

At the PSS conference such current Chinese statements as the following were particularly cited. The *Kuangming Daily* of 27 August 1971 proclaimed a 'new course' in Chinese historiography – to utilise antiquity for the sake of our own day'. 'So', said the main speaker at the meeting in Moscow, 'we may expect further falsifications of ancient history in justification of Mao's "General Line". . . .' Other examples related to the Maoists' use of Confucian and Mencian concepts for the critique of the *Black Book on the Self-Education of a Communist* and other contemporary tracts. The Soviet Union especially needed a translation of the Analects of Confucius – 'nothing can give such understanding as the text itself'.

In sum, the insistence on counter-attack against Maoism is as prominent in this field as in any other. For the rest, Soviet work on Ancient China appears generally scrappy in comparison with the more impressive output in the rest of the world, though in recent years it has been drawing on the international stock of knowledge and ideas in this domain, and has acquired momentum of its own. The Soviet colleagues are, however, much bound up with Marxian concepts that seem obscure and not very illuminating to Western scholars. Marx and Engels have long been dead (since 1883 and 1895 respectively) and their contribution to social anthropology was never the most brilliant part of their work; harking back to that contribution, or just to its terminology, the Soviet discussants isolate themselves from the general current of worldwide thought.

The main strife is, however, between the two Communist powers, Russia and China; that is where the 'contradictions' are most 'antagonistic', while each of them seems to be compacting in its own way with the capitalist rest of the world. Meanwhile, archaeological excavation and study have developed prodigiously in China – witness the exhibition in London at the end of 1973 – and the paradoxical situation is developing that new knowledge or understanding from China itself may mainly reach the Soviet Union via the 'enemy camp', the West, or through useful entrepôts such as Hong Kong, which it is in everybody's interest to maintain.

In so far as the crux is a doctrinaire dispute within Marxism, the ancient heritage of China is certainly skeletal and arterial to the body politic of that nation; the Soviet side would make a 'kill' if it could prove that Mao is some Frankenstein who has reanimated this gigantic corpse of the East Asian Methuselah to use, like some huge zombie, for his own nefarious purposes. The odds seem, however, to be against this being proved, at any rate on the academic plane; the Soviet side has been at this for only a decade or so, the Chinese for some centuries. The Chinese effectives are similarly more numerous than the Russians in this field – and the Chinese have full control over the supply of evidence at its source.

The Soviets must fall back on the conviction that 'thrice armed is he who has his quarrel just' and his doctrine sound – or perhaps on the more material reassurance that, at least at present, the USSR is also 'thrice armed' (in relation especially to China), in terms of modern weapons. The present writer would, however, consider *per contra* (on the academic planes) that the above reasoning may be too quantitative; in the *rafale* of literature and assertions, now massive but of generally low quality, one judicious and well-aimed shot may strike home where thousands of others fall wide. In the verbal warfare, the Soviets' salvoes are less hysterical and bombastic than the Maoists'; moreover, they have at present better access to Western work in this field and are more attuned to understanding it and using it.

7 The Chinese Economy

G. V. Astaf'iev introduced the Economics section of the PSS with reference to 'the necessity for fighting Maoism', beginning with the identification of the 'objective and subjective factors' in China's long and complicated transition from feudalism through capitalism to socialism. 'The key is economic history', in which there is much good Soviet work [104, 334, 220]. The second sphere of inquiry in the USSR concerns the economic views of Mao himself [419, 415]. The inconsistency of Mao's views with Marxism must be demonstrated. This should be backed by deep study of his predecessors and intellectual antecedents, on which less has been done [462, 464, 491–7].

There is need for work on the views of the Kuomintang, of Ch'en Li-fu, 'also the bourgeois economists within the CPR (Ma Yin-ch'u and others)' with special reference to notions of China being able to lift herself by her own bootstraps. The next heading is the periodisation of Chinese economic history; most Soviet works are limited to consideration of specific features of particular periods ('Great Leap', 'Rectification', 'Cultural Revolution', etc.) or go by the swings of policy rather than the changes in the national foundations.

'We have', notes Astaf'iev with italics to emphasise, 'more or less full views about the socio-economic structure of the CPR, but an insufficiently concrete perception of the tendencies of development of the various classes and strata (especially the working class, the national bourgeoisie and the intelligentsia; the peasants are a little better studied).' Soviet institutions must specialise on these, with a 'division of labour' between them. 'There are divergent views' concerning the nature of socialism in China, which further study must clarify, especially the real nature of the production relations in 1957–58 and the effects on these of the subsequent 'perturbations'. Further clarified must be the 'social product and its structure, the social expenditures and reimbursements, the national income, its structure and distribution. . . . But [there is] no study of the process as a whole. The money and natural [barter] sectors of the production process must be studied in parallel.' Data accumulated in recent years on the distribution of industry in China, consisting largely of estimates, must be checked and corrected. 'The problem of the place of China in the socialist world and its [general] international relations is clear from the political point of view but the economic one is not so clear. Especially as the CPR tries to keep a certain balance and maintain an intermediate position'; this is an important area in which political and economic factors merge. 'Close inspection must be made of China's relations, not only with the USA, European countries and Japan, but with some socialist countries.'

The relations between internal pressures and international behaviour are shown by the extremely important population question. This is connected with the problem of technology, and that in turn with education. Technical institutes and industrial Ministries in the USSR must help studies in this field. Econometric methods and forecasting could be developed on the good information available for the base-period 1950–60, sufficient to enable some model of China's economic development to be devised, from which 'normatives' could be deduced. Even the later data, for 1958–70, are sufficient for some useful extrapolations, especially if computer techniques can be applied.

'A two-fold programme is possible : working from general indicators and working from particular indicators in particular sectors – i.e. macroeconomic and microeconomic analysis. All this will require 'the active participation of all our sinologists and economists' to co-ordinate efforts, mount specific collective studies, sequential programmes of conferences, etc., including re-examinations of past work. The IDV is engaged on a four-volume study of the economy of China; it should take the lead in this field, but also collaborate with other institutions. How are these requirements being tackled?

Good Marxism may begin with economic history (and so may good anti-Marxism). In this field the PSS was led by G. D. Sukharchuk, who stated that this subject, 'founded by K. Marx, with his great work *Capital*, is of obvious interest to Marxists but [to the forefront] also in . . . bourgeois . . . capitalist countries'. A 'great and many-sided work' had been conducted by Soviet scholars, but, as in other fields, 'with limited achievements' so that prodigiously more is required, to deepen knowledge and destroy Maoism. There are works on current problems, and works on economic history as such. The former, which also throw light on the latter, date back to the work of Mad'yar at the end of the 1920s [295], E. S. Varga's subsequent work for the Communist International, Maslennikov's 'outline information' just after the Second War [309], through the later contributions of Maslennikov [310] and the earlier excellent work' of Kovalev [253]. Titles specifically on economic history may date from 1950 with a general article by Astaf'iev [34] (published also in Chinese in Peking), continuing much later in a 'new wave' with work in the second half of the 1960s [334, 325].

A confluent group must be mentioned: works on China's foreign relations which refer especially to the economic configuration, by Sladkovski in 1953 [459] and Boldyrev ten years later [68]. The subject was also sustained by translations from the Chinese (Wei Tzu-ch'u's *Imperialist Investments in China, 1902–45*, 1956; Chin Pen-li's *History of American Economic Aggression in China*, 1951). Soviet work expanded in recent years with 'a few tens of articles and symposia': Khokhlov's series on capitalism and manufactures [218], the works of Nepomnin [334], and articles on manufactures by L. N. Novikov, S. M. Iovchuk, and on many subjects by A. Chekhutov and others. The most basic may be those of Sukharchuk, Meliksetov, Chudoyeyev, Mugruzin and Stuzhina.

The PSS congress noted the American efforts for major regional studies, admired their quantitative sweep, but thought Marxists should do better qualitatively (it is not, of course, admitted that the Marxist viewpoint and methodology could be known to or used by Westerners). Soviet scholars should take more interest (as foreigners do) in the Kuomintang period. Meliksetov and Chudoyeyev (with Nepomnin) are now working further on excellent foundations recently laid by Khokhlov and Stuzhina [483], but not yet focusing sufficiently on Kuomintang China. The cause of the lag in this respect, as the spokesman saw it, is noteworthy : 'The establishment of the CPR soon after the war led to our then modest forces [in sinology] being concentrated on the study of the

New China, and on propaganda for it. That was quite natural and correct in the first period of the CPR and in the condition of [the USSR's] successful co-operation with China, when study of the "past", the Kuomintang, seemed hardly necessary.'

Now things have changed, the past is not dead, Mao carries it on; the need is even mentioned in Soviet Russia to study Taiwan, where the period is still that of the Kuomintang, also 'the works of Chiang Kai-shek, Hu Han-min, Wang Ching-wei . . . Hu Shih, Liang Shu-ming' and many others hitherto shunned : 'The roots of the thoughts of Mao', a Soviet speaker said on another occasion, 'spread from every kind of undergrowth'. The economic history of Taiwan, the achievements of Hong Kong and the overseas Chinese in general – who evolved a strong bourgeois class – are also beginning to interest Soviet researchers.

POPULATION PRESSURE

Turning to the characterisation of China's problems at the present day, the greatest single factor in China's economic life is the enormous population; the IDV's estimate at the end of 1973 (verbally to the present writer) was 820 million. This looms large in the whole background of Soviet thinking. Yet no major work has been produced in the USSR on the demography of China; there have been some articles, among which the contributions of Ya. M. Berger and K. N. Chernozhukov are especially noted. A contributor to PSS 1973, E. A. Konovalov, came forward with a paper stressing the need for more scientific examination of the implications. He pointed out that, while the basic information was 'incomplete' and 'fragmentary', there was the census of 1953 (the only modern-style one ever taken in mainland China) and the Soviets had factual information on population movements up to 1958–59. He cited foreign work (Tauber, 1966, and Aird, 1968, in the USA and Nakano, 1968, in Japan). Konovalov then developed his own analysis, as follows.

Changes in the home and foreign policies of China in the 1950s and 1960s are clearly connected with the population problem. 'Extrapolators' see a 'population explosion' that will not only reduce living standards still further but press outwards on the frontiers against neighbouring States. Marxists reject Malthusianism on the one hand and racialism (the 'Yellow Peril' to the 'civilised world') on the other : 'None the less we must turn again and again to the demographic situation for an explanation of the economic difficulties and of the causes of the aggravation of the political conditions in China.'

Most commentators, complains Konovalov, widely pursue all the various implications – strategic, ethical, economic, ethnographic – without sufficient analysis of the intrinsic working of demographic pressure, tending to devote more attention to the symptoms than to the pathology. There is a subjective and an objective side to 'Chinese expansionism'; respectively, the 'Greater Han [Greater China]' feeling and the practical pressure of numbers. 'Some authors proceed from the assumption that sooner or later China will "overflow" its surplus populations across the frontiers, the time when this will occur depending on the rate and scale of population growth and the rate and the way in which economic problems will be solved.'

Konovalov asserts that there are 'many possible ways, possibly dozens of variants' of internal policies for solving the problem of feeding all these people. Basic economic solutions must be selected from these; 'palliatives' are not enough. Optimal use of the human and material sources is the essential : in Western terms, full employment. 'One-sided "stocktaking"', neglect of an integrated approach (e.g. the attempt to combine surplus labour with insufficient equipment) by the simple use of muscular labour, economising as far as possible on the (physical) means of production, will not only be ineffective, it will damage the whole subsequent economic development. On the other hand, remaining 'oblivious to the critical economic conditions, failing to use them adequately – or the reverse, squandering resources – may retard the development of production'.

In China there are some tendencies to make more efficient use of the mass of labour-power, for instance by the application of so-called intermediate technology (not too advanced, not too simple). The vital problem is the combination of modern large-scale production with traditional small-scale production. The use of manual labour is one of the principal problems of China's economic development. Manual labour means low wages and high intensity of work, also that the work is very seasonal and its 'rhythm' irregular, that the markets both for the inputs or purchases (materials) and the outputs or sales (products) are fragmented. Labour costs are large, the wage bill large, little remains over for acquiring equipment and raising productivity. 'Mechanisation of the processes of production, however, permits not only reduction of the expenditure of labour but, because the productivity of labour is raised, also the allocation of the remaining labour to more productive techniques.'

THE SCALE OF INDUSTRY

'In the CPR there have been at some times underestimation of the role of small-scale production and exaggerated construction of gigantic industrial objects, at other times overestimation of the role of small-scale production at the expense of modern industry.' In the former case there was inadequate diversion of the unemployed labour to the two hundred or so large plants (mostly provided by the Soviet Union). Investment was also concentrated on railway construction. When the new facilities came into production (at long term) the difficulties and disproportions grew. Soviet commentators have had much to say about this. In the latter of the two cases (excessive emphasis on small-scale operations and insufficient provision of modern industry) the Chinese proceeded 'with local resources, by hand, slapdash everywhere in every branch of activity [to proliferate] hundreds of thousands of primitive handicraft enterprises, in which it was proposed to employ tens of million of people. It was considered that any degree of inefficiency in production was better than "festive" idleness.'

The actual cost of setting up these 'backyard' plants was not considered; it was borne locally. The costs of raw materials, fuel and transport were duly clicked up on the abacus: anyone could see that such costs were much higher per unit of output than those of modern plants. While 'an extremely high pace and great intensification of the work and premature wearing-out of the equipment brought about the inevitable collapse of the "Great Leap" venture'. In the following period the extent of small-scale production was reduced, many of the 'Great Leap' installations were left derelict.

The Soviet observer does not, of course, consider that something like the Great Leap may have been necessary from the Marxist point of view because the large modern plants referred to had mainly – precisely to the number of the 'two hundred or so' mentioned by Konovalov – been installed on the advice and with the aid of the Soviet Union during the early 'honeymoon' days. Many of these were suddenly abandoned by the Russians when the breach came. The Chinese said : 'They took away even the blueprints; the dishes were removed before the meal was finished' (which metaphor makes clear that the Russians were the hosts, and they prescribed the menu and called the closure). In the circumstances, some spectacular stirring-up of national morale was perhaps the only 'positive' policy open to the Chinese Government.

From the late 1960s, Konovalov notes, the small enterprises began again to proliferate; but again the motivation is not that the appropriate basis of building materials, raw materials and equipment exists, but just that the human 'material' is available. The population of working age, of some 450 million, increases by 10 or 12 million a year. From the Soviet point of view, if the determinant of policy at any moment is either some particular surplus or some particular deficit in one or another factor of production, this is like 'the tail wagging the dog'. The proper basis is to interrelate correctly the technological criterion and the criterion of economic benefit.

For certain activities the small scale is inefficient (e.g. textiles, or continuous processes); for others it is recommendable, where the raw materials are dispersed or where there are local reserves of labour (e.g. the production of soda, fertilisers or bricks). These must be combined in a selective economic accounting; but in China the progress of the modern industrial sector must govern and lead the small-scale sector. The former generates new demands, brings out the dominant production possibilities. Electric pumps and motors or traction engines are the kinds of things to concentrate on, for local utilisation. The small scale is of course especially dominant in Chinese agriculture : 650 million persons on 125 million hectares of cultivated area means that 2·4 *workers* per hectare (one per acre) carry twice that number of local dependants. 90 per cent of the labour input in this agriculture is muscle-power; there are not even enough draught animals. 'The sole cause of this is population pressure in the countryside' where 8–10 million more people are added every year, a 3 per cent addition to the already large rural labour-force.

AGRICULTURE AND OVERPOPULATION

Labour-intensive development is therefore more and more resorted to in the countryside. Labour-intensive crops are selected though they are less productive. There is no programme for the modernisation of agriculture by the use of electricity, because the only means of development so far has been the utilisation of the mass of readily available labour. The peasantry creates – and receives – 70 or 80 per cent of the national output; the rest goes to the cities in tax-levies, all but 5–7 per cent of the rural output which goes to the extension and modernisation of activities. 'Meticulous working of the soil, ridge-bed cultivation, terrace irrigation, hasty patching-up of the village inventory, almost complete lack of specialisation and co-operation, self-containedness within the communes' cause the small scale to continue to be the typical form. 'Any contraction of the numbers employed in agriculture leads to sharp, possibly catastrophic, deterioration in agricultural production.'

This is interestingly opposite to some bourgeois economists' view that the marginal productivity of labour in this kind of agriculture is nil, or even negative (they actually get in each others' way). The Soviet economists perceive that the Chinese system largely commits specific groups of persons to specific unitary acts of production; the latter would be reduced, or become infeasible, if labour is drawn away from them. Marginalist theory applies in continuous-process industries (at the conveyor-belt) but breaks down where the 'doses' of labour are very irregular and uneven (e.g. in rice agriculture, where there is actually acute labour shortage at the planting and harvest seasons, general inactivity at other times).

The Soviet economists do not give sufficient credit to the Chinese concept of mobilising the labour in the slack seasons for infrastructural and civic work (hedging, ditching, road-making, etc.). They are right, however, in emphasising the 'zigzag' nature of the Chinese course in this sphere also, e.g. alternating between the building of ever larger and higher dykes (which breach even more disastrously in times of unusual flood) and excessive dispersal of efforts into parochial projects, each of which individually is uneconomic in scale; also on such matters as the chaos resulting from a large poverty-induced drift of rural population to the towns, while the authorities are exerting political efforts to 'send down' as many people as possible, temporarily or permanently, from the urban to the rural areas.

There have, however, been notable fluctuations in the CPR's population policy. From 1950 to 1959 the natural increase was large, owing to decline in the death-rate, though the birth-rate remained 'traditionally' high. The death-rate halved in the 1950s, from 25–30 per mille in the war years to 12–14 per mille, chiefly through control of epidemics and reduction of infant mortality (for both of which Soviet aid is credited). The death-rate remained almost stable, however, in the population of working age. Local shortages and famines used to be frequent; now supplies were more evenly distributed. However, the average age at marriage fell – helped by the land distribution, say the Soviet economists (much more, others would add, by the advent of peace after over twenty years of wartime disruption : the Japanese invasion, it should be remembered, began at least as early as 1937).

According to the CPC, however, the numbers per peasant household fell sharply in 1950–52, from 4·7 to 4·1. The total increase of population soared in the 1950s from 10 or 11 million a year to 18 or 19 million. From 1960 this changed. The Soviet commentator stresses 'the background of the "Great Leap" and the "people's communes", a worsening food situation, collectivisation of all land and stocks, "collective forms of consumption" and the whole moral atmosphere' which 'led to a sharp fall in activity. In a very short time the ideal of the large family was destroyed before people's eyes, it became a necessity to postpone having childen.'

In 1956 a nationwide birth-control campaign was organised. This did not have much effect at first, but 'in the conditions of instability, hunger, moral depression and the unsystematic switching of millions of persons from one type of work to another, the idea of holding back from marriage and from having large families soon gained support among the urban population, later the rural'. This time the parameters behaved differently; the death-rate remained nearly the same (10–13 per mille per year) but the birth-rate fell from 32–34 per mille at the beginning of the 1960s to 22–24 per mille at the end of that decade.

Konovalov reported that the deferment of marriage, beginning in 1961, to the age of 28 for males and 25 for females had a marked though temporary effect in reducing the birth-rate.

Women aged 20–24 accounted for 45–55 per cent of the total births; the 'ban' on women marrying before the age of 25 'economised' about 8 or 10 million children a year. The rule about the age of marriage continues to apply, but by 1968 the large rising generation reaching the age of marriage restored the problem to its former dimensions: the cohorts already born were advancing to the permitted age of marriage.

In 1957–60, according to the Soviet observers, the 'danger' of population growth was presented by some Chinese experts in a 'panic' manner. 'Representatives of public opinion in China, most of them educated and qualified in the West, partly upholding Malthusian views' advocated prompt restriction of the rate of growth of population. 'Disowning Malthusianism in words, [in practice] they saw no other way out but birth control by permitting abortion and sterilisation. Professor Ma Yin-ch'u proposed such measures.' Professor Ma did point to the economic and social desirability of population control, stressing especially that quality is better than quantity, also praising Soviet policy in this field – for both of which offences he was dismissed from the Presidency of Peking University – but it seems untrue that he specified particular methods. Others did so – even in the National Congress of Deputies. 'The Government's point of view remained, however', in Konovalov's words, 'as expressed in the phrase "Many people – that's good!" This dogma contains both the elements of feudal attitudes about the big family and about wealth, appropriate to the early feudal society in China, and the sinocentric view that a large population is a bulwark and a sign of the power and thrivingness of any State.'

The Soviet scholars have not carried studies much beyond what is summarised above. The PSS conference report of late 1973 takes matters no further. There is much – though complex, sometimes contradictory – evidence about family-planning policy in China in recent years, which appears to be broadly ignored in the Soviet Union. However, the Soviet analysis of the economic aspects of the demographic problem is of special interest; in view of the centrality of this topic, it is worth summarising here the concluding section of Konovalov's officially approved standpoint:

'The attempt on the one hand to structure production so as to support a surplus population, by using the maximum amount of labour, and on the other hand' – Soviet economists are as ambidextrous as their bourgeois colleagues – 'the policy of containing population growth by postponing marriages and restricting distribution [of goods] to large families, are intended to "optimise" human resources relative to material factors of production. This gives only a temporary escape from the critical situation, not a general strategy for leading China out of the conditions of poverty and technical backwardness. These efforts embody not only inhuman ideas, but notions alien to the modern tendencies of economic development. It can only be hoped that in future, instead of the pragmatic attempt to make use of the "poverty of China", radical but humane and economically far-sighted measures will be taken.' What measures? Of course, the Soviet Union is the relevant and available model. There must be something wilfully evil in Chairman Mao that he actually opposes the Soviet Union.

EXPANSIONISM

'That is why', concludes Konovalov, 'the failure to solve China's population problem by internal methods makes it possible for the enemies of the people to forecast that the drama of China must be "decided" by external means [action from – or towards – the outside] and even to evoke an ardent desire that this should happen. Knowledge of the working and living conditions of the Chinese, their life and traditions, must immediately show the multitude of limitations that expansionist plans inevitably encounter. It appears that expanding the living-space at the expense of neighbouring countries is not enough; what is required is enormous efforts, decades of preparation, a recasting of the whole foundations of the life of the Chinese nation.'

The next passage may perhaps relate to Siberia – the great 'empty quarter' actually adjacent to China. 'Climatic conditions unlike those of China, untilled lands and a sparse population, unreadiness of the territory for intensive irrigated agriculture, the economically arduous conditions render these territories unattractive, moreover for Chinese unarmed against the elements these lands seem mostly inaccessible, incomprehensible and undesirable. In comparison with the landscapes that are familiar to them, their own territories where they may exist more conveniently with many times less outlay, the neighbouring lands are very inferior.'

It is interesting that these utterances were included at some length in the published report. There is sensitivity about the eastern half of Siberia. Some of these aspersions on its attractiveness and its developability seem to go against Soviet patriotism which regards that area as a place fit for heroes and as the greatest untapped storehouse of resources in the world. The USSR is now guarding that border with more troops than it has on other frontiers. Scores of millions of Chinese settlers, on their side, have braved those same forbidding conditions to make themselves at home in Manchuria, Mongolia, etc. The speaker Konovalov continued, however, with further whistling in the dark. He avers that only a few localities in the world are really overcrowded – Bangladesh, Java, the Nile Delta, the lower Yangtse and Pearl rivers. Elsewhere in the same countries there is plenty of room; all would be well if everyone followed the (Soviet) policy of coexistence. 'The demographic problem by itself cannot engender expansionism', which is the end-result of wrong political thoughts ([*sic*] : a far cry, this subjectivism, from the original Marxian precepts).

M. M. Nikol'ski (PSS, pp. 204–14) certainly treats of the material base of the Chinese economy, on which the CPR has waged for twenty years a complex struggle – vitiated by changes in the external as well as the internal setting – to construct a new economic order. In that process 'the superstructural phenomena and processes have affected the course and forms of the struggle'; though on the whole the production process is socialistic and makes for a broadly 'progressive' tendency, there are large and dangerous aberrations. The restoration of the economy was accomplished in 1949–52, so was the primary stage of socialist construction during the first Five-Year Plan; but the subsequent 'stormy events' caused 'serious' economic difficulties and 'sharpened the political contradictions in the CPC'. The leadership forsook the socialist course, Marxists must show how all this refers back to the fundamental economic basis.

Besides works already cited, there have been contributions to this effect from the older generation [39], the 'middle' [138, 155–6,244] and younger generations of Soviet scholars ([525, 329, 243], also L. I. Molodtsova and Z. A. Pivovarova; it is curious that four out of five in this last youngest group are women). Officials in various Departments have also contributed. There were special conferences in 1969–71 by the IDV [179–81].

Certain conditions in pre-Communist China must be studied, such as bureaucratic capital and agrarian relationships (on the latter, [253], [103] and [325] are again commended). Agrarian themes and rural implications are much in fashion for Soviet postgraduate theses on China; but they do not go deeply enough into fundamentals, are descriptive or 'episodic'. To highlight the subsequent errors and disasters, rural successes in the period 1949–57 should particularly be defined and examined – land reform, co-operativisation, transformation of capitalist industry and trade, nationalisation of bureaucratic and foreign capital, strengthening of the State sector. These matters are 'unevenly' studied in the USSR; land reform, mutual aid teams and the like have had the best attention (works of V. A. Zhamin, Korkunov, Maslennikov and Sukharchuk) but there are many 'blank spots'. And the analysis is not carried much into the phase of the communes, neglecting 'the consequences of the forcing, the actual forcing [*forsirovanie*] of agricultural transformation since the second half of 1955' (italics in the original).

The transformation of the capitalist sector has been examined in some Soviet works (S. A. Voyevodin, V. A. Maslennikov and [441]); but these are criticised for not going into the sociological aspects. What happened to the declassed elements? Have the old classes died, or faded away? The processes of nationalisation have also been studied (Astaf'iev, Ganshin, Maslennikov), those of industrialisation more widely (by several of those previously named): the nature of the industrialisation, the methods, the tempo, the sources of capital accumulation, the role of Soviet aid. What is lacking is assessment of the consequences for the social and economic structure of Chinese society, the relationship between the forces of production and the relations of production. (Marx's terminology must be strictly adhered to: one wonders how it would be if Western economists were forced to restrict themselves to the vocabulary of Adam Smith, in analysing present-day phenomena.)

However, it is stressed that the conditions and the relations have '*partially* changed' in China since 1958: 'The State form of property has gradually come to lose the elements of "people's socialist" ownership, under a military-bureaucratic regime; the

D

distribution of the products of labour in the State sector is subject mainly to the egoistic political and ideological interests of the governing nationalistic clique [*grupirovka*].' The State-owned means of production come to seem to the worker something alien and opposed to him : the authorities are driven to military or 'command' types of administrative measures of forced labour. The rural worker faces the same kind of alienation. This militarisation springs from the superstructure, which is *actually now* (underlined in PSS, p. 210) dominating the economic base. The superstructure is so complicated that it will require the combined work of Soviet historians, philosophers and jurists, as well as economists, to solve this tremendous puzzle. One expression used to dramatise the change is especially interesting : China has turned from the socialist market in the world to the capitalist market. The role of the army is a significant part of the explanation; the changes in the armed forces both reflect the social processes and lead them. The 'People's Liberation' Army has become a main component of the State, no longer a workers' and peasants' 'Red' Army, really a 'Controlling the People' Army.

ECONOMETRIC PROBLEMS

The strictly economic assessment is difficult, as 'there are no reliable official statistics since 1960'. This can only be compensated by (*a*) logical (deductive rather than inductive) analysis, through the mighty tool of Marxist science, and (*b*) more exhaustive use of the better data available from the earlier period up to 1958. Those earlier data, it is significantly noted, were compiled according to the Soviet forms and methods, 'according to the methodology of statistical accounting used in the Soviet planning and recording organs. Moreover they were made up in preliminary variants, then modified variants, finally confirmed variants, for the First Five-Year Plan.' These can therefore well be used for econometric, extrapolatory and other techniques by Soviet experts. Thereafter the factual data became 'sharply restricted, their reliability declined catastrophically (especially for 1958–60). From 1960 to 1971 official statistics on basic economic matters have been simply non-existent.' In this connection, the PSS meeting was instructed, 'use may be made of the numerous estimates and evaluations of the Taiwan, Japanese, Hong-Kong and Western bourgeois specialists; *but we cannot take these as original and basic'* (underlined in the text : PSS, p. 213). The bourgeois technical methods are different, they are guessing as much as we are (though perhaps in different sectors) and we need to train our own personnel directly, not on second-hand materials; such is the gist of the rest of the argument on this point.

It is interesting that the greatest emphasis is on the relative excellence of the materials for the First Five-Year Plan. There were also the Second and Third Five-Year Plans (1958–62 and 1963–67) and a Twelve-Year Programme for the development of agriculture, which were to some extent formed before the completion of the First Plan, i.e. still in the Soviet presence. There were, moreover, some preliminary drafts for the Fourth Plan (1966–70) made in 1965–66. Reference to these and their utilisation for making retrospective calculations of what true socialism could have achieved, had it been adhered to in China, would confound the bourgeois critics in their two camps : the pseudo-leftist wing which proclaims there are various roads to socialism, with China pursuing her own special one (R. Garaudy was especially named in the USSR for this heresy), and the openly anti-Communist wing which represents all these failures as inherent in any kind of socialism. The former would see that there is only one effective kind of socialism, emanating from the Kremlin, the latter that true (Soviet) socialism did work wonders when it was applied in China.

RESOURCES AND POLICIES

Sections follow in PSS 1973 on the development of productive forces (meaning especially, in Soviet parlance, resources) and industrialisation policy. V. I. Akimov, opening on the former topic, noted that Soviet academic forces were absorbed, in the first years after the establishment of the CPR, in the immediate practical aspects – primarily an inventory of its resources for building socialism. The USSR Academy of Sciences' Institutes of Oriental Studies, Economics and Geography, the Ministry of Foreign Trade's Institute for Research on Economic Fluctuations (*kon'iunktur*), the Moscow and Leningrad Universities, the Institutes in Moscow for International Relations and Foreign Trade, were all drawn into that orbit.

The Institute of Sinology of the Academy of Sciences was established in 1956, having within it an economic section, with special responsibilities. However, 'for various reasons' work on this subject was 'sharply reduced in scale' from 1960. The Institute of Sinology – a central organ in this respect – was closed after only four years of existence. An equivalent focus was restored only at the end of the 1960s when the IDV was created, also an Institute for the Study of the International Workers' Movement. The story is, however, as before : much has recently been done, much more needs to be done. There should be many more chairs in universities and higher educational institutions, devoted to this field.

Meanwhile the same names recur : Avarin, Astaf'iev, Kovalev, Maslennikov, Sladkovski, Tikhvinski. Those who trained the cadres (such as K. M. Popov) should also figure in the honours-list. However, the list of contributors is much longer than this : to the names just mentioned and those referred to earlier in this book may be added such as V. I. Potapov, M. V. Fomicheva, S. L. Shirayev, N. N. Shmigol', Yu. V. Yaremenko, and others. Yet the USSR is short of cadres in this field, since it is a particularly difficult one, demanding good technical knowledge as well as general sinological competence. So – once again – Soviet performance in this field is admittedly 'uneven', also insufficiently integrated. The 1949–57 period is the best covered (little wonder, in view of what was previously said about its being the only period for which there are real data). 'It must be noted, however', states Akimov *ex cathedra*, 'that some of the works published in the 1950s saw [China] through rose-coloured spectacles', besides failing to cover all aspects of the subject.

Subsequently and more generally, Sladkovski is especially interested in basic resource problems, Astaf'iev in economic reconstruction and industrialisation, Maslennikov in socio-economic changes. Figurny and Sladkovski furnished a basic text [128], Ganshin another [138], in 1959. There was practically no academic work on the consequences of the Great Leap Forward. The CPSU printed a considerable documentation and commentary in 1963–64, on the 'Three Red Banners' discussion in China; but this did not lead to specifically academic handling of the subject. A few works pointed out the heavy damage done to the Chinese economy by the Great Leap [233, 535], with wide reference to Chinese materials. Still fewer are the publications concerning the 'Rectification' period. In contrast, the Cultural Revolution stimulated a considerable amount of comment – still, however, very mainly on the 'brochure' level.

Mao's chauvinism and his great-power policy, in the present context of assessment of the real strength of China, have drawn such writers as Sladkovski, Vyatski [528], Mikhailov [315] and Pamor [357], who stress that militarism was greatly strengthened from the Cultural Revolution onwards; the country was divided into two sectors, the military and the civilian, the former 'privileged' with all the facilities the Chinese State can provide, the latter having to subsist on local resources. This militarism is a real threat to China because externally it threatens world peace, internally it consumes the gains made by the Chinese people. The connection of these matters with the population problem has been noted earlier in this chapter.

This subject is further developed by V. I. Orekhov (assisted by L. A. Volkova and Z. A. Muromtseva) (PSS, pp. 220 ff.). As an initial contribution to the study of the dynamics of the problem (as distinct from an inventory treatment, leading at best to comparative statics), these writers praise the master's thesis of G. A. Ganshin in 1951 on 'Heavy Industry in the CPR : Problems of its Renewal and Development'. In the following years, interest was shown in the nature of the industrial leadership in the CPR, the place of industry in the national development, the relation of capitalisation to technology, raw material problems and industrial training. However, 'some works, appearing in 1958–60, were in some degree influenced by the Chinese propaganda of those years, which exalted the policy of the "Three Red Banners" '. Some of the contributions were brief, so far as this subject is concerned (e.g. [366], two chapters in a symposium), though indicative. In the 1960s – as noticed above in other connections – there was a great contraction in the work of the Soviet Union, where the experts were dismayed and disoriented by the apostasy of China. In 1961–63 it fell to Ministerial circles in Moscow to produce the solid current documentation [319]; though E. A. Afanasievski included in his study of Szechwan at that time [2] a useful vignette of the province's industry.

In 1963–64 the Soviet press presented 'a great many articles and observations, often of a polemical character, in which Soviet writers who had formerly worked in the CPR criticised the adventurist policy of the Chinese leadership' in various respects, and contrasted the preceding gains from Soviet aid. In the same years there were solid statements by the Central Committee of the CPSU concerning the consequences to Chinese industry of the recent events. On the academic plane, however, major activity did not revive until 1967 in the USSR. The earlier material certainly left a rich store of information on certain vital sectors of Chinese industry. The most voluminous is on fuel and power [51–3, 48 (though [48] too is now accused of being influenced by Chinese 'boastfulness') 196, 208, 380, 484, 66], in which category some well-known Soviet specialists and engineers contributed [75, 78–9, 543].

Heavy metallurgy was another topic [297, 366] and there were contributions in engineering [8, 294] and chemicals (in which papers are cited of one Zhavoronkhov, not identified by the present writer; this illustrates the important point that, in technology especially, documents not widely published may be influential). The general field of light industry was covered by the widely circulated works of F. L. Kovalev [255] and S. Nikiforov [338] and by some Governmental publications [479]. The handicraft industries of China are of special importance; they accounted for 18 per cent by value of the industrial output in 1953–57 and were a focus of the 'transformation'. Accordingly they received considerable attention from Soviet writers in the 1950s [265, 310 (a very well-known book), 138, 9]. Only occasionally, more politically polemical publications give insights into peasant or cottage-industrial production, e.g. V. Ya. Sidikhmenov's *The Great Victory* (1959). All this work ceased in 1960 and has not been revived.

Concerning agriculture – which is some 80 per cent of the livelihood of China – Soviet interest was concentrated in the 1950s on agrarian politics and land reform ([102–3], Zhamin in 1958; Zhamin and Volkova, Rubin, Gorlenko in 1959; [223, 244]). They were also busy following the voluminous coverage given to these changes in China itself. Some have commented that at that time 'one could not see the wood for the trees'; analysis of principles was submerged in a mass of current and ever-changing detail. China-watchers in other countries are familiar with this feeling!

The specific observations were good ([3], Zhamin on agricultural economics, [44]). In the 1960s the Chinese material orchestrated the Maoist proposition that 'agriculture is the foundation' – foreshadowed earlier by his dictum 'co-operativism first, technical reconstruction later'. Soviet writers rallied against this line [524], but were unable to make a massive attack on it. The present problem is to assess exactly the importance of agriculture in China. Chou En-lai told Edgar Snow that agriculture represented one-third of the total national production, indicating a considerable degree of industrialisation. This contradicts Mao's designation of 'agriculture as the foundation'. A value-estimate of agriculture conceals the real prevalence of subsistence farming and barter. The arithmetic of the Chinese, and their records, are crude; and so on (thus the Soviet economists).

The foregoing depicts the general setting, in the sphere of economic considerations. Two more aspects should be noted before leaving the subject. One is a technical matter, from which it is possible to see in closer focus the operational difficulties of Soviet econometricians coping with questions on the Chinese economy. The other is a less 'numerical' issue in applied economics: the appreciation of the practical policy of the Chinese in the organisation of industry. Soviet analysts are instructed to use the basic material of the 1950s – as being the only extensive and reliable material on the Chinese economy. Up to 1957, this is comparatively straightforward. For 1958–60 (a crucial period) it is more difficult. Some Soviet economists use for that period the figures given as the 'corrected' data by the Chinese statistical offices, others apply to these their own estimates and corrections; a third group is eclectic, accepting some of the official Chinese data, modifying it in other parts. There is no agreement as to which of those years was the peak year, the one in which production (or productivity) was at its highest, 1959 or 1960.

When they turn to 1961–73, the Soviet experts work on extrapolations and the like (sophisticatedly, of course, with advanced techniques), also building in all kinds of other evidence, from sources in other countries as well as China itself. Some deal in ranking coefficients, showing China's place in 'league tables' of world industrial performance. The results are, not surprisingly, very varied. The Soviet authorities are urged to 'centralise' – and indeed to collectivise – this work, (*a*) to enable the better application of computer and other techniques, (*b*) to establish agreed official 'indices' or 'profiles' of the Chinese economy and its main sectors.

Secondly, the 1950–60 data deal (so to speak) in differentials, the incremental changes in that particular decade, rather than the physical base (what exact stock of resources, factors, inventories, etc, in which these changes occurred); or, in the businessman's terms, the trading account without the asset position. Hence there is an equally strong desire and need to study and identify what China's operative resources were, are and will be in future. This too requires modern 'computer age' handling. Thirdly, the 'problem of cadres'; all this, with the innumerable research requirements noted in the foregoing pages, necessitates a numerous and specially trained personnel. Fourthly, the Soviets did much work in the 1950s on the actual and potential location of industry in China. Regionally, this was done in some depth and detail for the North-East, Northern, Eastern and Central Major Economic Planning Regions of China, which were designated on the Soviet model; but done to some extent also for other regions, particular provinces, etc., even for some National Minorities areas, cities and particular branches of industry. All that has since ceased (*svernulos'*); so the corresponding data for subsequent periods must be improvised by scanning all information from given localities and all official Chinese statements.

These considerations are closely connected with the study of China's industrialisation. Here too everything was 'on the black-board' (for all to see : *doskal'no*) until 1958. Manifestly the right course was then being followed by China – which would have led to a state of correct balance between industry and agriculture, as prescribed by the Soviet advisers. In 1958–60, however, according to Soviet assertions, the Chinese switched to the course of 'superindustrialisation' or 'hyperindustrialisation', to develop the productive forces 'in an unrealistically short space of time, at the expense of the backward small industry and handicrafts'. No reference is made, of course, to what Stalin may have done in 'an unrealistically short space of time at the expense of' somebody). The Soviet literature had much to say on this during the period of the Great Leap, but it is now criticised in retrospect for not having identified the levels of resources and factors available or utilised : for measuring (so to speak) the waves and currents rather than the breadth and depth of the waters. It is alleged, for example, that changes within heavy industry were qualified, but not the proportion between heavy industry and light industry.

In the later period of 'Rectification', the readjustments after the Great Leap, the Soviet experts offered only general commentaries. Clearly, there was a reversal of the 'Great Leap' policies : industry was largely occupied with making good the rural damage, light industry was developed instead of heavy industry, capital construction was reduced, though the development of a nuclear and rocket capacity was 'forced'. Soviet scholars and experts are being urged to pay much more attention to this period. Recently various established scholars and a rising generation of new contributors [329] have responded to this call.

Yet another formidable list of problems remains untouched, which the Soviet effectives are bidden to tackle. How efficient is the Chinese administration ? Directives, demands, claims pour out; how far are they realistic, either in the input or in the output ? In the 1950s the scientific and technological potential of China was studied, its developments planned; this too has since been 'folded up' (according to the Russians). Soviet scientists should revive their interest in assessing the scientific potential of the CPR. Sociologists should assess small-scale and village industries. The economists have neglected the 'unproductive' spheres of activity; in the Marxist view, these are internal trade, credit and finance, or services in general. These have not been studied, except in relation to foreign trade.

In terms of industrial policy, it may be useful to summarise here the official Soviet analysis [232]. China embarked on industrialisation in the following objective and subjective circumstances, with debits (dr.) and credits (cr.) : dr. an extremely narrow initial industrial base, cr. major means of production not in private ownership, cr. pressure of the USSR and the world socialist movement, dr. population problems. The overthrow of Liu Shao-ch'i's 'theory of the primacy of productive forces', replaced by that of 'politics as the leading force', meant the rejection of objective economic considerations and resort to a frenetic subjectivism, much coloured by 'moralistics'. A grave error : the backwardness of China could only be overcome by strict objectivism, the provision of a solid material base.

Maoism does not ignore the economic aspects, it asserts the primacy of politics in some combination of the two, 'in the sense, not that the productive forces engender specific social transformations but vice versa, the "perfection" of the relations of production [social relations] must be the stimulator of economic progress'. Mao's numerous social experiments hinder economic progress. Industrialisation in underdeveloped countries can only proceed by using the surplus labour, 'live labour and embodied labour' (Marxian for capital) existing in the traditional sector (agriculture and handicrafts). The backwardness of this sector severely limits the prospects of industrialisation; the food problem must be solved first. Foreign aid is an urgent necessity. The world market can also be tapped. Population growth constantly swells the work-force. Those sectors and enterprises must be encouraged in which the productivity of labour can be raised.

China's adherence to the socialist camp (so the Soviet argument proceeds) brought indisputable advantages. Aid, material and technical, was available from the new partners, the Soviets, with their successful socialist experience. They urged heavy industry – and began to provide it. 'The successes of those years are evident and indisputable. They are broadly illuminated in the pages of our [Soviet] press.' (Thus the Soviet lecturer; the Chinese seem to have concluded otherwise.) Soviet claims [329] are that the share of industry in the total product of industry and agriculture, by value, was raised to 56·7 per cent by 1957, the share of production of the means of production within the output of industry to 48 per cent, and there were corresponding qualitative improvements.

There were, however, 'disproportionalities' in the planning, notably as between extractive and processing industries, and too great a burden was placed on agriculture. The Second Five-Year Plan was due to remove those defects and start a new and higher round of development. At that point the Chinese broke away from the true and well-prepared path. (The Soviets furnish no 'positive' explanation of why the Chinese elected to do this, except in terms of 'the cult of personality', merely referred to in passing. Is this cult, we are obliged to ask, just something that may happen? Surely there is a Marxist explanation identifying it with some kind of 'class' basis? Only Trotsky and Djilas appear to have attempted such an explanation, in terms of a 'new' bureaucratic or technocratic class; but their views are of course anathema to the USSR.)

All the events of Mao's adventurist course in 1958–60, according to the spokeswoman Kondrashova (PSS, p. 236), show that Mao's economic policy is 'to solve economic problems by voluntaristic methods, counting on the maximum utilisation of the surplus labour power, ignoring the role of national stimuli in the development of production'. The emphasis on heavy industry was not wholly abandoned in the Great Leap, it is conceded, but it was narrowly interpreted to mean metallurgy, and based on small-scale undertakings which could at best represent mere quantity. Kondrashova quotes Muromtseva who, in her strongly anti-Maoist study [329], stressed the last point, as does Korbash [243].

Kondrashova notes that the heavy-industrial investment during the Great Leap was considerably greater than in China's First Five-Year Plan : 'With the help of wheelbarrows, they built not only thousands of reservoirs but also tens of hydroelectric stations, thousands of small furnaces but some tens of large ones.' Vyatski and Dimin [528] say that about 500 large enterprises were put into operation in the First Five-Year Plan, but in the Great Leap period 700 of the sort were completed and another thousand under construction. Muromtseva therefore goes too far in her assertion that this hyperindustrialisation 'neglected' heavy industry. More basically, it meant overestimation of small industry : big industry continued to figure, but was no longer dominant.

The colossal dispersion of labour over such a wide 'front' was a practical cause of losses that 'set China back many years' by occasioning disproportionalities, transport difficulties, shortages of equipment and materials, disruption of technical processes, elimination of material incentives. What followed was a forced retreat, not a deliberate abandonment of the aim to industrialise. The policy formula changed to 'agriculture as the base, industry as the leading force'. The Leap had assumed a linear development, its downfall brought in a theory of development coming in waves, with slumps in production. Industry serving agriculture was acknowledged to be the 'decisive link'. However, the slogan of 'relying on one's own resources' justified regional economic autarky and preference for 'universalised' units (i.e. those doing everything for themselves); also the State ceasing to subsidise small-scale activities. The people's welfare – raising the standard of living – though still the proclaimed purpose, is no longer a criterion of practice. Much capacity has been diverted to producing arms, including atomic rockets. The slogans are imprecise and ambiguous.

This policy is viewed in many ways: some regard it as temporary, other as a basic new strategy; some as support for agriculture, others as increased exploitation of the peasants; some as an admission of the helplessness of the Maoists, others as the calculated postponement of heavy-industrial development or a careful regrouping of forces in preparation for another Leap. The postponement of real (i.e. heavy) industrialisation is considered by the Soviet experts to be truly a long-term deferment: Korbash says 'for fifty to eighty years or more, according to the statements of some leading activists of the CPC' [243, p. 115]. This estimate is approved by the Soviet authorities, though they consider that 'agriculture as the base' cannot be a lasting or 'strategic' policy. Immediately, the Chinese have been obliged (some Soviet authorities note) to foster industries that furnish agricultural inputs: farm tools and machinery, chemical fertilisers. In other words, backward linkages have appeared. Small-scale industry is also diverted increasingly to serving agriculture. These two trends could work together, but actually clash – as there is a change in the meaning of what is meant by 'agriculture'; moreover the structure changes with the increased emphasis on military strength.

The 'Rectification' movement adduced the slogan 'agriculture is the base' as a means of diverting attention from the need for social transformation and concentrating it on the technical reconstruction of agriculture through State aid; but later the Maoists used the slogan as a prescription that agriculture must 'develop itself'. The 'good intentions of the advocates of the more sober course of increasing capital investment in agriculture yielded to the demand for still greater withdrawal of means from agriculture'. The accumulation of capital within agriculture was forcibly speeded, at the expense of consumption and production in that sector, the funds thus accumulated going to develop large-scale modern industries. This gives in effect two separate economies, an agricultural and small-scale one and an industrial one, the latter exploiting the former both through the commodity market and through direct intervention of the State with its taxes and levies [319].

The 'Rectification' brought about a definite rise in production, with consumption kept at a minimum, but established no new economic strategy. All the questions of the possible methods of economic development remained open. The decision on each of these questions 'depended on the outcome of the struggle for power, which took the form of the so-called Cultural Revolution'. Having convinced themselves of the difficulties of 'instant' economic prosperity, 'the Maoists planned first and foremost to establish an integrated military-industrial [economy]' – a completely different concept of industrialisation. 'Civil' and 'military' sectors in the economy were demarcated. The Soviet writings denounce the military-industrial sector as 'parasitic', draining the countryside of its subsistence, and note that it is being expanded to include more and more activities.

'War preparation' [*sic*] is now a major part of Chinese industry. Dialectical philosophy loves a paradox, however : it is noted that this very concentration on armaments will soon force due attention to be paid to heavy industry. The oil and automobile industries are being brought forward for military reasons, nuclear and rocket devices even more so. All these require steel – and good-quality steel regularly delivered, not the puddling in backyard furnaces. Possibly this 'drive' will fail, as its predecessors did, giving place to some different adventure; but the army is strong in the present power condition at the top, the situation is in any case dangerous.

In sum, Soviet economists naturally pay extensive attention to the problems of the Chinese economy, in which they have some special expertise; but they find it as complex and confusing as do economists in other parts of the world. Obscurity is perhaps confounded by both the Chinese and the Soviet Communists dealing in Marxist concepts and formulations that are defunct, or were never current, in the rest of the world. The economic basis is the main determinant, in the Marxian view; accordingly it has had to be considered at some length in this chapter. There is practically no Soviet work in this field of a quantitative and econometric character; the treatment is subjective, concentrating on economic policy. The organisational aspects are considered in Chapter 9; before proceeding to that subject, the psychology of the policies must be reviewed in Chapter 8.

8 Ideology and Politics

An understanding of China begins – and, the cynic might add, ends – with a study of the ancient philosophy on which the Chinese civilisation is deeply founded. The rapporteur on this subject in the PSS was N. G. Senin, who noted the pre-Revolutionary Russian work on Chinese philosophy to which Chapter 2 has referred. For Soviet work, however, the speaker had to leap some decades ahead : Chinese philosophy did not receive any considerable attention in the Soviet Union until the end of the Second World War. In the earlier period the USSR had little interest in the archaic and reactionary philosophy of China except for stocking museums and providing ammunition for atheist and anti-traditionalist campaigns. Radul'-Zatulovski's remarkable work in 1947 on Confucianism [399] was discreet in describing Chinese thought indirectly through the mirror of Japan; it was only an oblique precursor of the direct interest in Chinese philosophy which matured later.

The new wave could not rise until a better supply of original materials was available, through Russian translations. This began in 1950 with Yang Hsing-shun's rendering of the Taoist classic [533] and Konrad's of the *Art of War* (which he amplified eight years later [238–9]), also an inferior version by others of the *Book of Songs* [451]; but continued only in the 1960s, with Shutski's *Book of Changes* [452] and Shtein's *Kuan Tse* [450] to inaugurate that decade, Pozdneyeva's study of Yang Chu, Lieh Tse and Chuang Tse [390] appearing only in 1967, Perelomov's book on one of the founders of Legalism [370] in 1968. There is still not a complete library in Russian of the classical originals, despite more recent work to be mentioned below. Meanwhile, for the long period of 'medieval' Chinese philosophy through which the basic Classicism took root and branched, Soviet materials were practically limited to some general references [503] – as indeed were those on the nineteenth century [435].

The list of commentary and critical literature is longer. It begins as early as 1936 with A. A. Petrov's text and analysis of Wang Pi on the *Book of Changes* [373]. The same Petrov did his doctoral dissertation on Wang Ch'ung, but it was not published until 1957, after Petrov's death. A book of Senin's in 1956 defended Sun Yat-sen from falsifications of his views by 'ideologists in the anti-Communist camp'; it asserted that Sun's 'revolutionary democratism' showed the heritage of materialism in Chinese thought. Contrastingly, Tikhvinski in 1958 dwelt extensively on the 'utopianism' of the modern pre-Republican reformers [495]. In 1966 Bykov produced a wide survey [87]. Also broad, but deeper, is L. S. Vasil'iev's treatise [520] in 1970. More peripheral contributions were Yu. A. Zamoshin on ethics in ancient India and China, G. F. Alexandrov on sociology and V. A. Krivtsov on aesthetics. Another fringe is that of generalisation or popularisation [374, 86]. Naturally far more 'specific', but technical and usually available only in special libraries, are some good postgraduate theses [85, 436, 47, 259, 502, 534, 127].

Senin gives the official stress on Chinese materialism being in constant opposition, over centuries and millennia, to the Confucianism of the Establishment. Mao Tse-tung is deemed to be – in effect if not in intention – essentially carrying on the basic Confucian tradition, still in conflict with the true (Marxist-Leninist) materialism. Senin's starting-point is: 'The history of Chinese philosophy is that of the rise and development of two basic lines, materialism and idealism, of the struggle between them.' Each current of ideas 'expresses a given epoch' and follows socioeconomic changes in that epoch.

Soviet researchers, readers will not be surprised to hear, have adopted 'one of the most important methodological principles – the principle of partisanship' (the Russian word, *partiinost'*, has wider meaning, as, so to speak, 'party-ness'). Such party loyalty demands not only the identification of every thinker's class-standpoint, but also 'analysis and evaluation of each philosophical doctrine from the standpoint of the definite historically progressive class of the corresponding epoch'. Thus, in selecting originals for translation, Soviet emphasis has been on materials expressing the 'scientific and advanced ideas' – such as those noted above. (They

are of course progressive because they have been so designated by
the USSR authorities, who selected them because they are progressive.)

Nevertheless, there are opposing views (in the Soviet Union) on
a number of questions. L. S. Vasil'iev's work [520] even 'recognises
Confucianism as progressive, seeing it as having had an "affirma-
tive beginning", at least in the pre-Han period. His attitude to
the teaching of Confucius bears a clear imprint of idealisation,
an embellishment of Confucianism as a whole, with which we
cannot agree.' The idealisation of Confucianism is a main Soviet
accusation against the contemporary Chinese leaders, as will be
seen later in this chapter; this criticism against Vasil'iev is therefore a serious one. Senin followed it with an equally serious
charge against Vasil'iev of idealising modern Western scholarship,
too : 'Moreover', he continued (PSS, p. 159), 'in the work referred
to, the generally acknowledged attainments of Soviet and other
investigators are ignored, the very existence of materialist thought
in China is placed in doubt or altogether denied. What is astonish-
ing is not a difference in opinions, which is quite natural in learned
circles, but the unreserved attempts to buttress his position by
references solely to the tendentious utterances of bourgeois sinologues (R. Wilhelm, A. Forke, G. Maspero, H. Creel and others).
We cannot accept such a contrasting of Soviet scholars with bourgeois Western sinologists.'

Two pages earlier, Senin had laid down that it was essential
that Soviet Marxists be 'partisan' (or Party-ish), selecting 'progressive' ideas and tendencies. When one of their number refers to
some very solid Western writers – who are on other occasions denounced in the USSR for the very breadth of their interest, leading them to the confused eclecticism so characteristic of the bourgeoisie in its decline – those foreign writers are denounced as 'tendentious'. Tendentious, evidently, in all directions at once, judging
from the variety of exponents cited. It is discouraging that the
Soviet *apparatchiki*, in face of all their proclaimed readiness for
coexistence of the 'two systems' in lively competition with each
other, still insist on this kind of denunciation, which may appear
childish to the rest of the world, be an injustice to good and loyal
workers in their own 'camp' and obstruct intellectual progress
there. The only consolation is that it seems that in many cases there

is, to adapt the aphorism about the fat man, in every Marxist academic a scholar trying to get out.

The PSS discussions of 1971–73 were emphatically aimed at denunciation of Maoism and its bourgeois coadjutors; in the Philosophy section, there was first an overall attack, then a pressing of the particular charge of neo- (or ultra-) Confucianism. On the general plane there had been useful works in the last few years. Fedoseyev had exposed, in 1964, the 'sinification' of philosophy, the cult of Chinese philosophy as something *sui generis* [124]. In 1969 Rumyantsev had criticised Maoism in the light of dialectical philosophy [419] and Senin had defined Maoism as 'pseudo-dialectical' [437]. Altaiski and Georgiev had been more severe, dubbing Maoism as positively 'anti-Marxist' [30, 304], while Sidikhmenov attacked it as 'distorting' and exorcised it with extensive reference to Lenin [453–4].

These works 'many-sidedly' criticised Maoism, 'showing the complete groundlessness of Mao's pretensions to having developed Marxist-Leninist philosophy and raised it to a new level. The Soviet scholars sought to uncover the ideational sources of the Maoist philosophy. It is not particularly difficult for the non-sinologist philosopher to expose the anti-Marxist nature of the views and utterances of Mao Tse-tung, but to show its connection with Chinese traditional ideology requires not only circumstantial knowledge of Marxist-Leninist philosophy but calls for special knowledge of the history of Chinese thought. This problem has not yet been solved in our literature and demands further exertions.'

POLITICAL BIAS

K. Ivanov's article in 1970 [195] uses only a few of the necessary approaches. Others give only a non-Marxist, 'vulgar' presentation, e.g. Fyodorov's association of Mao's thoughts with feudalism [137], which takes the undoubted influence of 'feudal sources' in Mao's education and his thinking to 'prove' by 'mechanical association' his guilt in this respect. (Though more generally, it must be remarked, guilt by association is as much a politico-legal presentiment in the USSR as it was at one time in the USA.) Senin notes 'another kind of extreme' in Soviet criticism, regarding the treatment of Sun Yat-sen as 'one of the theoretical sources of

Maoism'. Sun's views were sanctified by praise from Lenin in 1912. Subsequently Sun 'moved significantly to the left, especially under the influence of the October Revolution and knowledge of the experience of socialist construction in the USSR. Sun's view underwent a serious evolution in the direction of convergence with Marxism, though he did not become a Marxist. Nevertheless, some of our critics of Maoism, postulating the influence of Sun's ideas on Mao, seek, against the logic of history, to impute the reactionariness of Maoism to the views of Sun. In other words they try radically to revise the valuation established in the Marxist literature of Sun Yat-sen's views as advanced for his time.'

This fault is instanced specifically by Meliksetov's article [312] which falsely concluded that Sun's views were 'reactionary'. Sun was 'the great Chinese revolutionary democrat'. (So the founder of the Kuomintang is now in favour in Soviet historical circles, as Meliksetov and others should have somehow realised before publishing. Westerners may wonder in what sense Sun was a great democrat; his second Principle, People's Democracy, was specified by him as a one-party system under which 'individual liberty' – which he equated with licence – 'must be broken down; we must become pressed together into an unyielding body'. Perhaps this formula does express the Soviet ideal of 'progessive' thinking.)

The main charge of the Maoist leadership's maintenance and intensification of the Confucian outlook was only incidentally developed by L. D. Pozdneyeva. This contributor brought into the discussion in 1971–73 some sharp criticisms of her Soviet fellow-workers. She praised the previous work in the translation of primary sources, repeating the names mentioned above in that connection and adding a few more (L. E. Pomerantsova's *Huai-nan Tse*, Golygina's book on aesthetics [158] and K. I. Razumovski's notes on portraiture). These have made the matter clearer by presenting to Soviet students, 'though still far from exhaustively', 'freethinkers' or 'heretics' who opposed the official outlook in China. However, Pozdneyeva complains that on Confucianism itself 'nothing new' had been done; matters have even gone backward, so to speak, in comparison with the critical orientations of the nineteenth-century Russian sinology, the work of Bichurin, V. P. Vasil'iev and Monastyrev. 'The cause of this, it seems to me', she said, 'is the uncritical acceptance of some Chinese works, e.g. our translations of the books of Kuo Mo-jo, also acceptance of West

European and especially American works, the numbers of which are striking.'

Pozdneyeva proposed to 'dissipate this fog' (of an excessive amount of materials and commentaries?) by inviting careful consideration of the most basic terms in Chinese, on the understanding of which depends a proper appreciation of the literature, folklore and philosophy of China. The greatest of these is *li* (rites). Rubin [414, p. 36] explains this as 'ceremonies, etiquette, ritual, rules of decorum or as what is contained in the proverbial expression "Chinese politeness" . . .' (in the Russian language – which means the insincere kind of 'oriental' ceremonious manners or 'compliments', exaggerated protocol, flattery, and the like). Thus *li* indicates 'not only the rules of courtesy, but also religious ritual, the ritual of the hunt, of diplomacy, of administration'. When *li* is combined with *yueh*, 'music' – *yueh* meaning 'ritual dances' – this indicates in the Chinese tradition the culture called by the word *wen*, "cultures" or "things cultural" '.

CONFUCIANISM AND RELIGION

It is the necessity of proving Confucianism to be an actual religion – a self-condemnatory term in Soviet parlance – that chiefly preoccupies this spokeswoman, Pozdneyeva. Rubin refers solely to those sinologists as opining either that 'Confucius was essentially a religious thinker', or that 'though Confucius approved the observance of religious (among other) rituals, the impression is that this ritual was for him on the one hand a symbol of respectability, on the other a means of access to tradition'. The term *li*, notes Pozdneyeva, has certainly a 'diffuse' interpretation; for a definition, the original sources should be re-examined. The first meaning given to *li* is 'actions to serve the spirits (gods), in order to attain happiness'. It appears thus in the ancient Shou Wen dictionary, in the eighteenth century K'ang Hsi dictionary and in contemporary renderings – the *Tse Hai*, the *Tse Yuan*, in P. I. Kafarov [206], the French of Couvreur, the English of Legge. The analysis of the character itself confirms this; on its right is its most ancient part, the ideograph for 'a sacrificial vessel' and the character 'fertility'. The dictionaries explain also the 'five *li*' as 'the range of ritual enactments in China', of which, Kafarov noted, the number was very great. Some of these – the ritual of 'putting on the hat' (initiation), marriage and burial – are rites that the whole human race considers religious.

'Analogy is', however, 'not proof'; it must be confirmed by observation of practice. For example, burial : note the greater and lesser mounds in China, even on the smallest and poorest farms, which have always impressed foreign travellers [24, pp. 156–7]. As Lu Hsun repeatedly said in modern times, 'China is one great cemetery'. Pozdneyeva asserts that 'in 1962' (inferably the last date of which she has direct evidence?) these private graves were still everywhere – and rising with the population growth – the 'communes' not having 'brought themselves to touch them, or institute communal graveyards'. There is still 'unshaken' belief in China, then, in the 'magic power' of the graves, the 'protection' of the ancestors 'ensuring the prosperity of the living'; when really it takes away their land and impedes their progress.

Opponents of superstition appeared in China as early as the seventh century B.C. Kuan Chung and Lao Tse, Lieh Tse and Chuang Tse, who denied any such immortality, while Yang Chu and Mo Ti denounced funereal pomps. Confucius had to retort : he chided one who regretted the sacrifice of the ram, saying he would deplore the abandonment of the rite. He stressed that filial piety demanded continued sacrifices to the dead, and so forth (*Analects*, III 17, 12; II 5; 1 9; III 11) These filial services were put by him on the same level of religious necessity as the actual burial, wedding and other ceremonies.

A similar commentary is pursued by Pozdneyeva at some length with reference to such terms as *hsiao* ('humility'), *t'ien* ('heaven'), *wu wei* ('do not disturb', or 'do not break'), *jen* ('compassion' or 'endurance') and others (*Analects,* II 5; IV 20; 1 2, 11; II 21). Turning to 'the test of all these in practice' she notes that a contemporary progressive view is given in Lu Hsun's *Twenty-four Portraits of Respectful Sons*; but the current cult of filial piety in Peking shows the present state of affairs to be no better. Today's heroes of Maoism are the reincarnations of the filial sons of the distant past. Lei Feng, the poor and simple soldier on whose priggish diaries a considerable cult of Maoist conformity and self-sacrifice was founded, is the most striking instance. The distinctions between ethics and politics, or the personal and the public conscience, were obliterated under Confucianism – and such continues to be the case in Mao's China.

Obliterated also – at least badly smudged – is the distinction between learning or science (*nauka*) and religion or faith. The fore-fathers of Soviet sinology were clear on this. Shmidt wrote in 1901 : 'Confucianism and *nauka* are almost synonyms to the Chinese' [443, p. 189]; V. P. Vasil'iev in 1873 : 'in China . . . *nauka* itself constituted a religion . . . and Confucianism is a reli-gion more religious than any other religion known to us' [521, pp. 160, 162].

'The best medicine against the idealisation of Confu-cianism', wrote Pozdneyeva in 1973, 'is the books of Vasil'iev and Bichurin : they knew very well what religion is, while all of us – who have been atheists since 1917 – have basically forgotten [what it is].' Evidently there is some idealisation of Confucianism among her Soviet colleagues, possibly some touch of religiosity towards the ancient core of Chinese wisdom, which she was con-cerned to warn so heavily against.

The example of Lei Feng is the only specific instance adduced, but the implication that the Confucian outlook still dominates in the thought of Mao had been so strongly emphasised that the Soviet scientific public was presumably expected to find its own instances; we must, it seems, do the same. The merging of learning or science with religion would presumably be exemplified by the cult of veneration of every thought and hint of Mao, the flourish-ing of the little red book and other breviaries, the injunctions to be 'both red and expert', the tales of the old man and the youngsters who moved mountains or solved engineering problems by taking thought (the thought, needless to say, of Mao Tse-tung), the unconquerable loyalty of the White-haired Girl, the innumer-able confessional and admonitory campaigns for self-abasement and collective worship, the Five Antis, the Four Goods, and all the other alarums and excursions which have constantly busied the Chinese people since their liberation. There has been much *luan* (turmoil) (due of course to the enemies of the people).

Other notions such as *huai* (destruction), anathemas, propriety of dress (in Mao tunics), in songs, commentary, deprecation of strange or foreign things (*ituan, i, hsieh shou, yin*) are among the conceptual words discussed by this Soviet writer which are con-sidered applicable to the Maoist philosophy of today. Would-be Soviet illustrators of this theme appear, incidentally, to be in danger of infringing Pozdneyeva's earlier dictum that analogy is not enough; but one possible analogy they have not hit upon is with the Confucian revival under the Nationalists in 1934–37, the 'New Life Movement' to reinculcate the basic Confucian virtues and the modern ones of hygiene and fitness, orderliness and cleanliness, by methods described by a foreign journalist as a combination of militarism with the YMCA. In contradistinction to the Africa of the Romans, there is always something old out of China. Failing further 'concrete' and correctly Marxist instances from the Soviet literature of the ways in which Maoism represents new wine in old bottles, or new trademarks on old things, Westerners can but speculate as to the exact nature of Mao's departure from Marxism and adherence to Confucianism, on the plane of detail.

The official Soviet account of the further development of Confucianism in the middle ages – to go back to that point in the story – is pursued by Pozdneyeva in the following manner. She draws particularly on a Chinese work published in Peking in 1958, *Materials on the Banning and Burning of Plays and Novels in the Yuan, Ming and Ch'ing Dynasties* – unfortunately, collections of such decrees began only with the thirteenth century – to show the State's use of these oppressive classical concepts. There were all sorts of punishments – a hundred strokes of the bamboo, cutting out the tongue, or the death penalty – but the *corpus delicti* of offences was less varied. Most commonly charged were 'licentious romances or novels'. Private persons petitioned for 'the burning of all heretical tales and dissolute songs'. China's most-loved book, *The Water Margin*, was banned because it 'teaches brigandage *(tao)*'. (It recalls, of course, the Russian ballad of Stenka Razin, even in its title : '*Iz-za Ostrova na Strezhen*'.) The 'most famous drama of young love', *The Western Chamber*, was banned as 'teaching debauchery'.

Pozdneyeva severely criticised the translations of these works and of the *Three Kingdoms* published in the USSR, in that their prefaces dealt in 'commonplaces' about the popularity of these works, without pointing out that 'their popularity held through centuries in despite of threats of punishment by death'. The censorial terms 'dissipation', 'banditry' and 'heresy' came from the *Songs of the Kingdom of Ch'en*, and were widely applied not only to novels and plays but to the mass of prose, all the *hsiao shuo* – 'small (plebeian, vulgar) words', all that Confucianism considered to be 'old wives' tales and gossip'. What this clearly expresses is 'the struggle in China of two cultures – the popular one and the State, Confucian, one'. (Perhaps this struggle still continues; the Soviet researchers might for instance refer to H. Evans's *Adventures of Li Chi*, 1967 – and compare it with the satires of Il'f and Petrov on the Soviet way of life.)

Pozdneyeva considers that some of her Soviet colleagues are thus continuing the 'idealisation of Confucianism'. The process is often shown, in China, in there being two variants of a rite, an official and an unofficial, two sides or parts to a ceremony. (Such a duality would indeed be truly Oriental.) Confucius 'did not want to see what happens after the libations of wine in the sacrifices to the First Ancestor' – though he was no teetotaller : 'at home he took wine without measuring it, but not to the point of intoxication' (which is another meaning of *luan*) (*Analects*, III 10; x 8). After the 'cupping' and the 'partaking' with the ancestors (which Pozdneyeva equates with the eucharist and the communion) the feasting 'went over into an orgy'; see item III 3 in the *Book of Songs* which is entitled 'Altogether drunk'.

The spokeswoman protests too much the sexual implications, proceeding to discuss the Chinese New Year festival when for three days or two weeks, coinciding with the celebration of spring and of fertility, not only is (or was) no work done, but one positive activity was what Engels referred to as 'the production of man himself, the direct production and reproduction of life' (*Collected Works of Marx and Engels*, Russian ed., vol, 21, pp 25–6) : in a word, fornication. Pozdneyeva is concerned with the intense clash between these popular activities and the official 'Confucian asceticism', of which clash, she remarks severely, 'evidently not everyone is convinced. L. S. Vasil'iev affirms that 'there could not be said to be any opposition between the secular and the religious principles in China' [520, p. 9]. The other Vasil'iev, V. P. Vasil'iev, had thought otherwise (in the nineteenth century already : 'mourning is a temporary Confucian monasticism' when 'one should not marry – or even procreate' [521, p. 43]).

Mo Ti had greatly opposed the pomps and restrictions of Confucianism; it is a great pity that there is still no Russian translation of his work. He stressed the economic waste – all the gear buried in the tombs, the loss of socially necessary labour time. The horrors of Confucian mourning, far surpassing any Christian Lent, are dwelt upon : a mourner must dwell alone in a special hut, sleep on a straw mat with a clod of earth for pillow, hunger and shiver in thin clothing, till 'his ears do not hear, his eyes not see . . . his limbs refuse to function . . . till he cannot rise without help or walk without a stick'. Mo Ti stressed how this would impoverish and deplete the race. He scheduled the required periods of mourning : three years each for the passing of a ruler, a father, a wife, an elder brother, a year for uncles, and so on (*Mo Tse*, chap. 25). The total could be twenty years at least; for the normal large Chinese family, thirty years or half a lifetime. The 'humanity' of Confucius, which Pozdneyeva accuses some of her Soviet colleagues of 'idealising', seems to extend to the dead rather than the living. The bitterness of the struggle must be noted.

On the intellectual plane, opponents were successfully anathematised, as Mo Ti and Yang Chu were by Mencius; Confucianism won. On the many-millioned plane of the working people, however, non-compliance steadily prevailed : witness the creation of the huge population of China. (It must be remarked here that the great rise in population really occurred in the eighteenth century onwards, i.e. after the 'middle ages' as defined in the Soviet discussion, and other factors were involved, besides the libido.)

Again the spokeswoman addressed L. S. Vasil'iev : here was the conflict between the secular and the religious which he 'did not find' in China. (The class-war is fought, we divine, on all fronts; and one at least of its victories has been gained in bed.) Unfortunately no specific extension of this theme was made to apply to current conditions in China; may we infer, for instance, that 'Confucian asceticism' is involved in the Maoist discouragement of marriages below the ages of about 25 for males and slightly younger for females?

In contrast to the contemporary Vasil'iev, K. I. Golygina is praised for her book [158], which demonstrates the strong continuation of Confucianism in the Fourth of May Movement (1919–, still lauded at the present day) in at least two respects : affirmation of 'the immovability of the ideas of the Confucian canon' of 'no heresy' and 'the exclusion from *belles-lettres* of all "low literature". . . .' The former 'included mainly narrative prose, drama, the song and story genres of the single people'. Soviet scholars should go deeply into these popular media. Pozdneyeva thinks, however, that it would be better to distinguish more clearly, even at that level, secular elements (popular poetry; *chi*, *fu*, perhaps) and ritual elements (threnodies and litanies, perhaps).

Even within a genre, in 'biographies' for instance, the secular productions of Liu Tsung-yuan are distinct from religious moralities – the tales of dutiful widows who do not remarry, sons who cut out their livers to feed their poor parents, and so forth. All this has been exposed by Lu Hsun in modern times; but it is creeping back in Maoist China, with such tales as those of the self-sacrificing Lei Feng. Soviet scholars must 'finish off' the cult of idealisation of Confucianism (a touch of which apparently persists in their own ranks) and develop the study of Chinese thought in terms of the 'secular versus religious' struggle, in the light of the Leninist teaching that 'in every culture there are two cultures'. (It is not clear whether this dictum applies to the current culture in the USSR, or whether the latter has achieved a new synthesis resisted only by a few persons in mental wards.)

MODERN COMPLICATIONS

Pozdneyeva's contribution may thus raise many questions. A more positive analysis of modern Chinese thought is given by V. G. Burov and V. A. Krivtsov (PSS, pp. 136–52). These comrades see that there is far more to combat than Confucianism. China's modern historical experience is very complex – opium wars, colonialism, the T'aip'ings, the Boxers, nationalism, Marxism. The intellectual influences of the bourgeoisie weakened meanwhile, the sheer arrogance of early expanding imperialism ending with a mere whimpering in its present state of decadence and defeat; but all this has left China with a baffling 'spectrum' of intellectual influences 'combining Rousseau and Montesquieu with social Darwinism, liberalism, pragmatism and positivism, irrationalism and intuitivism, anarchism and Trotskyism, and finally Marxism'.

The Communist Party was founded in China fifty years ago, but initially on one sound impetus (the October Revolution) and one less sound (the surge of nationalism under social pressures). Thus the Party included an actual minority of real or qualified Marxists, among bourgeois nationalists, anarchists and peasant democrats. Tsarist Russia was just as backward as China, but had a rich tradition of revolutionary social thoughts and movements. Only a little of such formed in China in the nineteenth century. Russia 'got Marxism through suffering', in a way China did not. Between 1920 and 1940 'Chinese democrats, and they were pre-eminently peasant democrats, were able *subjectively* to become socialists or even Communists', but rarely or only slightly Marxists; the *objective* situation hardly enabled this.

'Mao Tse-tung, above all, remained [based] on the standpoints of bourgeois nationalism.' He and his kind led the CPC, from the mid-1930s, 'with non-Marxist views in a Marxist envelope'. The struggle of the people was sharp on two fronts : against the internal feudalism and the foreign intervention. Various kinds of people went various ways under that strain. The T'aip'ings combined peasant utopianism with some Christianity, the bourgeoisie wanted to replace feudal methods of production with their own. Though believing they would have to bring other parts of Western culture in with the techniques, they clung to some parts of Chinese culture – as did not only such as K'ang Yu-wei but also revolutionary democrats like Sun Yat-sen, Ch'en T'ien-hua and Chang Ping-lin.

Senin's doctoral thesis [436] and articles traced the development of bourgeois ideology in two streams : one liberal, adding new elements to the old structure, the other democratic, seeking to replace the old structure with a new one. He considered the former as descended from Lin Tse-hsü through Wei Yüan to culminate in K'ang Yu-wei, the other's lineage to be through the T'aip'ings and Sun Yat-sen. 'Reform or revolution' were the alternatives. Tikhvinski, in 1959, had considered K'ang Yu-wei's reform movement 'progressive' for its time; but it was an attempt to combine Confucian and Western thought [495] and this was the course followed later by Feng Yu-lan and others. Tikhvinski finds K'ang Yu-wei's utopia of 'Great Unity' to express the longings of the peasantry – in 'harmony', then, with the philosophy of Tolstoy.

Ilyushechkin's work of 1967 [182] switches the earlier interest of Soviet students in the 'progressive' aspects of the T'aip'ing movement to a proper focus on their attempt to amalgamate aspects of Christianity and Chinese tradition. This was an anti-feudal movement trying to utilise parts of the feudal structure of ideas. As Plekhanov pointed out, lower classes sometimes imitate the higher ones – when they have not reached the level of class-consciousness to fight for their own emancipation.

Concerning the bourgeois reformers, Grigor'iev [168] and Chudoyeyev [97] have presented useful material further illustrating the great widening of thought in China from 'the narrow Confucian frame'. V. F. Sorokin's book of 1958 on *The Formation of Lu Hsun's World-Outlook* is also of interest in that connection. The 'progressives' are thus fairly well identified, but it is now time to broaden the inquiry, identify also the negative strains – and determine exactly the genesis of the thoughts of Mao Tsetung.

The first point is that all – reformers, revolutionary democrats, and even apparent Marxists – have been affected by such concepts as Kung Tse-chen's of the agrarian commune, or Chen Kuang-yin's of the confluence of Western and Chinese learning. Secondly, notions like social utopias and peasant socialism must be more exactly investigated. It is simply 'paradoxical' that the ideology of the T'aip'ings has not really been 'identified', despite all the attention given them, in the Soviet Union. Thirdly, a formidable array of modern Chinese thinkers remain to be thus properly dealt with : twenty are named, followed by 'and others'. Borokh's work [73] on Ch'en Kuang-yin and Wang T'ao is the only Soviet contribution, against this long list.

This does not, however, exhaust the desiderata. In the fourth place, the way in which Marxist and anarchist ideas came to be adopted in China must be studied. In the fifth, the sources and information on all this – foreign as well as Soviet – must be collected and systematised. This has been done for an earlier period to a limited extent in one collection by the Institute of Philosophy of the Academy of Sciences : *Selected Works of Progressive Modern Chinese Thinkers 1840–1898* (1961).

Sun Yat-sen has received considerable attention. Senin produced in 1957 the first 'systematic' analysis of Sun Yat-senism as representing the petty-bourgeois outlook, both rural and urban, 'approaching' Marxism though not embracing it [433]. The Founder of the Chinese Republic was 'the first to tread the path taken today by many leaders of the liberation movements in the countries of Asia and Africa'. He remained 'fundamentally an idealist' and 'fundamentally a materialist' – both in a single sentence of Senin's book. Sun's *Selected Works* were translated into Russian only in 1964, supplemented by a centennial volume in 1966 [486–7] – more than forty-five years after Lenin recognised Sun as a man 'subjectively' good but 'objectively' confused, like even the best of his countrymen, by the practical circumstances of China.

The spread of Marxism in China was considered more generally by Krymov in 1963 in his doctoral thesis [259] dealing with Li Ta-chao and Ch'en Tu-hsiu, the founders of the CPC, Tsai Ho-sen and Tsui Chiu-po. This thesis overestimated Mao Tse-tung's work in 1926 on *Classes in Chinese Society*, though saying that 'he called himself a Marxist some time later'; however, it deals usefully with the struggles of the early Chinese Marxists (or near-Marxists) with 'American pragmatism' (Dewey), Liang Ch'i-ch'ao's 'Oriental renaissance, Machism, vulgar materialism and behaviourism, eclecticism and anarchism'. Delyusin dealt in 1970 with the discussion in China (from 1920 onwards) about the 'choice between the West and Socialism' which 'laid the ground for the foundation of the CPC'.

Besides those already named, Li Ta, Li Chih and Shih Tsun-t'ung (= Shih Fu-liang) were notable champions of Marxism. Delyusin considers, however, that 'many saw the strength of Marxism, but not all, by far, could attain to an understanding of it. Some saw in it only the key to power, others the means to national salvation, not understanding the social class character of scientific socialism. [Such understanding] was not given to all, or given suddenly.' The Chinese Marxists were 'very weak' in that respect [105, p. 84]. The struggle was also against the Bakunin and Kropotkin types of anarchism, among other 'petty-bourgeois views', to which Ch'en Tu-hsiu, Li Ta and Hu Shih were inclined. Yevgen'iev recently gave a good account of this [542].

The foundation and development of the CPC (1920–40) has been the subject of many useful contributions, notably those of Glunin, Grigor'iev, Kartunova and Kukushkin in 1969 in a symposium on *The Comintern and the Orient* [169], which deals in some detail with the petty-bourgeois and nationalist trends. The latter included Li Li-san's view in 1930 of China as the centre of the World Revolution and Mao's ideas (*c*. 1940–45) 'of the necessity for a purely utilitarian adaptation of Marxism to Chinese reality and the replacement of Marxism-Leninism by a "sinified" Marxism'. Bourgeois social thought was dealt with as early as 1954 (when Maoism was not yet being impeached in the USSR) by Batalov in his master's degree thesis [47], centring on the discussion in the 1920s about the philosophy of life and science – Chang Shun-mai, Liang Shu-ming, Ch'en Li-fu, Feng Yu-lan's 'new neo-Confucianism' and others – showing again the two influences, Western idealism and Chinese traditionalism. Batalov's is still almost the only direct work in this field, Krymov [258] and Yan Khin-shun [532] are the other contributors.

In the 1950s there were only a few articles on Chinese thought. Again, bumper crops can only be recorded in the last few years. Kyuzadzhan in 1970 gave an extensive review of the Maoist 'drives' in the CPR (prior to the Cultural Revolution) without presenting any very profound theoretical explanation of 'the contradictions with a socialist society' [273]. There is a book about the Cultural Revolution by A. E. Bovin and L. P. Delyusin, *The Political Crisis in China* (1968).

MAOISM THE ROOT EVIL

This extensive review prepares the ground for the major attack – the criticism of Maoism, which only developed massively after 1967. There are broadly two wings, it might be said, in the Soviet alignment, though they are overlapping. Some find Maoism 'anti-Marxist' because of the 'anti-socialist' character of the domestic and foreign *policy* of Mao. Others present it as a distinct system of ideas, a general *theory* on its own. Is it a direct negation of Marxism, a deviant or an alternative? A dozen current books straddle these questions [82–3, 275, 30, 453–4, 302–4, 276]. The summing-up is roughly as follows.

The class character of Maoism is determined by the petty-bourgeois peasant structure of Chinese society, but is intensified 'by the low level of political ideation of its adherents, which largely determines its national[istic] limitedness' [304, p. 59]. The sources of Maoism are 'Chinese traditional, utopian socialist and sundry non-Marxist foreign doctrines, above all anarchism and Trotskyism', though 'not consolidated into a finished *Weltanschauung* or a more or less structural theory. [Mao's views] are a conglomerate of various ideas borrowed according to needs as they arise from the most heterogeneous sources, beginning with the conversations of Confucius and ending with the works of Kropotkin' (ibid, p. 9).

One focus in all this eclecticism and opportunism is, however, the aspiration that China should be a great power – the greatest power in a Sinocentric world ruled by the CPC. Mao's 'Leninism' was always 'superficial and pragmatic'. He turned to Marxism as part of a general turn of Chinese nationalism towards Western ideas, selecting Marxism as suiting his own purposes best – and as his rivals had not picked it up. Mao borrowed only the phraseology of Marxism, not understanding its historical and philosophical principles. He follows a slogan widely heard in China in the second half of the nineteenth century : 'Make the basis what is Chinese, use what is foreign as the means.' Mao uses Marxist terminology 'as his own kind of code, a cipher concealing the real content of his "thoughts" . . .' [30, p. 110].

This raises the question of the application of Marxism to 'backward' countries such as China. Marxists must not be so 'sectarian' as to ignore national peculiarities, the specific needs of 'tying-in with' working-class movements in each different country. Lenin bade the 'Communists of the advanced countries' to 'speak the language of each people' (*Works*, vol. 39, p. 330) but on no account to distort the principles of Marxism thereby, or to allow the intrusion of ideas alien to it. Another of the errors that beset the subject on every side is to attribute too much to the personality of one man alone, in this case Mao Tse-tung. This contributes in effect to the magnification of the hero-worship of this individual.

Soviet commentators should certainly not forget the 'Marxist-internationalists' of China (i.e. those who kept, to some acceptable extent, to the Marxist line). Those usually named as such are Li Ta-chao, Tsui Chih-po, Teng Chung-hsia, P'eng P'ai, Fang Chih-min and Wang Ming. But all these – with the single exception of Wang Ming – were active as far back as the 1920s and early 1930s. Soviet researchers are bidden to seek evidence of good comrades or 'better elements' in the record of more recent years : Bolsheviks and Bolshevism cannot have died out in China completely, or done so more than thirty years ago. (Mao won control of the CPC early in 1935 – and was not, of course, significantly criticised in the USSR until a quarter of a century later, though his defects are now supposed to have been obvious from his beginnings. The only significant exception, on the Marxist side, is the unmentionable one of the Trotskyists, who noted in the 1930s many of the strictures now raised in the USSR against Mao's credibility.)

Soviet activists are now directed to trace the whole complex of evolving ideological trends in China, including many that were ignored, or simply dismissed with abuse, in the past – even the evolution of Kuomintang views and the recent history of Taiwan. 'If we formerly limited ourselves to stating the fact that the Kuomintang concepts were reactionary in nature, the task today is to show what constituted their reactionary character.'

Burov and Krivtsov appropriately concluded with an admonition to 'raise the critique of Maoism to a new and qualitatively higher level. Hitherto we have, so to speak, gone at it in breadth. Now it is necessary to go to it in depth . . . to show the social conditioning' of Maoism. The review in the last part of this chapter illustrates the very considerable broadening – in the last few years only – of the debate, in contrast especially with the narrower purview insisted on, with some unpleasant side-kicks at named colleagues, by Pozdneyeva in her study of Confucianism which was reviewed in the middle part of this chapter (though it must be emphasised that her contribution appears after those of others, which she might take to have already covered the broader 'directives').

Many contributors do take a fairly wide view. The reader may well agree that more 'depth' is required; but it may be noted that a comparatively large licence is being issued to Soviet sinologists for greater efforts, which presumably carries some inference of more official support for their endeavours. Perhaps the Soviet Union may begin more substantially to 'catch up and outstrip' the capitalist world in the output of sinological work. The quality of the output is another 'problem'. Soviet work in other fields of China studies must be reviewed in further chapters, before a general conclusion can be justly attempted.

After these lines were written, a great *anti-Confucius* campaign was launched in China, illustrating the 'kaleidoscopic' nature of changes there. The Soviet commentators are not disconcerted; they brand this as a new 'manoeuvre', a fresh ruse on the part of Mao.

9 The Organisation of China

Central to the study of organisation is the subject of law. PSS 1973 included a brief consideration of the legal system of the CPR [171]. The subject substantially interested Soviet jurists in the 1950s, almost solely, however, in the aspect of public law (in Russian, State law). Eminent names in that connection are L. D. Voyevodin, K. F. Kotov and A. E. Lunyov. Other branches of jurisprudence received only fragmentary attention, in relation to China, with the exception of one extensive monograph in 1959, on criminal procedure [98]. This was mainly because material was comparatively available in the field of State law, whereas the rest of Chinese (CPR) law was not yet codified in those days.

One or two Soviet lawyers could read Chinese, but none could follow verbal proceedings in People's Courts and the like. The Soviet jurists are competent and keen, but L. M. Gudoshnikov (PSS, pp. 182–5) adduces two criticisms of their work in the 1950s: it was of 'too general' a character and 'shared failings common to all our prolific literature about China in that period' (the early days of enthusiasm about the new ally), 'namely painting everything that went on in China in [rosy] colours.' Furthermore, in this field as in others, there was the deviation of attributing to China a character of its own: 'Whatever the researchers were unable to fit into their accustomed concepts, they treated as national pecularities of China'. 'Though', chides Gudoshnikov, obviously 'what was involved was commonplace voluntarism and arbitrary rule'.

Like every other sector in China studies in the Soviet Union, the analysis of the laws and their enforcement in the CPR fell sadly away in the early 1960s. In Moscow in 1960, Gudoshnikov produced an important work on the higher organs of the State [172], and a very interesting treatise on the national-minorities of China, unfortunately published only in Ukrainian, appeared in Kiev in

1962 [490]. (Ukrainians are of course sensitive to questions of nationalism.) In 1964 a symposium defending the 'purity of Marxism-Leninism' against Maoism [308] included a key article by V. M. Chikhvadze [95], who came similarly to the fore six years later in another 'counter-attacking' symposium [96]. The salvoes from the big guns of Moscow became heavier, in this field of fire as in others, from about 1967. The official journal *Soviet State and Law* (1967, no. 6), published an article on "Politico-Legal Ideology and the Crisis of Political Power in China" by G. S. Ostroumov, followed by two other notable articles [372, 173]. There were also at that time articles in academically less 'central' journals (*Soviet Legality* and *Soviets of Workers' Deputies*) by F. Kalynychev and I. Gavrilov; but in 1970 and 1971 there was a curious lull, with no articles at all on China, so far as the legal journals were concerned. Efforts seemed to be switched to the Academy of Sciences, whose Institute of State and Law renewed in 1968 work on China which it had ceased exactly ten years earlier. The fruits of this resumption soon began to appear [96, 173].

Cadres proficient in both law and sinology continue to be extremely few. Yet a determined effort must be made to trace and analyse legal developments in the CPR since the 1950s, or rather earlier (the cadres are instructed), since the study of what happened in the 'liberated areas' even before the CPC came to national power would be most illuminating. At the same time, events after 1958 must be followed as far as possible – granted that there are no published legal statements (*akty*) or 'normatives'. For this important period we 'must mobilise all possible sources for getting material, including the personal papers and memoirs of our workers in China, [also] Western, Japanese and Taiwan sources' (PSS, p. 184).

The subject of greatest importance is the class character of the CPR (also of the liberated areas that preceded it) in the various stages of their development, and the political machinery by which they operated. 'The weak point in our past work on China', pronounces Gudoshnikov, 'has been a passion for studying the situation of the State apparatus without due appreciation of its interrelation with the party-political apparatus and the army. What was written in the legal norms of the CPR has usually been presented as the actual [practice], although much of what

E

was on paper did not [really] exist, or was heavily distorted in practice.' It is necessary to study the mechanism of the military-bureaucratic dictatorship through the processes by which it took shape and by which it functions, the role of the army in the political structure, the system of 'revolutionary committees', the economic administration, the penalties and sanctions.

The difficulties of such study are enormous, particularly because administration and law-enforcement (with the legislative and the punitive not too clearly separated in China) is now in the hands of organs or persons not formally charged with powers of State. (Gudoshnikov says: 'Indeed, Mao Tse-tung himself does not hold any State post.' This may not be quite true, as the Chairmanship seems to have some institutionalised significance; and the same point might be made about Stalin, or even some of his successors.) Legal decisions or directives are usually not published in the CPR; only extracts appear in the press. This is likely to continue to be the case; the 'military-bureaucratic dictatorship' will not trammel itself with a legal framework – at least until it feels its power secure, when it may prefer to dress again in the 'parade uniform' of a formalised legal system. Full study will only be possible if that occurs; meanwhile, indicators and instances are only to be sought in the hurly-burly of the tempestuous political and social life of the CPR, which must be watched and interpreted as closely as possible. (Once again, the Western reader may feel that historically these remarks could apply in some degree to the USSR.)

GOVERNMENT

The 'political organisation of society in the CPR' is considered more generally by N. N. Konstantinov [242]. The basic distortion of Marxism by the Maoists is, in his view, its perversion of the dictatorship of the proletariat. The 9th Session of the CPC and many official statements stress Mao's 'great contribution' in averting the restoration of capitalism in China', 'strengthening the dictatorship of the proletariat' and 'carrying through the socialist revolution' (*Hung Chi*, 1969, no. 5). Nothing does more to inspire the 'revisionist opportunists' and revive the hopes of the bankrupt anti-Communists than Mao's falsification of this most basic part of Leninism. Yet, on this as on so much else, Soviet scholars have until recently done sadly little (PSS, p. 175). To understand the 'regression' in China, the class structure in that country must be keenly examined.

The CPR was born of an anti-imperialist and anti-feudal revolution; Mao seized upon certain basic elements to shape it into a new political system. The revolution was embodied in a People's Political Consultative Council, as a united front of constituent 'soviets', workers' military and social organisations 'and other organs of power'. The Maoists at first concealed under this broad cover 'the class content, structure, role and methods of work of the Party, of the organs of power in the liberated areas and the other elements of the revolutionary political organisation that was coming into being'. Soon Mao began to introduce unsound 'thoughts'.

The Maoists' campaign for 'rectification of the style of work' was a wide purge, enabling them to strengthen their hold at the 6th Congress of the CPC in 1945 and set their line on the 'New Democracy'. They ousted their opponents from the leadership positions and avoided admitting proletarians to the Party in sufficient numbers to give it the correct class-foundation. Instead they drew their cadres of party workers increasingly from military personnel of non-proletarian origin, and trained these in 'military-police methods'. The strategic position from the conquest of power in 1949 until 1953, and the path towards socialism that the circumstances indicated, must be clearly defined. Some writers consider it a start in non-capitalist development through a 'revolutionary-democratic dictatorship'. The CPC was designated the ruling party and charged with ensuring the evolution of the revolutionary-democratic dictatorship into some form of dictatorship of the proletariat, also with securing the basis of the people's power in and through the People's Consultative Committee, the assembly of deputies of the people and through the pyramid of consultative committees in the localities and in industries. (The broad analogy here with the soviets in Russia is not much mentioned or closely identified in the USSR.)

The non-Soviet reader should be apprised that the apparently self-contradictory term 'democratic dictatorship' is used because this is a dictatorship that is a dictatorship of, in the name of or the sake of the people as a whole. This is, of course, the common pretension of all dictatorships; but to proceed with the Soviet argumentation, a transitional dictatorship seems to be envisaged. Two states could follow from this 'revolutionary-democratic dictatorship'. It could evolve, guided by a Leninist Communist Party, into a dictatorship of the proletariat; or, without such proper guidance, 'be transformed into one of the forms of reactionary authority'.

'Despite the obstacles placed in the path by the Maoists, in the first decade of the CPR some of the functions of the dictatorship of the proletariat were successfully implemented' in China. But 'the Maoists utilised the enormous difficulties of shaping a political organisation and applying a socialist policy in a backward peasant country' to divert China into the 'reactionary' course. 'Lenin considered that a repetition of Bonapartism was possible in our day', states Konstantinov – without, however, any page-reference to the works of Lenin. He notes that the working class was small and weak in China, the masses conditioned through centuries to despotism, with no democratic traditions, not even bourgeois ones. Yet all these 'objective difficulties' need not have been fatal'; 'subjective factors played the decisive part'.

The present socio-economic structure of the CPR has 'a socialist character' because the means of production are owned by the State and by co-operatives. But there are other institutions, of a political nature, which are 'intermediaries' in shaping the ideology in a less healthy direction. The way of living is socialistic, but the way of thinking is poisoned by influences steering towards a system of the opposite kind. The reasons are : firstly, that the situation is new, socialism is novel and not yet rooted; secondly, that the Maoists deliberately distort socialism; and thirdly, that the workers' consciousness of their interests is 'weak and twisted' so that they do not see through the Maoist plot.

The state power is of course the supreme focus of political relationships; the State is an 'all embracing' organisation. The holders of direct power tend to be alienated from the society, even from its ruling class. In China there is notably a 'one-way' flow of authority – from the 'Great Helmsman', both directly and through the military bureaucracy *downwards*, to 'the masses who have no rights'. Mao introduced some special institutions and controls in this chain of command : 'democratic consultations' to form 're-volutionary committees' and the like, 'struggle meetings', campaigns for 'criticism, struggle and re-education', for 'correcting the work-style', the 'three togethers' (live together, eat together, work together).

MILITARISM

Evidently the army is a main pillar of the structure, but the Maoist Party organisations also 'fulfil a role that is not that of proletarian power'. Konstantinov lays down that the army cannot rule the Marxist-Leninist party in a country that is building socialism, for it cannot give truly socialist objectives or ensure a 'broad democracy for the toilers, without which socialism cannot be attained'. 'In China, Mao's group took to itself full power, not regulated by legal norms. Its sole will is unwritten law for the action of the executive and the unquestioned subjection to it of all Chinese citizens.'

Though the Mao group and the military bureaucracy 'catch on to and make political use of the views and inclinations of various strata of people in China', its 'concrete' basis is physical and administrative oppression. It is necessary to identify the degree of coercion – and the forms it takes. A proletarian power coerces only the exploiters. The more the latter are liquidated, the more the State's non-coercive functions come to the fore – economic, organisational, cultural and educational dispositions. Of these 'creative' functions Maoism makes no mention, except to distort them radically, as for example in calling 'Cultural Revolution' what was really a wave of vandalistic coercion. Konstantinov's contribution concludes like all the others with a list of tasks. A full evaluation must be made of the present political system in the CPR as 'petty-bourgeois in its class nature, authoritarian and militaro-bureaucratic in its form and in its method of political sovereignty'.

A closely connected question is, how socialistic is this society? 'In China today the political superstructure has lost its revolutionising effect on social relations and become deeply inconsistent with its infrastructure. Contradictions between the base and the superstructure have taken on an antagonistic character. Development and functioning of a socialist superstructure, on a new base, does not proceed automatically.' The Maoists have 'revised' the laws of socialist transformation of society in this context, intruding the individual military and bureaucratic dictatorship of Mao. A reactionary group subordinates the interests of the working people, the workers and peasants are no longer masters of the State- and group-owned property, which has already lost its socialist character. 'The socialist principle of "to each according to his labour" is abrogated, the working class disorganised, it does not have the leading place in society. The peasantry is dismembered too, its alliance with the working class destroyed. The intelligentsia is set off against the workers and peasants.'

Marxism gives the reassurance that the infrastructure must in the end be decisive, forces will break through which will restore the balance and set China back on the socialist path. 'But at what a cost, and when this will come about, is hard to say,' writes Konstantinov in a somewhat *diminuendo* conclusion; 'for these laws do not operate automatically under socialism, they need regenerated and organised social forces to make them effective, above all a change in the nature of power, to give it a proletarian and socialist quality. The task of the Soviet scholars is to disclose and evaluate the factors on which the doom of Mao's personal dictatorship depends.' (We are given, as yet, no precise indications of the internal forces that might unseat Chairman Mao, or his successor. Perhaps an external force, the Red Army, may have to take up this role, of which it has had some experience in Eastern Europe.)

THE WORKING CLASS

The internal alternative would of course be the working-class movement in China itself. On the present position and possible future of the Chinese proletariat, however, as distinct from some studies of its earlier history, Soviet scholarship provides us with scanty information. Thus in the PSS the sole contribution on this subject (by T. N. Akatova, pp. 129–36) is placed in the historical section and is largely political and declamatory. Her treatment is on the following lines. The workers' movement began in China as a reflection of the success of the October Revolution and the cordial support of the Soviet workers, the Comintern (the Communist or Third International, 1919, suddenly dissolved in 1943) and the Profintern (the Red International of Trade Unions, 1921, faded out of existence in 1935–37).

The movement in China was naturally a main focus of Soviet 'publicity' in that revolutionary period; in fact it was the subject of a large output of highly unacademic propaganda. Many participants have left their works and memories of those heroic days :

Geller, Voitinski, Lozovski, Dalin, Mif (this name, ironically, means 'myth' in Russian), Iolk, Al'ski and others. Yet this movement was soon defeated : 'In the conditions of the fall of the workers' movement in China in 1927, the specific weaknesses of the work of the CPC among the toiling masses were distinctly revealed.' In the following twelve years much more was published in the USSR on this subject, some of it of a serious kind; the most basic contributions were, however, descriptively historical rather than analytical [299, 359]. (Political analysis was a very risky pursuit during the reign of Stalin.)

In 1941 China studies, like many others, were obliterated by the war with Germany. Four years of neglect of this subject (plus some depletion of the ranks of specialists and of possible new recruits who were victims of either the Nazi or the Stalinist terror) left a gap which it took a few years to fill. The restart, except for the most general statements, came with university theses and articles. Many of the former were never published, but some works of the 1950s are well known : I. I. Gerasimova's thesis on the beginnings of the trade union movement in 1921–25, N. P. Vinogradov's articles on the events of 1923, Akatova's on those of 1924–27 [5–7], Kartunova's on the same period [213] and Pentkovski's on the Nationalist era [367].

The brief period of friendly access to China in the 1950s yielded a new supply of original materials which were worked into 'deeper' studies in response to the current demands of the situation – which meant, however, especially the filling of many serious gaps left by the earlier work. (Akatova is frank about these perspectives, more so than most of her colleagues. These comments about the reasons for the variations in the academic output in certain periods are interesting; they must apply generally in all fields of Soviet intellectual effort.) Akatova goes on to say : 'Thus Soviet historians have in recent years set themselves on the road of minute investigations of particular fragments of the history of the workers' movement in China, restricted not only by narrow chronological limits but frequently also by regional ones' (e.g. [213] is on Shanghai, [5] on Canton, for the same two years). This 'led not only to fragmentariness but also to a certain one-sidedness' as these dissertations concentrated on selected periods of special significance and on the materials that happened to be particularly available concerning them.

The period most studied and remembered is 1925–27, because this is hailed as 'the first colonial revolution in the world'. Nevertheless, 'these [studies] give only partial material'. (It is in fact a little difficult to establish in more than partial detail the comparison that some Soviet enthusiasts would desire to draw, that 1925–27 was 'China's 1905'. Akatova, for instance (PSS, p. 132), considers that study of the 1924–27 period in South China should throw light on the role of the working class in a revolution . . . the union of the workers with the peasantry . . . the tactical basis of united fronts . . .' and many other things, in fact most of the topics in the Leninist's handbook, which really were not very integrally applied or tested in that 'Canton phase'. The Chinese working-class movement appears as having been relatively weak in that sequence of events, in which it and the Communist Party with its Soviet advisers were heavily and rather summarily defeated.)

Work is continuing on the Chinese labour movement (Yu. N. Kostousov on Shanghai in 1945–49, Kartunova on the Profintern in pre-Liberation China, V. I. Khor'kov on 1927–37, and the Institute for the International Labour Movement on the recent period), but this is still mainly 'in process'. The subject is 'resolved in an oversimplified way. The CPC's leadership is taken as an adequate leadership of the working class, though the Party itself departed gravely from proletarian positions, in its composition, ideology and practice'. The Party 'led' to only a limited extent just before 1927, when it was 'ridden' by the Kuomintang; after 1927 it 'headed towards serious tensions, primitivism, finally to infringement of the historical truth' (falsification of history). The Chinese Party pursued all kinds of visions, to the neglect of its most basic function, which is to lead the working class. (What happens in a case like China's where the urban proletariat is (*a*) very small and (*b*) does not want to be led by outsiders? Apparently the only practical answer is Soviet occupation, which (i) proletarianises large masses of the people and (ii) ensures development towards true socialism, i.e. the present Soviet type of society.)

Akatova complains of the over-emphasis, even in Soviet publications, on the weaknesses of the Chinese proletariat. Did not Lenin, as early as 1907 (*Works*, vol. 3, p. 13), 'lay down that the role of the working class is immeasurably greater than its ratio to the total population'?? This is all the more true in the new conditions of the time after Lenin's October Revolution. As in Russia, the proletariat is 'concentrated' in China, in a few major industrial districts. Its heroism is on record. The fault is not theirs, it is their Chinese leaders'. The 'primitivism' referred to earlier is connected especially with 'dogmatism', of which the Chinese historiography in this field is guilty, though 'it has to some extent also shown itself in the Soviet researches'. The Chinese historiography gets this, however, from its own party leaders, who showed it most sharply – under Ch'en Tu-shiu – in 1921–27 in the form of 'so-called rightist opportunism'. After the defeat of 1927, on the other hand, the mistakes were those of left opportunism : weakening the links of the party with the mass of workers, breaking those between the industrial centres, the peasants and the Red Army in the Chinese areas.

At the same time, Akatova notes, the Kuomintang enemy is underestimated. 'In most of the articles, all the Kuomintang measures are described as anti-worker, or just demagogic. Indeed the KMT's "worker policy" was broadly social-demagogic, but at the same time it was fairly complex, flexible and manoeuvring; and in a certain measure it was based on real concessions to the working class. Thus it was much more dangerous than mere demagogy. Such a simplification implies underestimation of the development of national-reformism in the Chinese labour movement.'

Moreover, regarding the initial period of the CPC, many Soviet writers suppose that the Chinese working class was immune from reformist influences, because it was so poor; there was no 'labour aristocracy' such as Western countries have. 'This simplified assumption', comments Akatova, 'was mistaken after 1927 when the KMT, invoking the peculiar nature of the Chinese conditions, was able to spread national-reformism widely among the workers.' (Cf. the present writer's comment, pp. 20–1 above.) It is most important to study this kind of nationalist-reformist propensity, because it has gravely affected China and is a deeply embedded feature of Maoism; furthermore it is ubiquitously 'typical in subjugated or dependent countries, where the spirit of nationalism is strong not only in bourgeois circles but also in the working masses'.

The logical conclusions seem to be, for this chapter, that the

Chinese working class – on which the Marxist must intrinsically rely as the only force that can break through the impasse into which Maoism has allegedly brought China – is hardly strong enough for such a task, or poised to undertake it. Yet a burning faith in the Chinese proletariat seems to be about all that the Soviet reader is given to sustain the expectation that China will be brought peacefully back to the correct path towards socialism. The other aspects of organisation in the CPR seem to have been found entirely flimsy, by the same criterion. The legal system is sketchy, unable to defend the toilers, designed rather to subject them than to be serviceable as a sphere of change. The Communist Party of China is now similarly the creature of 'Mao and his group'. The latter have made the legislature and the executive, as well as the judiciary, part of a construct of their own. They have emasculated other socialistic institutions, such as the co-operatives, and set up a variety of permanent or *ad hoc* organisational devices of their own, such as meetings for 'struggle', public accusation or confession.

The Soviet expositions seem hardly to have adduced any counterweights to these Maoist machinations, let alone 'antitheses' likely to defeat them, or something 'concrete' with which to replace them. Previous chapters have in turn revealed a similarly hopeless view in the fields of foreign relations, the Chinese economy and ideology. The next chapter will address itself to a rather different horizon – the cultural life of China. This is so vast and rich a subject that it may seem impertinent to give it only a single chapter; but the reader will understand that the prospectus here is not to examine all these subjects exhaustively, it is merely to note the state of studies in the USSR. In the Soviet Union, it will further be borne in mind, the approach is in principle broadly that the economic realities are 'basic', the rest 'superstructural', while every subject in this curriculum is prefixed by 'politico-', as politico-economic, politico-social and so forth – even politico-cultural.

10 Chinese Culture

N. T. Fedorenko provides [121] a general survey of Soviet studies of Chinese literature. Soviet researchers must relate this literature to the basic socio-economic processes in Chinese history and to the general laws of cultural development that hold for all mankind – no country can plead to be a special case. V. M. Alexeyev, the founder of Soviet sinology, had recommended taking some famous writer (he instanced T'ao Ch'ien, alias T'ao Yüan-ming) for exhaustive study, when the context of his social period, even if previously unknown, would be fully exposed. 'It is necessary to begin, not with general surveys, but with particular sharply limited investigations – monographs' [16, pp. 56–7]. This chimes with Chuang Tse's saying that 'people read what is known and do not realise that learning begins only when, on the basis of what they know, they start to investigate what is not known'.

Alexeyev had firmly distinguished broader categories of specialisation – 'history, philology, philosophy, linguistics, art studies, etc.' – which could on the Soviet Marxist basis be co-ordinated as never before, a co-ordination both within sinology and between sinology and the other 'sciences' [22]. Fedorenko outlined the difficulties which tend to favour extreme specialisation and impede 'co-ordination' in the case of sinology : the archaic, varied and difficult language and scripts, the extent of the source-materials (extremely few in old times, swelling to an unexplored plethora later), a wide range of interpretations and terminologies among sinologues. It is particularly regrettable from a Soviet point of view that there is no agreement as to the periodisation of Chinese history. Until the present century there existed even in China no proper history of Chinese literature, though there could be no country in which literature was more important. This is noted by Ch'eng Chen-to in his great *Study of Chinese Literature* (in Chinese, Peking, 1957, vol. 3, p. 1138). The nub of the question is, what is Chinese literature? There is the term *wen hsüeh*, but what does it comprise? The content varied in different historical periods, also the term : *wen, wen chuan, wen hsüeh*. All were 'subjectively' selected and interpreted; a new 'objective' treatment is required, relating it to contemporary realities. There was not even a term for 'the history of literature', but there were expressions showing the way it was treated : *shih hua* (words about poetry, *wen t'an* (conversations about literature), *ts'e t'u* (vocabularies), *wen-yuan chuan* (tales from the garden of literature), *i-wen ch'ih* (descriptions of literary remains), etc. Thus there was commentary in plenty, but no synthesis of ideas.

On the other hand, a concept of 'pure literature' was enhanced : writings which 'exalted sentiments . . . the expression of aesthetic emotions'. These are the words of Hu Yun-i, whose *History of Chinese Literature* (in Chinese, Shanghai, 1936) influenced some Soviet specialists. Hu excluded severely from 'literature' not only the classics, histories, philosophies and natural histories, but also the literary aspects of historical narratives such as the *Tso-chuan*. Indeed he went further, in excluding from 'pure literature' the T'ang and Sung masterpieces of Han Yü, Ou-yang Hsiu, Su Tung-po and the rest. Such one-sidedness was counterbalanced by the work of Fan Wen-lan, translated into Russian much later [120], which praised such works as the *Tso-chuan* as good prose and rich in popular history. Alexeyev, in 1920, had, however, stressed that Ssu-ma Ch'ien (for instance) was 'above all a stylist' [14, p. 287]. The *Tao Teh Ching*, for another example, was in an entirely new poetic form.

Thus Fedorenko is concerned to defend Chinese literature as a valuable field of study, firstly for its intrinsic merit and secondly as a key to the understanding of China. He correlates the evolution of the various genres with basic historical changes : in poetry the original *shih* was followed by *fu*, the T'ang *lü shih*, the Sung *ts'e*, the Yuan *ch'ü*. The first lasted until the end of the T'ang, the fourth until the Sung, the last until modern times. Peking University produced a collective *History of Chinese Literature* in two volumes in 1958, revised into four volumes the following year, which took the right directions, but it was too 'schematic', 'exaggerated the role of folklore and simplified that of some great writers'. The periodisation suffered from the same 'sociological distortion'. This shows the ways in which work in China began to go wrong at the time of the split with the USSR.

Fedorenko expands on these points, emphasising that 'literature is a special category of social creative activity, not synonymous with philosophy and science but interconnected with them, using many of their methods: concepts, symbols, forms, measures, rhythm, euphony'. It must be taken broadly, not as 'old dusty texts' but as showing the development of life; for that it must include all the worthwhile contributions of elegance and useful criticism on the more sophisticated plane. International and cross-cultural studies are essential : Marxism affirms that the same laws apply to all mankind, there are differences only in circumstances. Fedorenko at this point notes the usefulness to Soviet scholars of Japanese work, instancing Kondo Moku's synoptic treatment of *wen hsüeh* in his large *Dictionary of Chinese Art* (Tokyo, 1959) p. 1108.

Historic social currents and changes are admirably reflected in the changes ('differentiation') in what is considered as worthy of being termed 'literature' and in the composition of what is included as such. Indeed the former determine the latter; though the latter are secondary elements, a superstructure on the former, and there may be a time-lag in the adaptation of the superstructure to the changes in the base. It is further stressed that the 'pecularities' of the situation in China be recognised : the 'uncommonly long period of feudalism, over two thousand years' and the specially strong role of violent rebellion as the machinery of change, bringing down one dynasty after another. This means, however, that a new periodisation is now acutely lacking; a Marxist basis of periodisation is essential.

Nevertheless, this commentator gives the impression that the new Marxian strain should be superimposed on the old traditional chronology rather than displace it : 'It is hardly suitable, in the process of establishing the new one, to ignore altogether the old "dynastic" periodisation [which has been] greatly serviceable both to our predecessors and to ourselves.' Alexeyev is again cited (in a later work, of 1958) to stress the necessity of respecting the broad nature of Chinese culture : 'The Egyptian civilisation was characterised by the cult of life beyond the grave, the Greek by the cult of beauty and art, the Roman by that of the State and law, but the Chinese by the cult of the written word, of literature'

[24, p. 301]. It is striking, adds Fedorenko, that there have been 'no special researches' in the USSR to follow up the great lead given by Alexeyev. As the Soviet novelist K. A. Fedin has put it (platitudinously enough), the development of literature is innately connected with the development of society.

These themes having been illustrated at some length, Fedorenko makes clear the application. 'Meanwhile', he continues, 'the magnificent masterpieces of national and world literature, the pride of humanity, are anathematised by the Maoists as "deadly growths", "harmful weeds", containing "feudal poison, bourgeois and revisionist views of the world. Maoism thus denies that literature and art are specific individual forms of social consciousness. This Maoist line is enormously damaging. . . .' The Maoists have raised up mass movements of vandalism, the Red Guards and the rest, 'to do nothing but defile everything and leave only ruins. This is now a historical fact.'

Lenin's precept that the revolution should take over the heritage of the past and give it to the whole people has been 'consigned by the Maoists to oblivion'. They have condemned the *Books of Songs and Poetry*, that record of the earliest development of the Chinese people, their *Iliad* and *Odyssey* and Ramayana and Mahabharata, their Igor' the *Elegies of Ch'u* the *yüeh fu*. . . . A two-page catalogue follows – in sum, practically the whole literary heritage of China fell to be 'burnt like weeds' by the vandal 'hordes' of the Maoists (especially their youth – which does not augur well for future generations taking a better course, as some optimists expect). A Chinese 'revolutionary sculptor' is quoted as saying : 'Armed with the thoughts of Mao Tse-tung, we boldly despise all that has been called the summits of world art. However much the Renaissance and the "Golden Age" of T'ang in China have been praised to the skies, the former was bourgeois, the latter feudal, neither of them proletarian. And there was nothing really remarkable in them, nothing that we could not surpass.'

In this way China under Mao reached a crudely destructive stance, after a long process of campaigns, of pressures and persecutions, which had already destroyed the artistic confidence of China. This goes back to the Yenan conference of 1942 where Mao affirmed the line of 'proletarian realism' pronounced by the League of Left Wing Writers of China in 1930–36. In the 1953 reissue of the *Collected Works* of Mao this term 'proletarian realism' was replaced, in the Yenan 'statement', by 'socialist realism'. Subsequently the 'zigzags' in the Great Helmsman's course widened. In 1956 he declared 'let a hundred flowers bloom'; all kinds of free and critical artistic and other expression were briefly permitted, but this proved to be a trap, for any nonconformist productions were swiftly punished. In 1957 the counter-attack against the 'rightists' followed, with the campaign for the 'rectification of the style of Party work'.

In 1958 Mao produced a different formula, 'a combination of revolutionary realism with revolutionary romanticism', in deliberate antithesis to socialist (Soviet) concepts of art. At that time there was the 'Great Leap' in the economy and the communes were forced ahead; literature and the arts were also to 'leap' into a new and frenzied profusion. From 1963 to 1965 the 'Great Proletarian Cultural Revolution' already loomed, the subjection of the arts to Mao's notions was extremely intensified. In 1963 Chou Yang had in fact gone back to the Yenan declaration of 1942 to 'revive the idea of an opposition between the professional writers and artists and the amateurs, the non-professionals . . . reducing the artistic intelligentsia to the position of "superfluous people". . .'. On the eve of the 'Cultural Revolution' in 1966 the *Kuangming Daily* laid down that 'the victorious proletariat does not need professional writers, artists, composers or painters : it needs half-writers/half-workers, half-artists/half-soldiers, half-painters/half-peasants . . .'. A totalitarianism by infinite schizoidisation – which, no doubt, the Party will do nothing by halves to attain – is a fascinating formula for the Brave New World.

The Soviet intellectuals' task is thus to preserve Chinese culture, 'as [one that is] inseparably bound up with the appeal to traditions, with centuries of popular culture in all its richness and diversity. There is, however, no question of retreating into the past, into contemplative or exoticist interest in other periods, into antiquarianism . . . not to escape from the present but . . . to realise in it the organic continuance of the national traditions, the further development of the culture. . . .' Only Marxism can do this, reaffirmed Fedorenko in his conclusion.

THE PRESERVATION OF CHINESE CULTURE

Soviet sinology, then, is to step forward to preserve Chinese culture for the World Revolution – the real Chinese culture, in all its breadth and depth – as a living entity for further development, against its destruction or perversion by the Maoist vandals. (This has not yet been dubbed conservative revolution, but perhaps that is the dialectical sense of the tendency.) How well are the Soviets able to take up this great historic responsibility? The answer lies, first, in their stock of resources and skills in this field, the account of which is pursued by L. N. Men'shikov in PSS (pp. 259–67). He sets out a number of requirements, interspersed in heavy type among some availabilities for meeting them, for 'the study of Chinese literary memorials'. There is little analysis of Pan Ku's *Han History*, not to speak of subsequent dynastic histories; the prime requirement is for 'specialists in the bibliography of Chinese history' to list what exists, evaluate what has been done in the USSR, then identify the gaps.

There has been some success in tracing lost works and making new discoveries. There is a collection of materials from the Tun-huang caves, the Chinese portions of the Khara Khoto, the cata-logue of the xylographs in the Leningrad branch of IVAN; there are works on 'lost' Chinese literature by B. L. Riftin, V. I. Semanov, D. N. Voskresenski 'and a few others'. K. K. Flug pro-duced in the 1950s a study of *Printed Books of the Sung Period*; since then the evidence from archaeological work has been much further examined, but the more general situation is most un-satisfactory. 'There are no catalogues of the xylographs in such major collections as the Oriental Library of Leningrad University and the [Moscow] Lenin Library, not to speak of lesser ones. The description of the Chinese manuscripts in our collections is also incomplete. The provision of a Union catalogue of holdings of archaeographic works is the second task, one that is not to be postponed.' All this is far from enough. 'To consider just one country's holdings renders learning one-sided, condemns it to provincialism. A full guide [*svod*] to materials kept in various countries is required. Academic forays [*komandirovki*] abroad are necessary *with special bibliographical and archaeographical aims*' (emphasis in the original). Even more important than basic texts are abundant commentaries, notes and the like.

Following the great example of the *World History* series [529] the translation of the basic texts should be pursued; yet not one of the twenty-four dynastic histories has been rendered into Russian. The translation of all these should be pressed, it is similarly emphasised. Much is made of the 'Sung project', an international move in which Soviet sinologists are participating. For such work, the latter need better resources in the way of the indices and other facilities mentioned above.

Men'shikov next stresses the importance of using Chinese characters in all relevant discussions and publications. Some appear 'without a single hieroglyph', which is *'simply inadmissible'* – underlined in the original. (Agreed – where the ideographs are necessary. The facilities for this are as scarce and, in real terms, as expensive in the USSR as in the West.) Men'shikov notes that 'not all sinologues, by far, understand the need' for using the ideographs, at least in cataloguing and giving references. This neglect of the study (of written Chinese) is one of the reasons why some of 'the basic classics . . . remain untranslated and uncommented [in the USSR] and we still turn to Legge's translations, why books on the Chinese philosophical tendencies are not translated and studied'. There are of course notable exceptions (e.g. [478]). The characters are only part of a more general requirement – that the index reference should give sufficiently full indications regarding the book, or other artifact.

Men'shikov makes an interesting plea that workers in this field should be to some extent 'inventors, experimenters' – just as the first 'translations of poetry [in Russia] in the early nineteenth century and the translators of European symbolism in the early twentieth century' had to be complete innovators. An example is the rendering of the Chinese tones, or their interchanges; no one has yet shown ways of doing this in Russian. Much depends on the translator's talent, as well as that of the sinologue. (The two should obviously be combined. Translations into English, too, mechanically perfect as such, are often vitiated by ignorance of the subject-matter; a random Western example is a Frenchman's denunciation of a certain detestable 'People's Police' in which the latter is rendered into English as 'the hated popular police'. With proper names, 'in-group' allusions and cant-words, the cross-cultural pitfalls are more dangerous.)

VULGARISATIONS AND SERIOUS WORKS

Men'shikov claims that 'in the last twenty years or so an enormous quantity of translations of classical Chinese literary works has appeared in the Russian language'. (The other 120 Soviet languages are not mentioned by the speaker. Some of the important ones, and a large part of the total population – an actual majority of which, overall, are now non-Russian – are Asian.) 'It is possible', adds Men'shikov, who is in flat contradiction here to what many of his colleagues have said, 'that in the number of [translations from Chinese] we are already in first place in the world'. He proceeds, however, to criticise severely the quality of these. One interesting complaint is against the popularisation and romanticisation shown in the renderings. Contemporary fashions in 'glamour', as well as the long-standing propensity to strive to appear 'exotic', are reflected in the packaging of popular translations.

'Under one title, people will read it : under another, they won't. So instead of the demure title "Popular Tales from the Metropolis" we have "Fifteen Thousand Pieces of Eight".' A 'collection of stories' becomes 'How Chui Nin was Executed by Mistake'. Well-known late Ming and early Ch'ing novels are blurbed as 'seductive' and titled accordingly 'Tricks of the Festive Dragon'. 'Instead of *The Western Chamber* we have *The Spilt Cup* . . .', complains Men'shikov; yet 'no one would permit himself to call the *Decameron* "Ten Nights of Passion", *Madame Bovary* "The Tragedy of Carnal Love", the *Odyssey* "Wanderers on the Boundless Seas" or "The Vengeance of an Outraged Man". It seems that all this is "commercial", these are a sort of commodities; that means fostering bad taste and false concepts of literature.' (There is certainly a very small but perceptible degree of convergence between Madison Avenue and the Kalinin Prospekt, but not yet to the point, for example, of some strait-laced classic being covered – in paperback – by a nude harlot. This has happened in the West, but the process has only begun very mildly in the East.)

Apart from a ban on flippant book covers and on spicing the text itself, the speaker demanded that serious translations be produced (e.g. of *The Dream of the Red Chamber*) with indices of names, indications of changes of scene, glossaries also of dresses, furnishings, explanations of current allusions, staging techniques, etc.; and 'all this *must* [in bold type : *obyazatel'no*] be given in Chinese characters. . . . Three steps : translation, commentary and [this] scientific apparatus.' One model, long used, is the more than a century-old German *Paulys Realencyclopädie der classischen Altertumwissenschaft*; the latest is the Harvard–Yenching series of indices, and there are others in China, Japan and France. For Japan, the *Taisho Tripitaka* is specially mentioned as the largest index of Buddhist texts broadly fulfilling the given requirements; and there is Hatano Taro's guide to the Ming period. The Sung project – to create a 'universal guide' to the period, with participants from Asia, the USA, France, Germany and the UK – is again mentioned in the same context. In the USSR there is currently the series of 'Literary Memorials of the Orient', with its yearbook; and works of Perelemov [370], Vyatkin and Taskin [489], Fishman, and Munkuyev [327]. 'For the large number of sinologues in the USSR, that is too little.' There are, however, project proposals coming forward which the editorial boards hope to be able to accept.

The main account of Soviet studies in Chinese literature follows, with L. Z. Eidlin as the spokesman. It is long (PSS, pp. 267–93), detailed and wordy, in an elegantly patchworked style. The definition of 'medieval' is crucial, in Eidlin's opinion, and within it the distinction of its 'early, developed and late' stages [472]. The term 'medieval', originally applied to the fifteenth and sixteenth centuries in Italy, is relative [529, chap iii, p. 7]. The Moscow University experts in 1968 (*History of the Countries of Asia and Africa in the Middle Ages*) and those of Leningrad University in 1970 (*History of the Foreign Countries of Asia in the Middle Ages*) agreed that China's middle ages began with the fall of the 'slaveowning' Han Empire, but disagreed as to its ending, the Moscow group finding that 'recent' history begins in the middle of the seventeenth century, the Leningraders choosing the end of the eighteenth.

The diverse interpretations of 'medieval', says Eidlin in his characteristically metaphorical style, 'are like those wineskins in which we need not pour one and the same wine'. The relative terms need special and expert study for China, as each country's culture expresses itself in a different way. Concretely, insufficient attention has been paid to the pre-T'ang feudal period. There is a master's thesis by B. B. Bakhtin on the *yüeh fu*, two books

[89, 116] and some partial references [279]. 'Work done in Japan and the West does not absolve us from doing our own work.' Gusarov's thesis [175] usefully stressed Han Yü's championship of 'a return to ancient times', which was 'based on fundamental Confucian teachings'. Since Alexeyev's work of 1916 [12] there has not been anything on T'ang poetry that can be compared with it: there have been translations of Li Chin-ch'ao, Lu Yü [439] and Hsin Tsi-chi, a collection of 'Sung poetry', some of Ou-yang Hsiu, a few articles on others – 'and that's all'.

Bel'gus and Tsiperovich presented the only item of Chinese 'popular stories' available for many years [50], followed by Sokolova [469] and Zhelokhovtsev's treatises on the 'prompt-books' of the storytellers and on T'ang novels [546–7]. Fishman's treatment of Chinese satire [133] is noted, but her belief that there was an 'actual' renaissance in China is rejected. There were useful new translations [514–15] and reissues of older works. Manukhin's translation of the *Chin P'ing Mei* [300] had not been printed, though it is much required (the administration may consider it pornographic, but it is a vital social document). Riftin [403], Semanov [430] and Tsiperovich [506] made useful contributions. The Tunhuang caves material provided a new rich store of *pien-wen*, 'monkish tales', for which Men'shikov, Gurevich and others of the Leningrad branch of IVAN are to be thanked.

DRAMA

Over a hundred and forty Yuan and Ming dynasty plays are available, of which only one has been properly rendered into Russian – Wang Hsi-fu's *The Western Chamber*. The post-Ming drama is thus also badly served, because its base-period material is so largely unavailable. Some, notably Hung Sheng and K'ung Shang-jen, are 'inaccessible to non-specialist readers' and 'inconvenient' for Soviet researchers; but 'who knows [even] the names of the Ming plays of K'ang Hai, Wang Ch'u-shih, Hsü Wei? Can we judge the dragon of Chinese drama and make any generalisations when we have at our disposal only one little scale from this hidden dragon's body?', declaims Eidlin in his inimitable manner. There is a master's thesis by T. A. Malinovski on the sixteenth-century Hung Sheng and his play *The Palace of Longevity*, also Sorokin on the Yuan theatre [474], S. A. Serova on

Peking Opera and I. V. Gaida on *The Chinese Traditional Theatre*; and a few articles. On the whole, there is very little on the Yuan drama, and the available material is partial and 'detached from its context' [474, p. 340].

CLASSICAL RENAISSANCE AND MARXIAN MODERNISM

This completes Eidlin's survey of the Chinese theatre. He turns to the basic Confucian trend, to stress the background to the general development of Chinese culture. Alexeyev complained in 1920 that 'until now we have not had a readable translation of any of the Chinese classics'. He went on to speak of 'the Chinese renaissance' [14, pp. 20–7]. He used this term, however, to refer to the Neo-Confucian movement of the eleventh to twelfth centuries, when it greatly clarified the classical form; it was replying to the challenges of Buddhism and Taoism. Later Soviet sinologists postulated a Chinese Renaissance with a capital R, more or less analogous with the European original – incidentally misinterpreting Alexeyev to that effect. This led to a considerable controversy, still apparently unsettled; L. D. Pozdneyeva wrote on this in *Problems of Literature* (1971 no. 5).

'After T'ao Ch'ien Alexeyev rated highly 'the three Hsiehs – the famed fifth-century poets of the landscape lyric', Lin-yun, Hui-liang and T'iao. These, Eidlin notes, 'remain unkown and unstudied' in the USSR. He praises both the prose and the verse of Han Yü : the latter's poems, those of his nearest contemporary 'the extraordinarily interesting poet Meng Ch'ao, also those of Tu Fu, the greatest poet of the late T'ang, are not available' in Russian. For the Sung poets Alexeyev wished to begin with a full volume on Su Shih before making a more general anthology. Almost nothing has been done in that direction, though Basmanov recently translated the Sung poetess Li Chin-chao. Eidlin concludes, therefore, by asking : 'Have we done much, or little? Is there a direct answer to this question? If there is, then it is very little; so little that one stands embarrassed at what remains to be done.' The injunctions and the leads given by Alexeyev, the founder of this branch of Soviet sinology, have been very scantily implemented. On the credit side 'indexes and collections of critical material on the poets T'ao Yuan-ming, Tu Fu, Po Chu-i, Liu Chun-yuan, Lu Yü and Fan Ch'eng-ta, dictionaries, reference books and findings by Chinese scholars are bringing us nearer the goal'.

'We have to look our difficulties in the face.' The greatest is that the methods of research in aesthetic matters are thought by some to be 'unscientific, subjective'. In fact there is much science in the modern approach : psychology and the accurate, even 'objective', grading of values, of what used to be left in the air as 'matters of taste' beyond the reach of dispute, moreover the possibility of explaining the causation or the morphology of taste. Something of this has been done on the Russians' own classics; Eidlin instances Bondi's recent study of Pushkin [69]. Why not do the same with the major Chinese writers? Limited credit goes, in this respect, to the studies of an 'outline' nature produced in the Soviet Union on Chinese literature ([115, 472, 240, 283] and some of Fedorenko's work).

Especially important, in the Soviet view, is the question of a correct periodisation; Eidlin reverts also to this topic. Chinese comments in the 1950s on this subject are approved (e.g. Yeh Yu-hua in *Wen-hsüeh Yenchiu*, 1957, no. 3). The Moscow University textbook [283] covers the following periods of Chinese literature : 'I. Early middle ages, 3rd–7th centuries. II. Renaissance, 8th–12th centuries. III. Mongol conquest, 13th–14th centuries. IV. End of 14th to mid-16th centuries and to the early Enlightenment.' Besides wrongly taking it for granted, notes Eidlin, that there was such a thing as a Chinese Renaissance, this is very confused; it obscures, above all, the fact that key periods were those of 'reunification' of the country under the T'ang and Sung (seventh to tenth and tenth to thirteenth centuries – not fitting into the above schema at all). Eidlin criticises this textbook on many points. He proceeds with a great number of colourful comments and allusions, so closely packed that there is not space for them here; and they would be of interest chiefly to specialists. He cites further works on many aspects [474, 431, 358, 43, 40, 353] but mainly to reinforce arguments already mentioned.

Eidlin's contribution is fatiguing in its lack of arrangement by subjects; it moves from one topic to another – which is, however, basically justified, because the various arts are interrelated, and is more refreshing than the heavily specialistic concentration of some writers. Eidlin is also stimulating in his breadth of reference – from Gorki on Russian handicrafts [165] to a Sherlock Holmes story for a moral on discretion [99] – in his encyclopaedic coverage of Chinese literature and his very lively phrasing. Such scholarship and wit could lighten the heavy pabulum of the Soviet discussions; but it might be more effective if it were organised in a clearer sequence of presentation. V. F. Sorokin joins in the general praise of V. M. Alexeyev and finds little progress in the Soviet study of Chinese literature until 1960, when the Institute of Sinology in the Academy of Sciences made a 'pithy' collection of 'heterogeneous' materials [122] on cultural revolution in China (using that term in a general sense, unconnected with the later Maoist application). 'This work was the first to elucidate systematically, albeit briefly, the state of the theatre, cinema and education in the CPR and to adduce interesting materials on other aspects and on the ideological struggle in that sphere. However, its brevity and its jubilee character [for the tenth anniversary of the CPR] told against completeness and objectivity in its exposition.' Subsequent developments alerted Soviet academics to the 'seriousness' of the situation of Chinese culture after Mao's 'Cultural Revolution'.

Sorokin thus turns to the present situation. 'Now literary, artistic, scientific and humanitarian activity in China is reduced to a minimum, militant anti-humanism thrives, the peaceable, spiritual native population is discredited or perverted.' The educational system has reverted to more normal conditions after the Cultural Revolution, but still within the Maoist framework and far from being on true socialist lines. A number of Soviet works [331, 100, 276, 302–4] present much information and show the growth of studies on contemporary China among the younger generation as well as the older. 'This was possible after a certain interruption' – when relations between the two countries were extremely reduced, during the early 1960s – 'of the study of such important aspects as education, the cinema and the reform of the theatre', also because conferences were held and studies promoted. 'More and deeper is, however, required.' For one thing, the resumption of the flow of material after several years' break produced 'many hitherto unknown sayings of Mao, on this theme [culture] as on others'. These 'exposed' Mao to 'a wider public', but mean more work for the academics. Secondly, the 'Peking propaganda' is constantly revising the interpretation and application of Mao's thoughts, 'preparing' (i.e. doctoring) classical or other texts; there is a heavy and continuing duty on this account, besides that of clearing the backlog.

According to Sorokin, the CPR policy of mass campaigns in the domain of the arts and literature began with the criticism of the film *Life with Hsiung* in 1951, officially for the re-education of the intelligentsia but later directed into general indoctrination of Mao's ideas. Accurate interpretation of such campaigns is difficult, because 'the ringing phrases sometimes conceal the underlying aims and measures', the accusations are a mixture of truth and invention. 'We must not leap from one extreme to another – if we formerly accepted the accusations as true, we need not now reject them indiscriminately . . . utilising also the material which appeared during the "Cultural Revolution", we must try to form an objective picture.'

Mao strives to 'depersonalise' the intelligentsia, to typecast them as 'those who know nothing but dead books, who can do nothing but get under the feet of the people'. This is Mao's way of closing the age-old gap between the educated people and the 'un-enlightened' masses. He wishes to put everyone in the dark, or the moonshine of his own thoughts, and to eliminate any thinkers, as potential oppositionists. Sorokin admonishes that the main task is to be thoroughly versed in the basic texts of Marxism and Leninism; these are fully proof against Maoist attacks, whereas the usefulness of the lighter special-purpose arms varies when the enemy shifts his tactics, as Mao is likely to do.

Some Soviet observers construed Mao's campaign of 'let a hundred flowers bloom, a hundred schools contend' as bourgeois ideology, others as a manoeuvre to attract the intelligentsia, still others as a ruse to trap dissidents, a provocation. Evidently Mao, 'overestimating the result of preceding re-education campaigns, counted on rallying the intellectuals to his policy, in preparation for a Great Leap. Besides, the aim was to make a favourable impression on progressives in foreign countries.' However, many intellectuals were 'uncomprehending and ungrateful', showed non-socialist or 'revisionist' tendencies; this 'provoked a stormy reaction, first a struggle against "rightists" – both real and imaginary – and so-called "revisionists", followed by the essentially anti-intellectual "Great Leap" . . .'.

THE COURSE OF THE BATTLE

The struggle is between the two lines – the Maoist versus the Soviets' 'internationally proved and tested socialist orientation'. (Proved where, we may ask? Not in Spain, Hitler's Reich, Chile, or now China; it is in fact 'oriented' only where the Red Army stands.) It did not begin in 1949 in China, Sorokin notes; it revealed itself in the late 1930s and during the 1940s, though its major growth was later with the growth of Maoism. 'As usual, these tendencies did not appear in a pure form', emerging only here and there. The opposition has been similarly confused, mixing Marxist with dogmatic or 'bourgeois-liberal' standpoints.

Sorokin, for the concrete programme, would give priority to the study of *contemporary* literature. (Others, we have seen, regard the traditional heritage as the heart of the matter.) The Maoists concentrate on current production, he considers, though 'working back' in many ways towards the past. They do this at a low level – full of 'schematism, illustrativeness, over-simplification, evasion of real difficulties and contradictions, of superficial optimism. [Their] criterion is only of the external, incidental aspects and not of the writer's purposes, not for plumbing the thoughts and feelings of the characters. The social yardstick is often vulgarly taken as the need to express one or another campaign or order of the day (for a perfect example, see Kuo Mo-jo's *Ou-yang Hai*).'

It is not enough for Soviet scholars to record or depict this state of affairs; they must identify its causes – which are diverse. They are 'not all to be attributed to Maoist plants or plots, nor to the novelty of the subject-matter and the inexperience of the authors. Experienced authors who do not have Maoist convictions have also produced uninteresting works.' Tradition weighs heavily against innovation in China; it stifled socialist realism at the start, only a few writers or artists with genuinely socialist propensities and skills have yet been born in China. Some with those qualities should, however, be detectable. They must be looked for 'in the current conditions', i.e. with fresh eyes – not in the mirror-image of past visions or lapsed standards. (Can this be a veiled plea for a complete break with Stalinist habits of mind?)

Sorokin adds that, if the Soviet reading public does not have a 'flattering' view of China, this could in some part be the fault of the translations which are often ill-chosen and badly rendered.

He would put 'the best novels, stories, plays and poems from the Fourth of May [Movement, 1919–]' urgently on the agenda, for better treatment. 'Critique of the critics' should also be developed, i.e. publication of the reviews and assessments made in China, tainted with Maoism as these may be, with due corrective commentary on them.

Sorokin gives much more emphasis to literature than to the other arts. Of the theatre, he says : 'Everyone knows the vicissitudes it has undergone in the CPR. At the beginning the attempt to reform the old theatre was correct in intention, but hasty and sweeping; then a period of rectifying the previous extremes, increasing the repertoire and reviving forgotten styles; then a new and still more radical "reform", or even "revolution", in which only "exemplary" plays were spared.' The only Soviet work being done on these periods is by L. N. Men'shikov of the Leningrad branch of IVAN, and it relates only to the first of them.

For other periods there are articles and surveys. Eidlin has written substantially about the acting of Mei Lan-fan and Chou Hsin-fan. Obravtsov's well-known books [346–9] 'give clear vignettes but cannot be a substitute for detailed scientific research'. Significantly, Sorokin adds that 'it can only be regretted that the best time has been allowd to slip by – not, we may only hope, for ever. But even now, when we [Soviet citizens] do not have the possibility of seeing performances, much can be done with the numerous scripts and pictures.' Not only the previous theatrical genres, but 'those that are new in China – colloquial plays, ballet and children's theatre – for it is in that quarter that the interesting problem arises of the mutual adaptation between those new modes and an audience brought up on the traditional theatre'.

THE CINEMA

'Still less attention has been devoted by our [Soviet] researchers to the Chinese cinema.' A 'young specialist, S. A. Toroptsev, is now working on that important branch of art', but meanwhile there is only a 'survey study' by A. N. Zhelokhovtsev. It must be realised, however, that Chinese stagecraft has an important, potentially very revolutionary, contemporary descendant – the Chinese film. A short note (two pages) on the Chinese cinema by the said young specialist S. A. Toroptsev is included in PSS 1973 (pp. 303–5). He notes that since 1966 the mainland Chinese screen has been used, like all other media, almost entirely to magnify the personal cult of Mao Tse-Tung. In the 1950s, however, the careful observer could already have identified the portents of the present situation. In the first years of the CPR the cult was 'modest – intimate, if you like (something like "internal monologue" in the 1950 film *The Steel Soldier*); thereafter it emerged into the category of evaluation (in 1954 in the film *The Great Beginning*) with a giant bust of Mao standing in the room to give a political and ethical characterisation of the personage; the "Great Leap" put an end to the psychological appeal and switched the motif of the cult to the footing of sloganeering (the so-called "light" documentary, 1958).'

This was marked in the first half of the 1960s; by the beginning of the "Cultural Revolution" [we had] such ardently personality-cult films as *Lei Feng* [that priggish and selfless soldier] . . . meetings of Mao with the "Red Guards" . . . [etc.]. . . . This was just the crowning touch to processes already maturing in 1950 to 1960.' (The young specialist writes graphically – from hindsight.) 'Unfortunately', he has, however, to complain, 'our possibilities of studying the Chinese cinema are sharply limited. The Chinese [ciné] archives are inaccessible, though it is known that they are being preserved. For example, there is not a single film of Mei Lan-fan in stock. Some of the extant plays of the Kuan Han-tsin were screened at one time in the CPR, but we were unable to hire even one of them, and it was just the same with the film on Kuan by Chang Hang. Today ,it is not only the art specialists and philologists who would like to see the film *Secrets of a Ch'ing Household* – but it is not to be had. Such is even more the case with pre-1949 productions.'

'We cannot always be satisfied', he continues, 'with a dubbed version. But the archives contain by no means all the films of past years in their original versions; among the gaps are the first film made in the CPR, *The Bridge,* also *The White-Haired Girl* and *Lin's shop. . . .*' He hopes 16-mm copies can be obtained and presented with commentaries to enlighten the Soviet public concerning the errors of Maoism. Available for this purpose in the Soviet Union are, for example, numerous copies of the 1950s film *The Haughty General* which was denounced by the critics in the

Cultural Revolution period as an attack on Mao. The success of the telecast in the Soviet Union in 1969 of the film *Praying for Happiness* showed the way.

In the middle of 1970 a succession of films of 'exemplary revolutionary plays' were screened in the CPR, led by the TV films *The Red Lantern* and *The Capture of Wei Hu Mountain*. Shortly afterward the Changchun (Manchuria) studio came to life again, having been out of action since the Cutural Revolution, with a few television films and colour films; in Peking, such have been produced for some time, for instance the ballet *The Red Women's Detachment* shown at the Venice Film Festival. In 1967 the popular-science genre of film had been condemned as 'bourgeois', but some were produced in Peking in mid-1970. Soviet critics wondered whether this indicated 'a breach with the past, just happenstance, or a new content? To answer that, we must have films'; the matter is an important one. It may be commented here that films provide a minor but significant illustration of the present difficulties of China studies in the USSR, on the one hand, but on the other of the Russians' determination to tackle such studies from every possible angle – and to do so in an organised or systematic way. How far have Western sinologists considered the film? What prospects of national or institutional support would they have for such studies? It will be interesting to see the scale and kind of support given for this and other new lines of inquiry in the USSR.

On the visual arts in the CPR there were a number of works in the 1950s by E. A. Zavadskaya, N. A. Chervova, N. A. Vinogradova and others, but thereafter a 'dead calm'. 'Certainly, the painting and sculpture of the 1960s in China is not the most interesting subject.' Soviet critics and public have usually had no politer comment for it than 'poster art'. One newspaper carried a piece of satire that is worth recording, headlined 'A visit to the Hall of the Ten Thousand Maocons', but most of the scanty references are not so humorous.

EDUCATION

It is rightly stressed that both the supply of worthwhile art and the demand for it depend greatly on the educational system of any given country. Education is treated, in Soviet sinology as generally in that country, under the rubric of culture (a word widely used in the USSR). On this subject, Sorokin has noted, 'Until now our [Soviet] list of activities shows only a few articles by A. Kirpish and V. Klepikov, though some others are now studying it.' We know only too well 'what part education plays in rearing generations imbued with the thoughts of Chairman Mao'. Like all the other speakers, Sorokin had to report (PSS, pp. 302–3) 'little or nothing' for Soviet work under various headings, including, in his case, the following: 'The state and trends of the development of science in China – not only the natural sciences but also the humanities – are hardly followed at all' in the USSR. There are no works of collation evaluating the development of historiography, of the study of political economy, of the study of literature or the arts, or of the study of social thought in the CPR. Nor are there any studies of the policy of the Chinese leadership at various stages towards science and towards the learned [professions].' A large collective effort is required to fill this gap. A similar deficiency exists in respect of library and museum matters, the press and publishing. Investigation of these is required 'not merely from the professional [functional or operational] point of view' but for the light they shed on 'the working of Peking's propaganda and the extent of its influence'. 'The cultural links of China with foreign countries are little studied. Now that such contacts have been renewed, their nature, extent and tendencies must be intently watched.'

Just at the end of his PSS paper, Sorokin sees a little recent progress in China; his peroration is worth quoting:

> In the last few months some, albeit weak, signs of an enlivenment of cultural life in the CPR have been observable. Higher educational institutions in the humanities are resuming work; there have been some new theatre shows; some expansion of artistic and scientific publishing is reported. Articles on cultural matters show a trend towards being very argumentative. This makes our task of criticising Maoist cultural politics more complicated, but more interesting. . . . It is extremely important, in particular, to seek ways of obtaining for ourselves a current supply of new publications in China. In a word, there are difficulties, and they are not small ones. Let us unite our efforts to overcome them and worthily fulfil our tasks!

Well, there are 'not small' academic facilities, and direct or entrepôt possibilities of importing from China, in most other parts of the world – if the Soviet Union can utilise these genuinely on the basis it proclaims in international exchanges, of 'equality and mutual benefit'. In these intrinsic respects, the rest of the world is to some extent open for China studies. There is, however, in any case an intrinsic technical factor which specially affects any country's or person's capacity for China studies : proficiency in penetrating one of the most awkward barriers, the Chinese language. This chapter must certainly include some notice of the progress and problems of Chinese linguistics in the USSR.

LINGUISTICS

The rapporteur on this at the PSS conference (pp. 305–13) was V. M. Solntsev. He notes the possible dual aims of studying the Chinese language : 'practical' and 'scientific', for utilitarian or 'abstract' purposes. On the plane here in question, a full scientific basis is required. In Russian there are such terms as *yazykoznanie* (knowing the language : cf. German *Sprachkenntnisse*) and *lingvistika,* the (science of) linguistics; it is difficult to use these terms exactly in English translation. However, 'Effective study of the language on a large scale is possible only on the scientific basis of a definite knowledge of its structure, i.e. a sufficiently high level of knowledge of phonetics, grammar and vocabulary. Vocabulary, particularly, depends on the availability of various kind of grammars, dictionaries, descriptions of phonetics and specific problems of structure', syntax and so forth. 'As an academic discipline, knowing the Chinese language is complex, having many branches.' Modern conditions enforce specialisation in one branch, or a very few of them : 'Phonetics or phonology, grammatical structure, lexicology, lexicography, etc.' Yet each learner should know at least the basics of all or several of the branches, and know the many points at which the language study as such impinges on so many different fields of science or learning.

To Soviet students, the social implications are paramount. The 'language situation' in China has tremendous social importance, including its direct and contemporary, its indirect or historical 'presence' and its influence in the whole area of South-East and East Asia. A 'typological' design of study is recommended, and some consider that it should take the whole 'Sino-Tibetan family of languages' together as one group. There are two large tasks, in principle : to apply to Chinese language study the methods of modern linguistics and to bring Chinese linguistics into the corpus of modern scientific language study. The structure of the language is the main Soviet emphasis in practice, more than the phonetics and vocabulary aspects. This seems understandable, given the highly inflected nature of the Slavonic, which may be said to make it essentially more different from Chinese than English is. These questions cannot be discussed here, but the foregoing may suffice to give the essential perspective.

The record of Russian and Soviet study of Chinese is long, the achievements very creditable. It has also 'its own traditions'. The great pre-revolutionary figures – Bichurin, V. P. Vasil'iev, A. O. Ivanovski, S. M. Georgievski, N. S. Popov, P. P. Shmidt *et al.* – were 'universalist' or generalist sinologues. Outstanding in the Soviet period have been V. M. Alexeyev and N. I. Konrad. By their time, the 'specialisation quandary' had begun to loom. Apart from that, there were two tendencies : one was to see the matter 'through the prism' of the effective Western work in this field. This led to 'Europeanisation', trying to fit Chinese into 'Indo-European' moulds, with their apparatus of cases, declensions, conjugations, genders or the like. But the other was to protest – as Bichurin did long ago in 1835 [59] – that these moulds did not fit the Chinese language. There was also a strain of 'Asianism' in this school of thought; a definite analogy exists here with the great division in nineteenth-century Russia between 'Westernisers' and 'Slavists'. Some went too far in concluding that Chinese was 'on its own', outside the 'norms' of linguistic generalisation. Neither of these tendencies – 'Europeanism' or a cult of the 'uniqueness' of China – has yet been fully overcome in the Soviet Union. The former is feared as a carrier of *embourgeoisement*, the latter because it is symptomatic of Maoism. 'The present situation makes the matter all the more complicated.'

The following list of notable Soviet practitioners, with summary indications of their specialisations, may be useful (see also the bibliography below).

Phonetics and phonology, lexicology and lexicography : Polivanov, Dragunov, V. M. Alexeyev, Kolokolov, Oshanin, Isayenko.

Grammar and structure : Polivanov, Dragunov, Konrad, Korotkov, Oshanin, Gorelov.

Ideographs : V. M. Alexeyev, Oshanin, Shutski, Bunakov, Koloskov.

Romanisation (this was a definite movement in the 1920s and 1930s): V. M. Alexeyev, Dragunov, Kolokolov, A. G. Shprintsin and B. K. Pashkov. These collaborated with Chinese colleagues Chu Ch'u-po, Wu Yüch'an and Emi Hsiao on a Latinised spelling of Chinese.

Textbooks : Oshanin, Korotkov, Gorelov, Isayenko, Sovetov.

Language-training : (*a*) 'Older generation' : Dragunov, Korotkov, Oshanin. (*b*) 'Younger generation' (these had generally longer academic training) : S. E. Yakhontov (general : specialist on the history of the Chinese language), M. K. Rumyantsev (phonetics), Rozhdestvenski (structure), Tyapkina (syntax), E. I. Shutova (conjunctions and syntax), S. B. Yankiver (auxiliaries), M. V. Sofronov (Central China dialects), V. G. Mudrov, V. M. Solntsev, A. M. Tsukanov, A. F. Kotova, N. G. Raninskaya, S. Kh. Ioffe (grammar), I. T. Zograf, Yu. M. Galenovich, A. A. Moskalev, N. A. Speshnev, M. V. Kryukov, I. S. Gurevich, T. A. Nikitina, A. G. Larin, A. A. Zvonov, S. B. Kishinskii, Yu. V. Novgorodski, B. L. Smirnov, T. N. Zadoyenko, M. G. Pryadokhin, I. D. Klenin, M. V. Sokolov, I. N. Gal'tsev, V. A. Voronin and V. M. Zherebin. This younger generation is thus a comparatively large cohort numbering more than thirty leading names.

The language work naturally centres on IVAN but draws on the experts elsewhere. There was some concentration of forces on Oshanin's great dictionary [356], subsequently on a definitive grammar (which may be finished before these lines are printed). The problem of dialects is important, for the study of the history of the Chinese language as well as for practical purposes, but the only work on it is M. V. Sokolov's on the Shanghai colloquial tones. 'Periodisation' must also be developed to clarify the evolution of Chinese speech. 'The reconstruction of the ancient sounds of Chinese words, begun by Karlgren, revealed the different kinds of combinations of consonants at the beginning of a syllable and the complex system of final consonants, which are often still preserved in the southern and central dialects. This led to the constructs being taken in Western works (Pulleybank, Bodman) and ours (S. E. Yakhontov) to be like prefixes, infixes, and suffixes.'

The work of Polivanov and others may lead to some reconsideration of previous judgements. It is, however, difficult to relate this to the whole background, because 'the development of sociolinguistic research as a whole is held back by lack of materials, the impossibility of doing field research in China itself and the scarcity of relevant publications in China. The Chinese words should be studied in both the written and the spoken forms; the characters and their evolution may tell as much as their vocalisation. The application of computer methods to this kind of work is being studied. Mention must also be made of confluent work on the other languages of the China area, living or dead; for example, M. S. Sofronov and Ye. I. Kychanov have continued the work of Nevski on the Tangut language.'

The Soviet linguists are certainly industrious and alert. The impression is also that this sphere of work is less 'politicalised' than some others. The Maoists do not seem to be accused of revisionism or anti-Sovietism in the domain of linguistics. The omissions are downright startling. The recent simplification of many Chinese ideographs is not mentioned, for instance. On Chinese literature and drama generally there is plenty of political comment, as shown in this chapter; but again with extremely surprising omissions e.g. there is practically nothing about current trends in literary style, the curious 'numerical' phrasing of slogans (the Five Antis, the Four Goods) and the like. Similarly for poesy, e.g. there is no reference to Mao's own poems.

On the other arts in China (music, painting, sculpture, etc.) surprisingly little comment is made in the USSR, considering the various interesting things that occur in those branches also (e.g. choral and choreographic propaganda, posters, the Stalinesque busts of Mao, etc.). Soviet scholars respect Chinese culture – as must anyone who knows it well. This is the field in which they feel most deprived of access to China. Yet it is probably the field in which they could most easily collaborate with – as distinct from merely coexisting with – colleagues and institutions in

F

all the other countries. The final dimension in an assessment of the position and prospects of Soviet sinology is thus the attitude of its practitioners to the profession in other countries and their links within the worldwide 'industry' of China studies. The next chapter reviews these aspects.

11 Soviet and World Sinology

Soviet scholars have in recent years become increasingly familiar with the work in other countries in most fields of learning – including China studies. (Not in all fields alike : their access to foreign political science, for instance, is rather limited, or they cannot make much use of what they may know of it.) The situation is exactly what has been described, with instances from so many fields, in the ten preceding chapters of this book. A pompously didactic and not-too-specifically enunciated official 'line', under an intellectually conservative politico-bureaucratic controllership which can only repeat vaguely the precepts of Marx, who died more than ninety years ago, and Lenin, who died more than fifty years ago, continues to be imposed on rising new generations of increasingly well-informed and questioning professional scholars, who are writing and discussing more and more searchingly and experimentally on their subjects, in situations which Marx and Lenin never envisaged. Thus the PSS report closes (pp. 313–44) with a rather weak report on 'Foreign Sinology'. It is only possible here to reproduce the argumentation and let the reader see for himself the highly uneven mixture of partial appreciation of the non-Soviet work and partial subjection to the two most basic political ineptitudes – being ignorant of or underestimating the opponents, and being (as Keynes expressed it) the mental slaves of 'some defunct economist'.

THE BROAD STREAM OF WESTERN THOUGHT

G. V. Yefimov contributed the section in PSS on European and American sinology. He stated that 'Soviet students of China have done considerable work in the last few years' on Western sinology, 'its organisational and political standing [*statut*]', with due criticism of its bourgeois conceptions. Yet he can only specify, for this 'considerable' work, three substantial instances [55, 254, 491]. He directed that the merits of Western work must be appreciated so far as it is genuinely scientific, but its deductions criticised in the light of Marxism-Leninism. He urges 'principled disagreement about methodology', in which Soviet scholarship is strong. That part of the Western literature which is 'nourished by a spirit of anti-communism, which is hostile to the movement for national liberation', must be 'relentlessly' combated. 'The cornerstone of [such] literature is the falsification of the historical process' (i.e. not accepting the Marxian historical schema). 'Exposing that falsification is the task of the Soviet scholars'; but the latter have failed to do this. 'Significant work has been done, but it must nevertheless be acknowledged that the struggle against militant anti-communism, especially against anti-Sovietism and apologia for Maoism under cover of the mask of scientific objectivism, is still at a stage of beginning. What is required from Soviet sinology is a line of attack against every falsifier of history; first and foremost on questions of the history of the revolutionary process in China, of Russo–Chinese relations and of the history of the CPP.' The stress is thus obviously again on recent or contemporary history and on the relations between the two countries.

Yefimov represents this as a concerted and organised Western development : in the West 'the time has long gone by when sinology was the province of particular specialists, or of people serving in China and becoming sinologues by a whim of fate'. It is now a component part of national policy, of the State machinery, an important element in the university system; 'the study of China problems is generously financed by the State and the monopolies'. (There may be a resounding hint here that the same integration and support should be effected in the USSR. The expression 'monopolies' is of course Sovietese for 'large capitalist companies'; in the Soviet Union, where the State owns and controls everything and everyone, there are of course no 'monopolies'.)

Yefimov thus emphasises the *integration* in China studies in the West; these words are in heavy black type in his text. 'There are more and more symposia, conferences and publications as joint undertakings of scholars and experts of the USA, Britain, France, West Germany, Australia, Canada and others'; especially on *contemporary* China, which is 'becoming a component part of a unified science' in the West, even though the development is new in such countries as Australia and Canada which did not assert themselves in this field before.

AMERICAN DOMINANCE

However, the USA has the 'commanding heights' in the academic sphere in the West,. as it has in the economic sphere. It is the United Kingdom, as usual, that is given the henchman's part in this respect. Yefimov's prime example is London University's Contemporary China Institute (London School of Oriental Studies.) This was established in 1968 with the help of the Ford Foundation and is headed by an American, Professor Stuart Schram. Professor Schram is indeed an American, but the facts that to the British mind this is only of more or less incidental interest, that British scholarship is universalist in spirit, without the acute sense of nationality that is constantly displayed by the First World-Communist State, and that Professor Schram's formative work has been largely in France and in French, are ignored by the Soviet spokesman.

Yefimov swings for his next example to the other end of the vestigial British Empire to find evidence of the American takeover : 'In the British Colony of Hong Kong there has been established an American teaching [and study] University Service Center.' This, *per contra*, was headed by 'the English diplomat Ford' (reference is to J. Ford, an excellent scholar, formerly a Foreign Office researcher and a consular officer, who has, it may be noted, no generic connection with the Ford Foundation). Other activities in Hong Kong, the British and Chinese universities, the various research institutes, groups and persons that have appeared in that great window into China are not mentioned; nor is the enormous amount of information emanating through the American Consulate-General, to which students of China all over the world, including those in the USSR, are massively indebted.

Yefimov continues with instances from metropolitan Britain. The Institute for Strategic Studies in London 'is, in its structure, an international (or rather NATO) organisation where foreigners are occupied on China studies, but for the discussion of problems [*sic*] Britons are broadly enlisted'. (Discussants in fact include Japanese, Africans, or whoever might be useful.) Then there is the *Cambridge History of China*, a joint Anglo-American enterprise, with Professors Twitchett of Cambridge, England, and Fairbank of Cambridge, Mass.

Three particular undertakings are next mentioned. *China in Crisis* (ed. Hou Ping-ti and Tsou Tang, 1968, from two five-day conferences in Chicago) had fifty-nine contributors, all but four of whom were Americans. Of these four, three were, according to the Soviet spokesman, Americans working in England – Stuart Schram, Roderick Macfarquhar and Ruth Macvie. (*Sic* : that is what Yefimov told the assembled Soviet sinologues. There is no space here to unravel all the misconceptions or misrepresentations, but examples are that Macfarquhar is on the whole British and now a Member of Parliament, and there is a striking failure generally to note the very large number of Chinese involved in all these Western activities, which are broadly devoid of the sort of flag-consciousness that is so marked in the psychology of the Soviet spokesmen.)

Next, A. Doak Barnett is editor of a study of Chinese Communist policy in action, similarly a joint Anglo-American affair but practically American (John Gardner of Manchester is mentioned as one of the British.) The third major project cited by Yefimov is the Contemporary China Institute's study of the CPC leadership, directed by Professor John Lewis of Stanford, with nine American participants and three British. A great growth of all such joint activities was anticipated by the Soviet speaker, who tends to imply that it is all a great American plot, expressive of the US grip on the UK in particular and the Western world in general. His auditors are widely aware of the freedom of movement and conversation, the liberal internationalism that mainly prevails in academic circles outside their country, but the official spokesman cannot publicly acknowledge such a feature.

This massive effort in the West, Yefimov continued, is evoked by the great developments in Asia and duly emphasises contemporary China; it is deliberately harnessed to the needs of policy-formation. 'The official-service [*sluzhebny*] character of Western sinology, its dependence on the government and on monopoly-capital is screened by a semblance of scientific objectivity.' The *China Quarterly*, London, is named as having been established under American subsidy, transferred in 1968 to the London University School of Oriental and African Studies with David Wilson replacing R. Macfarquhar as editor; in 1971 (no. 45, p. 1) it declared itself independent 'of any financial assistance from outside sources'. In fact, Soviet practitioners believe, such cannot be the case. However, they appreciate the way in which this central journal has helped to establish and define sinology 'as a definite academic discipline'. They equally appreciate the rise of radical opposition to bourgeois approaches in Western sinology. A critical 'Association' of the 'New Left' was formed in England in 1970. Vyatkin, especially, has commented on this [527] as essentially a dangerous deviationist movement. 'The substantial successes of Western sinologists cannot be denied, including publication of sources, major researches, accumulations of factual material' (including microfilm of Red Guard and other papers which the Soviets were less well able to obtain elsewhere, Who's Who in China, etc.); 'but their acquaintance with the Soviet literature is slight'.

Works like Fairbank and Reischauer's history of Far Eastern civilisation pose such fundamental questions as the nature of Far Eastern society, the heritage of colonialism, the prospects for socialism and the Third World, but they heavily develop the concept of a 'traditional' Oriental society transformed by the (generally) beneficent impact of the West since the nineteenth century. This 'denies the existence of a feudal society in China . . . and thereby argues against the normality [*zakonomernost'* : scientific lawfulness] of a revolutionary transformation of society. This is still another attempt at a "refutation" of Marxism.' The same basis sustains various Western efforts, all markedly under American auspices or control, such as those of F. Michael or the 'Wentworth concept of the Nationalist Revolution' (from the conference on the subject at Wentworth, USA, in 1965 and Mary Wright's *China in Revolution* (1958) which is accused of 'ignoring the revolutionary struggle of the masses' and presenting the Revolution mainly as the work of 'moderate elements', stressing its weaknesses.

The Western scholars in this stream 'try artificially to link the past (1911) with the present ("Great Leap"', or voluntarism)'. Fairbank stresses Chinese 'traditionalism' in the sphere of foreign relations, in the book on that subject which he edited in 1968 from symposia in 1963 and 1965; its *leitmotiv* is Sinocentrism. The main topics of Western study lie, however, in the 'most recent' or 'contemporary' periods: Yefimov gave a detailed analysis of the approximately eight hundred projects or themes noted in the

International Bulletin in August 1970 and February 1971, the most important of which were as follows : the Cultural Revolution, 17; history of the CPC, 17; 'personalia (other than Mao)', 9; Mao and Maoism, 18; militarism and the PLA, about 12 (mostly as biographies of commanders); Sino–Soviet relations, 30; Sino–African, 10; Sino–Japanese, over 20; and Sino–American, very few (the notable exception being Fairbank). The Soviet's own lists, the speaker seemed tacitly to demonstrate, were comparatively small. He stressed moreover the large flow in the West of press and broadcast summaries, interviews and statements of refugees, visitors and others, Chinese *belles-lettres*, even secret CPC material (e.g. the army material in 1961 and the *Kung-tso T'ungshün* documentation), the several journal series (*Current Scene, China News Analysis, Far Eastern Economic Review*).

Yefimov is also impressed with the variety of approaches and methods. For example, Edgar Snow (*The Other Side of the River*, 1961) describes, from his visits to China, a vast country in the throes of industrialisation; Franz Schurman (on *Ideology and Organisation*, 1966), using press sources, 'sees China through the eyes of Mao as a society seething with contradictions'. Doak Barnett (on *Bureaucracy and Political Power*, 1967), from conversations with Chinese cadres, 'depicts a country with an extraordinarily involved bureaucratic apparatus'. The conclusion from all this is that, while it is completely true as a generalisation that 'the standpoints of bourgeois sinology are anti-Communist, which they strive to cover as far as possible with a mantle of scientific objectivism', the effect is to 'fan the flames' of 'national communism'. This tendency is traced particularly to Isaacs's *Tragedy of the Chinese Revolution* (1952) (mentioned in this connection and not as 'Trotskyist'), Brandt's *Stalin's Failure in China* (1958) (incidentally, the only mention of Stalin's name in the whole of the proceedings of the PSS is in this section by Yefimov), North's *Moscow and the Chinese Communists* (1953) and the same author's *Chinese Communism* (1966).

'In the most general terms, the essence [of such work] is that, while not denying the foreground influence of the October Revolution, of the Soviet Union and of the ideas of Marxism-Leninism, the bourgeois falsifiers of history are inclined at the same time to attribute the responsibility for the destruction of the Chinese Revolution in 1927 to the Comintern, to the mistaken leadership of the Comintern – which did not know China but tried to impose its conceptions on the CPC, which could only result in failure.' This, continues Yefimov, is a revival of the catchwords about the 'hand of Moscow, Kremlin and Comintern agents, etc.' which the bourgeoisie had previously been forced to drop, because the 'powerful historical events' made it so obvious that the Revolution in China was 'deep-rooted . . . not something imported'.

The foregoing summary in no way distorts what this speaker developed in a few short paragraphs; a full analysis would be lengthy, but some interesting Communist techniques of argument may be noted. One is the 'Aunt Sally' gambit : asserting that the opponent has stated an absurdity, in order triumphantly to knock it down. The 'Moscow gold' dramatisation was a journalistic theme of some long time ago. It hardly involved the academic investigation in the West, which has given a far better and deeper appraisal of the efforts of the Comintern than anything done in the USSR; but Russians are of course conditioned to believe that anything printed expresses governmental views.

The admission that the Chinese Revolution suffered 'destruction' in 1927 is interesting. Who (to adopt the Khrushchevian style of rhetoric) buried whom? Among the 'powerful historical events' that profoundly affected world opinion were some of the funerals arranged by Stalin, including those of his agents in China and the liquidation of the Comintern and the Profintern themselves. In the present writer's view, true scientific progress can only come in the Soviet Union when the whole phenomenon and history of Stalinism is investigated by the Russians themselves – beyond the lone voice of the exiled Solzhenitsyn – in full frankness. At present it remains swept under the carpet, and sometimes is seeping out again at the edges.

Meanwhile we must continue with Yefimov's review of Western sinology. He next mentions George Kennan's views in 'Stalin and China' (*Atlantic*, May 1961) on the 'contradictory' and 'hopeless' nature of the collaboration between the CPC and the Kuomintang, the subsequent position of Mao as 'an ally but not a satellite' of Moscow, and the development of this notion by North, Jerome Chen and others in the 1960s who represented Mao as correctly appreciating the situation in China, the Sino–Soviet conflict as rooted in the whole history since the seventeenth century and 'nationalism as [being] stronger than inter-nationalism'. Harrison Salisbury is mentioned as carrying this tendency to the extreme, journalistically but with academic acceptance.

John Rouet in the preface to his *Mao Tse-tung in Opposition* (1961) represents Mao as having 'adapted the Marxist teaching of old Europe to the requirements of [China]'; Joan Robinson in *The Cultural Revolution in China* (1970) and other works puts 'directly the Maoist interpretation of events'. The collective Oxford work *Party Leadership and Revolutionary Power in China* suggests, apparently to the surprise of the speaker, that struggles for power and purges (including the Cultural Revolution) are normal features of a totalitarian regime, and makes invidious comparisons with like events in the Soviet Union in the 1960s. It satisfies bourgeois 'decorum' that Maoist nationalism is so integral, and pleases the aggressive Western mind that it is anti-Soviet, rather than being pointed in some other direction.

This pill is coated, however, with some praise from Yefimov of perceptive bourgeois comments on Mao's 'considering the Party only as a tool of his policy', shattering the Party and making it no longer a 'revolutionary brotherhood', destroying the 'general world-view' that constituted its spirituality, substituting his own 'individuality and nature', but finding the Cultural Revolution did not bring him 'the fruits he sought'. Nevertheless, the Oxford work is 'in abstraction from the class-struggle . . . the role of the masses . . . the basic processes . . . the ever-growing role of the world socialist system'. These are evidently self-explanatory condemnations; no further elucidation is vouchsafed as to which classes are struggling and how, what the task of the masses is, what is the world socialist 'system' and its 'role'. Thus ends Yefimov's *doklad*, with more peroration than prescription.

IN THE UNITED STATES

A much shorter section (five pages) follows in PSS by R. V. Vyat-kin and B. N. Zanegin on China studies in the USA, noting their great increase and prominence in the humanities, well equipped and engaging a total of some 30,000 persons; though the US has no unified (i.e. uniform) academic system in the Soviet sense. The functions of the relevant institutions are outlined; a 'network of secret and semi-secret special' organisations exists 'to fulfil the directly political and military-strategic work for the government and leading circles of the USA'. (Thus does one see others in one's own image.) Some of these deal more or less constantly with China problems : Rand, Hoover Library (Stanford), Brookings, MIT, General Electric (Santa Barbara), etc. Then there are universities, whose principal centres and institutes are briefly noted; their interests are mainly contemporary and political, with some backing of general sinology, 'on the one hand a clearly expressed anti-communism, on the other an urge to utilise the mistakes of the Chinese leadership for playing up to the nationalism and anti-Sovietism of the Chinese policy. At the same time the serious work done in the USA on China's economic problems, on the CPC and army cadres and some of the social processes, cannot be denied.' Historical and cultural studies are also acknowledged, with some names cited.

These authors thus leave themselves little room for comment or evaluation, between these ambidextrous acknowledgements; they seem slightly dazzled by the profusion of 'unplanned' enterprise on the one hand and the lavish central provision on the other. 'In our view the stronger side of American sinology lies in : 1. Its polycentrism – tens of large centres well equipped with libraries enabling studies on a wide front. 2. A greater actuality of the themes of study, concentrating on twentieth-century problems. 3. Constant care to replenish sinological staffs and effectives, with hundreds of postgraduate students ensuring a constant flow of young faculty and researchers, fertile work of schools led by scholars of calibre. 4. Splendid material and technical basis of apparatus, rich sinological libraries, special teaching and information centres in Taiwan and Hong Kong. 5. Staffs include many persons of Chinese nationality, a help to students. 6. An atmosphere of broad consideration of important issues in seminars, also numerous conferences both in the USA and abroad.' (At last a handsome tribute on some of these points.) Technologically at least, this seems to be the standard the USSR would like to attain. The rapporteurs proceed, however, to list the main debits : 'The following are, in our view, the weak and negative sides of American sinology' :

'1. Ideological weakness and *porochnost'*.' (This word means, in the scientific context, 'fallaciousness', but it may also imply 'viciousness', 'depravity' or 'wantonness'.) Thus the Americans cannot form a 'correct general conception'. '2. The *konyunkturny* character of many publications.' (This expression relates to the economic sphere, meaning 'fluctuating' like the vagaries of the market or, more sociologically, 'reflecting changing taste or the like', or just that it is a literature of periodicals making current comments.) '3. Duplication in publications and research, repetition of the same data, etc., especially where information is short : on the armed forces, the [state] apparatus, the economy.' '4. Unspoken rivalry and competition between the centres, luring professors and young specialists' (from one place to another). An eclectic view must be taken by Soviet scholars of this complex activity, selecting whatever is good. (There is no need to labour here the contrasts with USSR, where the 'line' is usually laid down, all turn when told to do so, and go where they are posted; or to note again the intrusion of a note of envy when the open society of the West, or the lavishness of American resources, are contemplated.)

CHINA STUDIES IN JAPAN

The PSS survey concludes with a section by B. V. Pospelov on 'Japanese sinology and the Problems of the Chinese Revolution'. This title certainly precludes a truly comprehensive review of all the vast amount of work in China studies of all kinds in Japan; nevertheless, this subject is given nearly two and a half times the space allotted to the paper on the USA (viz. twelve pages). The treatment is more highly political, with a limited factual basis. The Soviet scholars' understanding of Japanese work seems inferior to their grasp of the trends in America. Japan is of course a country with a large and prominent Communist Party, not to mention other leftist and fellow-travelling movements on a mass scale. (Italy and France come to mind in this connection, but the PSS did not note China studies in those countries, or in others not mentioned above, including East European countries.) Pospelov's account has therefore only to take the comparatively simple course of referring approvingly to a number of Japanese contributors who are more or less reliably in the 'correct' camp, some of whom are better known to the rest of the world than others, while simply polarising the view by referring in contrast to the strains of

Japanese thought which are equally indentifiable as 'reactionary', largely ignoring the enormous mass of work and thought in the middle ground.

Pospelov finds that thinking on China is at any rate more 'integrated in Japan than elsewhere. China is the huge neighbour – and the parent culture'. Add the two nations' 'practical involvement in the age of imperialism'; so contemporary studies of China have 'an incomparably greater significance for Japan than for other capitalist countries'. And the class-struggle has been reflected in such studies, strongly dividing Japanese sinology into 'two basic lines, the reactionary bourgeois and the progressive'. The latter have used the scientific, i.e. materialist, methodology. The history is recapitulated. In Shanghai in 1890 a research Institute for Sino–Japanese Trade was established, forerunner of the Combined East Asia Library which arose in the 1920s as 'a scientific and ideological centre for Japanese penetration of China'. According to Miyazaki Toten, the Director Yarao Sei and his staff were all 'advocates of the seizure of China'. The main studies were by militant Japanese nationalists of the Genyosha and Kokuryukai ('Black Dragon' : properly Heilungkiang) societies. Typically, the 'mystic and obscurantist' Kita Ikki (in his *External History of the Chinese Revolution*) denied the democratic nature of that revolution, and worked against Sun Yat-sen for a monarchical restoration in China, for 'despotic government in a Western sense'. This line of criticism has been elaborated by Hasegawa Yoshinori in his *Kita Ikki* (1969).

'Derogation of the Chinese people's national-democratic movement and justification of Japanese intervention' increased with the Japanese pressure in the 1930s. Professor Mitsukawa Kametaro of the Takushoku University, lecturing on the problems of the Orient (*Toyomondai Juhachiko*, Tokyo, 1931) 'lauded Chiang Kai-shek's *putsch* as a turning-point in the history of the New China'. (The fury is of course because this *putsch* drove the Communists into the wilderness. Incidentally, this passage confirms suspicions that Soviet experts are not always strong in the Japanese language, as this writer mistranslates the title of Mitsukawa's contributions, '*twelve* lectures'). Pospelov instances Ebi Saikichi, 'a Japanese philosopher and journalist who worked for many years in China'. This Japanese *Kulturträger* estimated the situation in China to be 'stagnant' at a time when it was 'in the flames of the national-liberation revolution' and diagnosed the trouble to be that 'Confucian culture had grown over-ripe'. The Japanese called for 'syncretism', i.e. to join nationalistically and racially with Japan. The slogan 'eight corners under one roof' was used by Mitsukawa; earlier, Ebi (in his *Future of East Asia and Japan*, 1925) proposed that 'China be taught . . . in a united culture . . . spiritual co-operation with Japan'. Okawa Shumei's numerous works (such as his *History of Japanese Culture*, 1922) denounced the spread of utilitarianism, hedonism, etc., in China and urged that it be replaced by the 'moral life' of military Japan. Doctrines of Pan-Asianism or Greater-Asianism proliferated.

The 'nadir' was reached in the 'period of preparation for the Second World War'. Japanese sinology still concentrated on the 'spiritual' plight of China and 'placed itself at the service of monarcho-fascism'. (All this seems a long disquisition, but the point will soon emerge that these tendencies are still alive in Japan, already recrudescent.) The Soviet account continues with representation of the situation in China before the Pacific War as a struggle of national *revolutionary* fervour, opposed by a close collaboration between Japan and Chiang Kai-shek. (This hardly reflects the situation at that time, when only a minority on the nationalist side were revolutionary, but Chiang and Japan were fighting on a very large scale; however, such are the fundamentals of the Soviet version and the attempts of the bourgeoisie to 'falsify' it must be resisted. For comparison, another instance of historical reversal may be remembered here : the Soviets emphasise that the present 'collusion' between the Maoists and the Americans began during the war period, when some American officers penetrated to the Communist hideout in Yenan.)

Pospelov concedes that some Japanese sinologists were not 'openly at the service of monarcho-fascism' at that time, but only to the extent that there were also 'liberal-bourgeois conceptions in Japan of the Chinese revolution'; and of these he presents centrist rather than radical exponents, such as Miki Kiyoshi who thought the China question would have to end in 'compromise', 'a third path' on the basis of 'Oriental humanism' – which is almost as bad a 'distortion'. However, the true dawn lay below the horizon : a socialist movement, gropingly conscious though brutally suppressed, was developing in Japan. Kotoku Shohei is hailed as a pioneer in appreciating the quality of the Chinese people and its revolutionary prospects. He translated the *Communist Manifesto* of 1848 into Japanese. He wrote in 1908 that 'the Chinese people is not "mortally sick" . . . it is a sleeping lion . . . the situation is analogous to that in Russia in the 1860s. . . . In the history of the World Revolution, China will in the not distant future be a second Russia' (see *Gendai Nihon Shiso Taikei*, no. 9, Tokyo, 1968).

After this prophetic voice in 1908 there seems to have been a gap of more than twenty years until the foundation of a Marxist centre, the Proletarian Science Institute, which published some works but was suppressed by the police. 'Many' of its members (in fact about eight) went into exile in China and resumed their work there, notably in Tientsin and Dairen; but admittedly they were 'very diverse in their political convictions and their scientific interests'. They included Ozaki Hidemi (*A Critique of Contemporary China*, 1938) and Funekoshi Yoshio, who directed the Institute in Tientsin. In 1969 one of these veterans, Nakanishi Tsutomu, in his *Chinese Revolution and the Thoughts of Mao*, claimed wide influence for this group in his time. Certainly, 'in 1943 the Research Department of the [Japanese] South Manchuria Railway, with a staff of over a thousand, was actually emptied, most of the members arrested'.

After Japan's defeat and Mao's triumph, everything changed : 'An Institute of Sinology was established, China problems loomed large in the attention of the Historical Research Association (Rekishigaku Kenkyukai), there was eagerness to understand the motives and reasons of the Chinese Revolution.' This Association's *History of the Pacific War,* published in Tokyo in the 1950s and in Russian translation in 1958, became well known in the USSR, but has recently been severely criticised there. Nagawa Yutaka's *Sun Wen and the Chinese Revolution* and Fuji Shozo's *Study of Sun Wen* (both 1966) explained Sun Yat-sen's contribution and his Pan-Asianism. At the same time the Soviet account has to stress the chronic disputes in the Japanese left wing : 'bitter struggle proceeds', though 'naturally its forms have varied'.

In the 1960s 'an especially stormy polemic arose concerning the theory and practice of Maoism. We must give the Japanese scholars their due : on some questions they were among the first to unmask the traitor face of Maoism . . . stripping him of the halo of a philosopher purporting to make a contribution to Marxism.' Niida Kazuo, for instance, showed that Mao's works on *Practice* and *Contradictions* were a step back, not forward, in philosophy. Nakanishi Tsutomu's *Chinese Revolution and the Thoughts of Mao* views these matters widely in terms of Mao's tactics and strategies. Such torchbearers fight valiantly against bourgeois Japanese sinology and the 'left' revisionist tendency, which actually join in unholy alliance 'to utilise the problem of China for combined practical struggle' against Marxism and the working class in Japan. The 'pseudo-leftist' tendency in Japan has closed ranks with the new reactionaries. Professor Niijima of Waseda University is 'one of the most pro-Maoist. His many works on China aim at justifying Maoism as the "peak" of Marxism-Leninism.' He has a 'petty-bourgeois unscientific understanding. . . . His work, *A New Socialism,* is permeated with unprincipled demagogy' in praising the communes, etc. He denounces 'urbanisation' as fostering bureaucracy (which, he asserts, Mao's drives ably checked); what he is really denouncing is the formation of the proletariat and its increasing power.

In Niijima's works on *Mao's Philosophy* (1970) and *Mao's Thought* (1969) he 'divides Marxist philosophical materialism into a "first" and "second theory of knowledge", setting Engels and Lenin in opposition to Marx – with Mao as the direct successor to the latter'. It is in this context that Pospelov gives his sole quotation from the works under discussion, from p. 163 of Niijima (1969), viz. : 'The old Marxism (after the death of Marx, this was Engels, especially) perverted dialectical materialism. Emphasising only that consciousness is the expression of existence, it ignores the relationship by which consciousness operates on social practice. Mao's work *On Practice* fills this gap. Reverting to Marx, it combined the materialism reflected in . . . the philosophers from Feuerbach to Engels (the first theory of reflection) with Marxian dialectical materialism (the second theory of reflection)' [*vtoraya teoria otrazheniya*]. However, it is not explained what exactly is wrong with this statement; the position of Niijima is simply denounced, labelled as 'long ago exposed'.

Finally, Pospelov denounces Japanese sinologues who interpret the concept of 'sinification' as a 'process of combining Marxism with traditional Chinese . . . moralising-ethical theories . . . Mao's thoughts as "sinified Marxism" among the "national variants" of communism.' He instances Yamaguchi Ichiro's *History of Contemporary Chinese Ideas* (1969). At the same time, Pospelov points to others who have an opposite approach, saying 'Communist ideas are in general alien to the Chinese mode of thought, so any "sinification" of Marxism is impossible; Marxism exists and is represented by Mao's thoughts, but the Chinese people will not accept it.' An example is Kuwahara Jujo's *Mao Tse-tung and Chinese Thought* (1969).

The spokesman concludes with the injunction to seek out the considerable good there is in the plentiful Japanese work, but to avoid its pitfalls; for 'Japanese sinology has been and remains an arena of acute strife about the problems of the contemporary Chinese Revolution . . . defined by the class aims of the political forces involved'. Thus, a ground thoroughly infiltrated by all sorts of left-wing as well as right-wing deviationists would appear to be dangerous terrain for the Soviet sinologue; even more dangerous than the lush pastures of the West. He must 'converge', even collaborate, with his colleagues in all these alien lands, but be ever wary of his Marxian innocence, keeping a quick eye on the Soviet Party leadership which will pilot him safely through this world of what the Chinese call 'ghosts and monsters'. Such is, by clear implication, the closing message of the marching orders from Moscow.

12 Conclusions and Inferences

The Russians made substantial contact with China in the first part of the seventeenth century, as a result of their swift penetration at that time of the whole of Siberia. The Muscovites were motivated in their expansion, like the West Europeans, by prospects of economic gain, by a spirit of adventure and by the ebullient self-confidence characteristic of nations which are young or in process of formation. They moved easily through Siberia – easily, at any rate, in the political sense. For, despite formidable physical obstacles, they met there practically no indigenous people numerous or powerful enough to halt them : until they came to China – comparatively a very populous, well-organised, highly cultured State, so self-confident as to be arrogant.

The presence of China deflected the Russians on to the northward fork of their road to the Pacific, but they developed trade, military, diplomatic and cultural relations with China and pressed (like the Far Westerners, but more continuously over a longer period and more contiguously as physical neighbours) for dominance over, if not actual occupation of, China to their southward. Accordingly there is a tradition of China studies in Russia going back to a comparatively early date, fairly well sustained through the eighteenth century, strikingly enlarged and modernised in the nineteenth and early twentieth centuries by not a few Russian scholars, explorers and commentators; so that Tsarist Russian names figure prominently in the roll of honour in this field of work.

The Bolshevik Revolution in 1917 initially took as its be-all and end-all the worldwide extension of Communism, not least in the poor and oppressed lands of Asia; it switched all the resources, accordingly, to political propaganda and action in that quarter. In Russia many good scholars obstinately (the academic everywhere is a persistent animal, with his own techniques of survival), though necessarily quietly, were able to keep – as Pasternak expressed it – 'a candle burning' in the red glow of the stormy dawn or sunset and through the long night. However, Lenin began and Stalin extended a major (if fluctuating and unsuccessful) involvement with China which necessitated information and analysis as well as propaganda. The profession of sinology soon came forward again to some extent, though with trepidation. For under Stalin's Terror – compulsorily treated as a non-event in Soviet Russia today – the *métier* was a dangerous one for its practitioners, their families and friends.

The Liberation of China in 1949 by Mao Tse-tung suddenly presented China as the Second Great Communist Power, to which the Soviet Union was deeply committed to extend every kind of support and assistance. In this situation the USSR found itself short of cadres in the field of sinology, which had suffered as much as or more than others in the massacres during the reign of Stalin. But that grim dictator lived on for another four years, and it was a further decade before the situation was clarified, before everyone could be moderately certain that Stalin was really dead, metaphorically as well as literally. There was therefore some upsurge of China studies in the USSR in the 1950s, but not on a scale commensurate with the country's gigantic political and economic involvement with the New China, or of a quality to cope with the requirements of that commitment.

This was, however, only a brief second act in the great drama of Communism in Asia. From the latter part of the 1950s the union between the two leading Communist countries was broken, as sensationally as it had been created. The relative shortfall of effective resources in sinology in the Soviet Union had been acute in the preceding situation. In the 1960s and the beginning of the 1970s when the two countries became deadly enemies politically and even militarily, the shortfall became desperate. From 1970, therefore, when the third act of the drama began (the *Götterdämmerung* of Communism in Asia?) the Soviet Union reacted to the situation, in this field, in a characteristic way. On instructions from the highest quarter, it became known that a great 'drive' was to be made to enlarge and improve China studies in the USSR.

Though Ministries and other bodies were duly involved and the whole political and educational structure related, the focus and the leadership would be in and through the Academy of

Sciences. The key persons in this high 'circle' had of course been alerted and contacted at an early stage. A large number of meetings and discussions were held throughout the country; the body of opinion on the subject and the formation of the effectives were consolidated. Organisational measures were taken, notably the establishment of a new Institute of Far East Studies (IDV) of the Academy of Sciences in Moscow for practical working in this field, alongside the Academy's existing Institute of Oriental Studies (IVAN), which is more generally concerned with orientalism in a broader and less 'applied' sense, including Central Asian and South Asian studies.

This new dispensation and the resultant activity constitute a major event in the intellectual (and necessarily the political) life of the USSR, which has been strangely neglected by foreign observers. Soon the stage was set for the explicit inauguration of the new era in Soviet sinology, in the form of a general gathering in Moscow of relevant experts at a national conference, at the end of November and beginning of December 1971, for briefing and discussion of the 'Problems of Soviet Sinology' and definition of the tasks, in all subject-fields, of the workers concerned. The exact number attending is not known to the present writer, but the proceedings are known to him in some detail (as outlined in this book, with his own commentary). The discussion papers were published towards the middle of 1973, but of course only in Russian, for a distinctly limited circulation (only one thousand copies were printed) and not normally for export, under the title *Problems of Soviet Sinology (kitaevedeniya)*, here abbreviated as PSS. Its contents are extensively examined in the foregoing pages.

This PSS conference assessed all the 'problems' of Soviet sinology (this term being used here for studies on China in all the disciplines) and the consequent 'tasks' for Soviet sinologists. These words 'problems' (*problemy*) and 'tasks' (*zadachi*) are frequently used in the Soviet Union, and give very much the pitch of life there. The PSS and the accompanying and subsequent literature contain at least scores, if not hundreds (according to how closely one distinguishes their categories) of problems; and thousands, rather than hundreds, of more or less specific 'tasks' which the various practitioners should have tackled in the past, ought to be working on at present, and will be at risk (professionally at least, and nowadays morally rather than corporeally) if they do not very definitely get down to in the nearer rather than the remoter future. The taskmasters expressed complete, or anything more than very partial, satisfaction with what had been done or was currently contemplated in respect of no single one of this profusion of desiderata and obligatoria. The auditors were, indeed, given labours of Hercules which it is lengthy merely to catalogue, let alone to discuss or perform. The myriad problems and assignments are reviewed in this book; here, our own task is to attempt to summarise them.

The *leitmotiv* is, however, clear : the injunction by all means, at all times, to combat the real, basic and supreme evil of our age – Maoism and all its works; to substitute, every day and in every way, true Marxism-Leninism. Neither the evil nor the antidote are very explicitly or clearly defined, but presumably the reader may keep in step day by day by following *Pravda* and *Izvestia,* and month by month or quarterly by following the appropriate journals. One very curious incidental point is that not once in this discussion, in a land where *Realpolitik* is so pronounced a feature, is there any speculation as to what happens after Mao dies, such as is commonplace in the rest of the world. The more one reads of this Soviet material, the more one is given the impression that Maoism is something permanent, or likely to stay a long time, if not endemic in China.

The Soviet analysts do stress the power of the Chinese proletariat to counter or eradicate Maoism, but they seem unrealistic in believing that this class is the most powerful one in China, and they give no specifics at all to to *how* it can assert itself. They invoke a wide category of 'progressives', too, but this is a shifting category, for which no truly Marxist rationale seems easily detectable.

The whole bourgeois 'camp' – a camp is apparently a rather disorderly layout, in Soviet thinking, since the bourgeois are represented as extremely confused, limited in perceptivity and chronically divided, though collectively bent on destroying Communism and the Soviet Union – receives much attention but little fundamental respect from the Soviet spokesmen. Some good work has been done by the bourgeois exponents, who are rather well equipped materially; balanced, if not outweighed, by the support they give (so the allegation explicitly asserts) to Mao, whose anti-Soviet stance is warmly welcome to them. They are broadly discounted, in any case, the postulate being that bourgeois thought is by definition at best not fully 'scientific' and is incapable of correct 'solutions'. The heretics are far worse than the pagans; especially, after the Maoists, the spurious 'leftists' (non-Moscow Communists, dissident Marxists, etc) who put up a more misleading 'screen'. Such is the general approach, a fuddle of part-truths conveyed in a tireless stream of vituperation. Such, at any rate, is the 'general line' from the speakers' platform. Under this air-stream, however, much serious and competent sinological work proceeds in the USSR, the exponents of which are intelligent and honest colleagues who greatly wish and are worthy to contact similar persons in other lands and work with them. They must somehow be helped to do so; but this will remain difficult until 'coexistence' becomes more of a reality. The present book gives an outline of a general survey of the Russian and Soviet material, with passing reference to hundreds of items that are of particular interest. It has further been attempted, in the foregoing pages, to clarify to some extent the subject-fields in which the Russians are especially interested or competent, adducing some indications as to the official and personal priorities involved. The reader must form his own conclusions, but the following may be indicative.

There is a focus on 'recent' (or 'most recent') history, presumably a natural interest of contemporary men and women, but reflecting also the official Soviet concern to raise the debate effectively against the present regime in China and its personification, Mao. Exactly the same glosses – both of them – may be put on the fact that equal emphasis is given to the study of China's international relations, and the specific concentration within this subject is almost exclusively on China's relations with Russia. Logically and suitably enough, present-day polemic needs to be backed by the evidence, the insights and the arguments obtainable from history.

That the current polemic is both the starting-point and the clinching-ground, history being dipped into primarily as a store of ammunition for it, is nevertheless clear from the fact that the Soviets go backwards through history, taking next (after contemporary history) the 'medieval' phase. This is fitting, on the one hand in so far as the medieval stage is possibly of special interest in the case of China and on the other because the Marxist categorisation is obliged to give this stage as the longest and the most formative in China's case, extending over very many centuries (if the starting-point and the climax are not very clear in your theory, you are obliged to leave almost everything in the middle stage). To complicate matters, there is unclarity about the appellation 'feudal', about Marx's concept of the Asian mode of production, and other aspects.

Precisely similarly, the Soviet purview moves next to Ancient China, well known to be even more basically 'formative' or 'definitive' of Chinese thought or usage right down to the present day, but involving difficulties of Marxian explanation as great as, if not similar to, those noted in respect of the preceding period. It is only when all this 'ideological' foundation, this massively 'subjective' consideration of the quintessence of the Chinese outlook, has been well (or exhaustingly, if not exhaustively) covered that the Soviet preceptors turn to what might have been thought to be the first and infrastructural concern of the Marxist – the Chinese economy. This subject, though not reached until the seventh chapter in this book, provides its fullest chapter. The reader may discount that spatial emphasis by the fact that this subject is the present writer's special interest, but may agree that the Soviet comments on China's industrialisation, planning and population problems are especially significant and formative.

One point of interest here is that it is in this connection, not in their discussion of the ideational, traditional or other aspects, that the Soviets specifically raise their accusation that Maoism is especially admixed with or connected with *militarism*. Maoist militarism is adduced by them in the economico-social context. (Apologies : it is impossible to go into all the dialectical paradoxes, for instance the fact that Maoism is denounced also as 'voluntarism', in some contradiction to the charge against it of 'commandism'. Of course, Mao sins in various ways at various times, if not in all ways at once.)

Naturally, once the basic principles have thus been established, a conspectus and an interdisciplinary synthesis are appropriate. Chapter 8 in this book attempts to reflect this phase or aspect of the Soviet discussion, which relates to many facets of the Chinese scene, but principally philosophy and the development of social and political thought, filling in the 'directives' to the Soviet scholars in those sectors. By all the foregoing, the essentials of correct thinking have been laid down for the Soviet sinologists. They are aware of what (in the Soviet view) makes, so to speak,

China 'tick'; the next step is to inspect the clockwork more functionally. This, as in Chapter 9 of this book, implies the administrative and organisational concepts of China. Under that rubric the spokesman can further do battle with the concept, shared by Maoists and bourgeois, that Chinese ways and Chinese institutions are generally peculiar to China, and reassert the Marxian view that the laws of social science operate, like those of natural science, all over the world and to all that is in it.

The next subject to be considered is the culture of China, the widest and deepest topic of them all. This grand theme has already been treated with unseemly cursoriness in Chapter 10 above, and it would be an ultimate disrespect to encapsulate it further here. As before, however, some review is given of indicative Soviet work on the literary and linguistic aspects, the drama and cinema, of China. In all these the Soviets acutely feel their estrangement from China, hence their lack of access to current materials. It is salutary to realise that, as China is beginning to form cultural linkages with all other countries, the only country still completely debarred in this respect from China is its giant Communist neighbour.

The survey closes with a glimpse of the Soviet cognisance of and attitudes to China studies in other parts of the world, which is revealing not only in its reiteration of the preceding basic themes but in giving additional sidelights. The Soviet colleagues are increasingly aware and appreciative of the work in other countries in China studies (though not always with perfect accuracy). There seems to be a touch of envy concerning the sumptuousness of the equipment and facilities in the United States in this field, particularly in matters technical. The assumption that all this is a concerted and integrated effort, by and for the national Grand Policy aims of the US, appears, however, to be mistaken; there has for instance been no PSS in the USA. The dominance of the United States in other countries is similarly exaggerated, especially in the case of the United Kingdom, regarding which the PSS makes considerable play of a large presence there of US sinological personnel, and much joint work between sinologists of the two countries.

There are other intriguing reflections: the following, for example. The Soviet commentators are imbued with a strong consciousness of nationality, surely unfitting in Communist internationalists; they clearly label individual Western scholars by their passports, whereas to a contemporary Englishman it appears in the main irrelevant that (for example) Professor X is an American citizen working in England (and, though the Soviet spokesman seems ignorant of this fact, did much of his basic work in France). Lenin said something, in any case, about working with the devil's grandmother if it was useful to do so; but apparently only a bourgeois would actually follow such a precept. Soviet mannerisms can be more irritating to other people than the Soviet colleagues apparently realise : for example, referring to Great Britain as England and any inhabitant thereof as English. It is more risible if, in ignorance, the person is described as an American when he is, say, a Scot.

Nevertheless, when it is a question of actual publications and institutions, the Soviet sinologues have a fairly good knowledge and estimation of American and British work in their field, vitiated only, among their official spokesmen, by a propensity to use vulgar techniques of debate such as the 'Aunt Sally' method of misrepresenting an opponent in order to demolish him. America and Britain appear to be the most important countries, in the Soviet purview; there is no presentation of the important contributions of the French, the Germans or other Europeans, nor – strikingly – of the significant activity in fraternal socialist countries such as Czechoslovakia and Poland. The Soviet profession and public are left in the dark as to what these partners in Marxism are contributing in the domain of sinology.

There is, however, one other country to which the Soviet account gives marked prominence : Japan, the only Asian country to figure in their tally. The Soviet appraisal of the situation in Japan is not the best informed of their country surveys. Principally, it polarises two extremes in Japanese thinking – the extreme left and the extreme right – and exaggerates the significance and influence of both, ignoring the obvious fact that the huge mass of Japanese work lies largely in the middle and side grounds between and around these. Full weight is naturally given to the Moscow-oriented Marxists in Japan; since these are relatively numerous, in comparison at least with the virtual non-existence of such on the academic plane in the other countries, it is possible to give the Japanese 'Moscowists' some prominence.

It is equally possible, in the very proliferant Japanese work in this field, to find examples of almost anything : so, in contrast, a few devoted 'apologists for Maoism' on the one hand, a few clearly 'feudal-minded reactionaries' on the other, are easily adduced as typecasts. There is much less work done on Japan in the USSR than on China; and regrettably it is, though not all bad, sometimes not spectacularly good. Industrial capitalist Japan inspires some of the same reactions in the Soviet Union as does the USA. Such is the *Weltanschauung* of Soviet sinology. A reviewer must inevitably draw attention to the defects, and has not the space to enlarge on the merits of all the work, in many overlapping subjects, of a legion of participants in a large country, or to explain fully the rich intellectual heritage of that country, which necessarily differs from that of others. However – significantly, that word 'however' recurs very often in this appraisal – it is hoped that due credit has been given above, if only in passing, to Soviet sinology, which is an impressive and important body of knowledge, served by an estimable body of practising and aspirant sinologists, of whom the world would like to see and know more.

The Soviet practitioners, for the part, would like to see more of the work in the rest of the world; but the doorkeepers of the Soviet Union are still not allowing, in this domain as in others, anything like the free ingress and egress that Westerners take for granted. Yet the final paradox may be that, the two Communist great powers not being on speaking terms with each other, each feels increasingly obliged to turn separately towards the Western world, where 'synthesis' in China studies is evolving far more happily than in the lands of the Marxian dialectic.

Bibliography

These works are in Russian unless otherwise specified. M = Moscow, L = Leningrad (PGD, SPB = Petrograd, St Petersburg). If place of publication is unspecified, it is Moscow for works in Russian, London for those in English. See also the entry 'bibliography' in the Index below.

A. A. (KHMELEV, APEN) :
  1. 'Three Shanghai Risings', in *Communist International*, no. 2, 1929.
AFANASIEVSKI, E. A. :
  2. *Szechwan*, 1962.
Agricultural science :
  3. *Some Problems of the Development of Agricultural Science in the CPR* (collected articles), 1958.
AKATOVA, T. N. :
  4. Article on history of working-class movement in China, in PSS 1973.
  5. 'The Hong Kong–Canton Strike and the anti-British Boycott in Kwangtung, June 1925–October 1926' (master's thesis), 1957.
  6. *The Hong Kong–Kwangtung Strike*, 1959.
  7. *The Working-Class Movement in China: The Revolution of 1924–27 (a collection of documents, etc)*, 1966.
AKIMOV, V. I. :
  8. 'The Main Branches of the Engineering Industry in the CPR' (article), 1954.
  9. with Voyevodin, S. A., *The Fate of Small-Scale Production in China: Kustar' Industry and its Co-operativisation*, n.d.
  10. with Orekhov, V. I., 'Development of Productive Forces in the CPR', in PSS 1973.
ALEXANDROV, V. A. :
  11. *Russia in the Foreign Far East (Second Half of Seventeenth Century)* (monograph), 1969.

ALEXEYEV, V. M. :

12. 'A Chinese Poem about a Poet : Sykun Tu (837–908), Translation and Notes' (master's thesis), 1916 (2 vols, with Chinese text).
13. 'Immortal Twins' (on Chinese folklore), in Russian Academy's Museum of Anthropology and Ethnography's symposium, vol. 5, II, 1918.
14. 'Chinese Literature', in *Literature of the Orient*, 2nd ed., vol. II, 1920.
15. *Liao Chai Chih I*, 1922 (cf. Herbert Giles, *Strange Stories from a Chinese Studio*, 1908). Also as *Liao Chai Chih I: Monks and Magicians*, 1923; and (part) *Strange Histories*, L 1934. Reprinted as *Selected Tales, Liao Chai*, 1973.
16. 'On the Definition of Chinese Literature and the Present Tasks of its Historicisation', in *Journal of the Ministry of Education*, new series, pt I, vol. XIX PGD 1917.
17. *Poetry and Prose of Li Po*, SPB 1911.
18. *Chinese Hieroglyphic Script and its Latinisation*, L 1932.
19. *Tales of Unusual People*, M–L 1937.
20. Chief ed., *China* (symposium), 1940.
21. 'Horace of Rome and Lu Tsi of China on Poetic Mastery', *Izvestia of Acad. Sci., Literature and Language*, no. 3, 1944.
22. 'Utopian Monism and "Chinese Politeness" in the Treatises of Syun [Su Hsün] (Eleventh Century A.D.)', in *Soviet Sinology*, vol. III, 1945.
23. 'The "Song to My True Heart" of the Thirteenth Century Chinese Patriot Ven' Tyan'-syan [Wen T'ien-Hsiang]', *Works [trudy] of the Military Institute for Foreign Languages*, no. 2, 1946.
24. *In Old China: Travel Diary, 1907*, 1958.
25. *A Chinese–Russian Dictionary*, 1948.
26. 'The Chinese Popular Theatre and Chinese Popular Painting', in *Chinese Popular Painting*, 1966.
27. *Chinese Popular Painting: The Spiritual Life of Old China in Popular Representation*, 1966.
28. *Literature and Culture of China*, 1972. See also Liu Dzunyuan.

AL'SKI, A. O. :

29. *Canton is Victorious*, 1927.

ALTAISKI, M. :

30. with Georgiev, V., *The Anti-Marxist Essence of the Philosophical Views of Mao Tse-tung*, 1969.

ANDERSEN, G. :
31. 'Tsarist Russia's Unequal Treaties with China in the Nineteenth Century', in *Struggle of the Classes*, no. 9, 1936.

ASHRAFYAN, K. Z. :
32. 'Problems of the Development of Feudalism in India', in *Peoples of Asia and Africa*, 1967.

ASTAF'IEV, G. V. :
33. 'American Expansion in China', in *Academic Transactions of the Pacific Institute*, vol. III, M–L 1949.
34. Survey article in *New Times*, 1950.
35. *US Intervention in China and its Defeat (1945–49)*, 1958.
36. 'On the General Direction of Economic Research, in PSS 1973.
37. with Yakovlev, A. G., 'Problems of the CPR's Foreign Policy and International Relations', in PSS, 1973.
38. Chief ed., PSS 1973.

AVARIN, V. YA. :
39. *The Struggle for the Pacific Ocean: Japanese–American Contradictions and the Freedom-Struggle of the Peoples,* 1947.

AVERINTSEV, S. :
40. 'Greek "Lierature" and Near-Eastern "letters" [*slovesnost'*]', in Problems of Literature, no. 8, 1971.

BAKHRUSHIN, S. V. :
41. *The Cossacks of the Amur*, L 1925.

BAKULIN, A. V. :
42. *Notes on the Wuhan Period of the Chinese Revolution: From the History of the Chinese Revolution of 1925–27*, M–L 1930.

BALASHOV, N. I. :
43. 'Problems of the Unity of Worldwide Literature of the Thirteenth to Sixteenth Centuries', in *Peoples of Asia and Africa*, no. 2, 1971.

BALEZIN, P. S. :
44. *Animal Husbandry in China*, 1959.

BARZOV, N. :
45. *The Betrayed Generation* (on youth in China), in English, Novosti, Moscow and Dresden, 1973.

BASMANOV, M. :
46. Foreword to *Li Tsin-chzhao, Strophes of Faceted Jasper*, 1970.

176   Bibliography

BATALOV, E. YA. :
47. 'Critique of the Basic Trend of Reactionary Chinese Bourgeois Philosophy in Modern Times (1919–49)' (master's thesis), 1954.

BAZHENOV, I. I. :
48. With Leonenko, I. A., and Kharchenko, A. K., *The Coal Industry of the CPR* (monograph), 1959.

BAZILIEVICH, K. V. :
49. *Guests of Bogdu Khan: Travels of Russians in the Seventeenth Century*, L 1927.

BEI'GUS, V. A. :
50. with Tsiperovich, I. E., *The Chinese Popular Story and its Epoch: Wonderful Stories of our Time and of Antiquity*, vol. II, 1962.

BERYOZIN, YU. I. :
51. *Coal Deposits of the CPR*, 1957.
52. *Natural Wealth of China*, 1958.
53. *The Fuel and Power Base of the CPR*, 1959.

BERYOZNY, L. A. :
54. *US Policy in China in the Period of the Revolution of 1924–27*, L 1956.
55. *Critique of the Ideology of American Bourgeois Historiography*, L 1968.
56. *The Beginning of Colonial Expansion in China and Contemporary American Historiography*, 1972.

BICHURIN, N. YA. (IAKINF) :
57. *Notes on Mongolia*, SPB 1828.
58. *The Oirats or Kalmuks*, SPB 1834.
59. *Chinese Grammar*, SPB 1834.
60. *A View of Education in China*, SPB 1838.
61. *Autobiography*, SPB 1838.
62. *China, its Peoples, Customs, etc.*, SPB, 1840.
63. *China's Civil and Moral Condition*, Russian mission, Peking, 1911.

BLAGODATOV, A. V. :
64. *Notes on the Chinese Revolution, 1925–27*, 1970.

BOBIN, A. E. :
65. with Delyusin, L. P., *The Political Crisis in China*, 1968.

BOGATYREV, A. P. :
66. with Voinov, V. V., *In the Coal Basins of China* (brochure), 1953.

BOKSHCHANIN, A. A. :
67. *China and the Lands of the South Seas in the Fourteenth and Seventeenth Centuries,* 1968.

BOLDYREV, B. :
68. *Loans as a Means of the Enslavement of China by the Imperialist Powers (1840–1948),* 1962.

BONDI, S. :
69. *Pushkin's Rough Drafts,* 1971.

BORISOV, O. B. :
70. 'The Historical Significance of the Destruction of Japanese Militarism' [in 1945], in *Problems of Peace and Socialism,* no. 10, 1970.
71. with Koloskov, B. T., Soviet–Chinese Relations, 1971; extended ed., 1972.

BORODIN, B. A. :
72. *The USSR's Aid to the Chinese People in the Anti-Japanese War, 1937–41,* 1965.

BOROKH, L. N. :
73. *The 'Union for the Regeneration of China', its Foundation and Activities, 1894–99,* 1971.

BOROVKOVA, L. A. :
74. *The 'Red Troops' Rising in China and the Fall of the Yuan Empire (1351–67),* 1963.

BRIL', R. YA. :
75. 'Development of [industrial] Power in the CPR' (article), 1957.

BRODSKI, R. M. :
76. *American Expansion in North-East China, 1898–1905,* Lvov, 1965.
77. *US Far Eastern Policy on the Eve of the First World War,* 1968.

BUDZKO, I. A. :
78. 'Rural Electrification in the CPR' (article), 1957.
79. *The Electrification of Agriculture* (general book), 1972.
80. *Oracle Bones from Honan,* L–M 1935.
81. 'Terms for [kinship] Relationships in the Chinese Language' (master's thesis), L 1935.

BURLATSKI, F. M. :
82. *Maoism or Marxism?,* 1967.
83. *Maoism: A Threat to Socialism,* 1968.

Burov, V. G. :
    84. with Krivtsov, V. A., article on modern socio-political thought in China, in PSS 1973.
    85. 'The World-View of the Seventeenth Century Materialist Van Chyan'-shan [= Wang Ch'uan-shan = Wang Fu-chih, 1619–92] (master's thesis), 1963.

Bykov, F. S. :
    86. with Yan Khin-shun, 'Chinese Philosophy', in *Philosophical Encyclopedia*, vol. ii, 1962.
    87. *The Genesis of Political Thought and Philosophy in China*, 1966.

Cherkasski, L. E. :
    88. *China Speaks: Verses of the Chinese Poets*, Chita, 1954.
    89. 'The Poesy of Tsao Chzhi (192–232)' [= Ts'ao Chih] (master's thesis), 1962; published 1963.
    90. *Red Surf: Poetry of the 'Fourth of May'*, 1964.
    91. *The Rainy Alley: Chinese Lyrics of the 1920s and 1930s*, 1969.
    92. 'New Chinese Poetry (1920s and 1930s)' (doctoral thesis), 1971; published 1972.

Chervova, N. A. :
    93. *Ku Yuan*, Iskustvo, Moscow, 1960.
    94. *Contemporary Chinese Prints (1931–38)*, 1960.

Chikhvadze, V. M. :
    95. 'On the Character of Democracy, Rightist Ideology and Legality in the CPR', in *For the Purity of Marxism-Leninism*, 1964.
    96. 'The Mao Tse-tung Group's Revision of Marxist-Leninist Teaching on the State and Law', in *The CPR*, 1970 ([100] below).

Chudoyeyev, Yu. V. :
    97. *On the Eve of the 1911 Revolution in China*, 1966.

Chugunov, V. E. :
    98. *Criminal [law] Proceedings in the CPR*, 1959.

Conan Doyle, Sir A. :
    99. 'Scandal in Bohemia', *Collected Works*, vol. i (in Russian), 1966 (from *The Adventures of Sherlock Holmes*).

The CPR :
    100. *The Chinese People's Republic: Economy, State and Law, Culture*, 1970 (see [96] above, [173] below).

Dalin, S. A. :
    101. *Outlines of the Revolution in China*, 1928.

DELYUSIN, L. P. :
102. *Great Changes in the Chinese Countryside,* 1957.
103. *The Struggle of the CPC to Resolve the Agrarian Question,* 1964.
104. 'Peculiarities of the Development of Feudalism in China' (review article), in *Peoples of Asia and Africa,* 1967.
105. *The Dispute About Socialism,* 1970.
106. with Myasnikov, V. S., *The First Russian Diplomats in China (P. Pettina's 'Catalogue' and F. I. Baikov's 'list'),* 1966.

DRAGUNOV, A. A. :
107. *Binomes in the Tangut Dictionary,* L 1929.
108. *A Tungan Grammar,* M–L 1940.
109. *The Grammatical System of Modern Chinese,* L 1962.

DUMAN, L. I. :
110. 'On Slavery in the Yin Period (14th to 11th centuries B.C.)', contribution to *Worldwide History* ([529] below).
111. *Outline of the History of China,* 1957.
112. 'Socio-economic Policy of the Mongol Khans in China', in *The Tartaro-Mongols in Asia and Europe* (symposium), 1970.

D'YAKONOV, I. M. :
113. Paper on the Hurrian and Urartean languages (in English), 24th Congress of Orientalists, Moscow, 1957.

EIDLIN, L. Z. :
114. Article on medieval Chinese literature, in PSS 1973.
115. *On the Chinese Literature of our Day,* 1955.
116. *T'ao Yüan-ming* [T'ao Ch'ien, 376–427] *and his Poetry,* 1967, 1972.
117. 'From the Editor', in A. Alexeyev, *Chinese Popular Painting,* 1966.
118. *Po Chu-i,* 1948, 1958 (1958 ed. had a foreword by Kuo Mo-jo).
119. 'Ideas and Facts : Some Questions Regarding the Ideas of the Chinese Renaissance', in *Foreign Literature,* no. 8, 1970.
120. *Theoretical Problems of the Study of the Literature of the Far East* (a *Festschrift* for Eidlin's 60th birthday), 1970. See also [281] below.

FEDORENKO, N. T. :
121. Article on Chinese literature, in PSS 1973.
122. Chief ed., *Problems of Cultural Revolution in the CPR* Acad.

G

180 Bibliography

Sci., 1960 (i.e. cultural revolution in general, not the specific event of 1966).

FEDOSEYEV, P. N. :
123. 'Current Tasks of Soviet Sinology', in PSS 1973.
124. 'Marxist Philosophy and the "Sinification" of Philosophy', in *For the Purity of Marxism-Leninism*, 1964. See also *Marxism and Voluntarism*, 1968 ([125] below).

FEOKTISTOV, V. F. :
125. *Marxism and voluntarism*, 1968.
126. Contribution to *Society and State in China*, 1971 ([189] below).
127. 'Philosophical and Socio-political Views on Sun Tse' (master's thesis), 1971.

FIGURNY, P. K. :
128 Ed., with Sladkovski, M. I., *Development of the Economic and Foreign Economic Links of the CPR*, 1959.

FISHMAN, O(LGA) L. :
129. *Li Po: [his] Life and Works*, 1958.
130. *Lying Does Not Stifle the Truth: Chinese Tales*, 1959.
131. Trans., *T'ang Novels*, 1955; republished 1960.
132. *Lyrics of the Chinese Classics*, L 1962.
133. 'The Chinese Satirical Novel of the Period of the Enlightenment' (doctoral thesis), 1966.

FITZGERALD, C. P. :
134, *Europe and China: An Historical Comparison* (in English), Sydney UP, 1969 (pp. 13–14 cited extensively in PSS, p. 290).

FOMICHEVA, M. V. :
135. 'Economic Construction in North-East China', (master's thesis), 1952.
136. *Outlines of Economic Contruction in North-East China*, 1956.

FYODOROV, V. P. :
137. 'Feudal Ideology and the "Thoughts" of Mao Tse-tung', in *Philosophical Sciences*, no. 4, 1971.

GANSHIN, G. A. :
138. *The Economy of the CPR*, 1959.

GEL'BRAS, V. G. :
139 *Mao's Pseudo-Socialism* (in English and French), Progress Publishers, 1968.
140. *Maoism and the Working Class of China*, 1972.
141. *China: the Crisis Continues*, 1973.

GEORGIEVSKI, S. M. :
142 *Old Chinese Coinage,* SPB, 1887.
143 *Analysis of Chinese Documents,* SPB 1888.
144. *The Importance of Studying Chinese,* SPB 1890.

GLUNIN, V. I. :
155. 'The Struggle of the CPC for Victory . . . 1946–49' (master's thesis), 1954; published as *The Third Civil War,* 1958.
156. *The Socialist Revolution in China,* 1960.
157. *Recent History of China,* 1972.
See also Perevertailo, A. S.

GOLYGINA, K. I. :
158. *Theory of Elegant Literature [belles-lettres] in China,* 1971.

GORELOV, V. I. :
159. *Methods of Studying the Chinese Language,* n.d.
160. *A collection of Teaching Assignments [exercises] on Chinese Grammar,* 1952.
161. *A Practical Grammar of the Chinese Language,* 1957.
162. *The Chinese Language,* 1962.
163. *Conjunctions in the Complex Sentence in Modern Chinese,* 1963.
164. *Handbook for Translating from Chinese to Russian,* 1966.

GORKI, M(AXIM) :
165. 'Talks on Handicrafts [*remeslo*]', 1st article, in *Collected Works,* vol. 25, 1953.

GREBENSHCHIKOV, A. V. :
166. *Forms of Manchurian Literature,* Vladivostok, 1909.
167. *The Manchus, their Language and Writing,* Vladivostok, 1912.

GRIGOR'IEV, A. M. :
168. *The Anti-Imperialist Programme of the Chinese Bourgeois Revolutionaries, 1895–1905',* 1966.
169. 'The Comintern and the Revolutionary Movement in China under the Slogan of "the Soviets" (1920–30)', in *The Comintern and the Orient: The Struggle for Leninist Strategy and Tactics in the National Liberation Movement,* 1969.

GRINEVICH, P. A. :
170. 'Questions of Chinese Feudalism', in *Problems of China,* no. 1, 1935.

GUDOSHNIKOV, L. M. :
171. Article on laws of CPR, in PSS 1973, pp. 182–5.
172. *Higher Organs of State Power and State Administration of the CPR,* 1960.

173. with Toporin, B. N., 'The Left-Opportunist Revision of the Teachings of V. I. Lenin on the State', in *Soviet State and Law*, no. 1, 1969. See also [100] above.

GUREVICH, I. S. :
174. 'Grammatical Peculiarities of the Chinese Language of the Third to Fifth Centuries A.D.', esp. on Buddhist literature (master's thesis), 1953.

GUSAROV, V. F. :
175. 'The Prose Heritage of Han Yü (master's thesis), L 1971.

IDV :
176. Ed. Sladkovski, M. I., *Leninist Policy of the USSR in Relations with China*, 1968.
177. *Social and Economic Problems of Contemporary China* (conference papers), 1969.
178. *Prominent Soviet Communists who Participated in the Chinese Revolution*, 1970.
179. *Socio-economic Structure of the CPR* (symposium), 1970.
180. *Foreign Policy of the CPR*, 1971.
181. 'Current Problems of the Socio-economic Development of the CPR' (conference), Nov. 1971.

ILYUSHECHKIN, V. P. :
182. *The T'aip'ing Peasant War*, 1967.
183. *System of the Extraneous Economic Demands and Problems of the Second Basic Stage of Social Evolution*, 1970.

INDUKAYEVA, N. S. :
184. *US Expansion in North-East China, 1920–24*, 1967.

International Communist Conference :
185. *International Conference of Communist and Workers' Parties (Moscow): Documents and Materials*, 1970.

ISAYENKO, V. S. :
186. *Experimental Chinese–Russian Phonetic Dictionary*, 1957.
187. Contribution to *Textbook of the Chinese Language*, ed. Korotkov, 1954 ([246] below).

ISAYEV, M.
188. *The T'ien Shan Province*, Frunze, 1958.

IVAN (Oriental Institute, Academy of Sciences) :
189. *Society and State in China*, 1970–71 (see pp. 97–8 of PSS).

IVANOV, A. I. :
190. *A View of the Chinese Nation*, SPB, 1860.
191. *History of the Mongols (the Yuan Shih)*, 1914.
192. *China and its Life*, SPB, 1914.

193. Translation (incomplete) of *Han Fei-tse*, 1912.

194. *Grammar of Present-day Chinese*, 1930.

IVANOV, K. :

195. 'On the Sources of the Ideas of Maoism', in *Maoism Unmasked*, 1970.

IVANOV, V. D. :

196. with Kazakevich, E. P., *Hydro-Power Resources of the CPR*, 1960.

IVANOVSKI, A. O. :

197. *The Buddhist Prayer of Repentance*, SPB 1887.

198. *On the Chinese Translation of the Jata Kamala*, SPB 1893.

199. *Outline History of Manchu Literature*, 1887–8.

200. *Copper Money in Manchuria*, 1893.

201. *Manchu Reader* (and others), SPB 1893–5.

KABANOV, P. I. :

202. *The Amur Question*, Blagoveshchensk, 1959.

KAFAROV, P. I. (PALLADII) :

203. Trans., *The Western Journey of the Taoist Monk Chan Chun*, 1866.

204. *The Old Mongolian Legend of Jenghis Khan*, 1866.

205. *The Old Chinese Legend of Jenghis Khan*, 1877.

206. *Chinese–Russian Dictionary, Parts I and II* (posth.; completed by P. S. Popov, 1888).

KALYAGIN, A. YA. :

207. *On Unknown Roads: Memoirs of a Military Adviser*, 1969.

KAPITSA, M. S. :

208. with others, *Development of the Economic and Foreign-Economic Connections of the CPR*, 1961.

209. *Soviet–Chinese Relations*, 1958.

210. with Ivanenko, V. I., *Friendship and Conquest in Struggle (Soviet–Mongolian Relations)*, 1965.

211. *To the Leftward of Sound Thinking*, 1968.

212. *Two Decades, Two Policies*, 1969.

KARTUNOVA, V. K. :

213. 'The Working-Class Movement in Shanghai, 1925–April 1927' (master's thesis), 1960.

214. *Blyukher in China, 1924–27*' (collection of documents), 1970.

KAZANIN, M. I. :

215. *Memoirs of a Secretary of Mission: Pages from the History of the First Years of Soviet Diplomacy* (I .L. Yurin's mission to China), 1962.

216. *On Blyukher's Staff*, 1966.

184 Bibliography

KHARNSKI, K. A. :
217. *China from the Most Ancient Times to the Present Day* (monograph), 1927.

KHOKHLOV, A. N. :
218. A series of articles in *Summary Communications* of INA and IVAN (1968–) on problems of agrarian relations in China from the end of the seventeenth century to the beginning of the twentieth, and on the genesis of capitalism in manufactures in China at the turn of the eighteenth to nineteenth centuries.
219. Russia's Military Aid to China at the end of the 1850s and Beginning of the 1860s', in *Countries of the Far East and South-East Asia,* 1967.
220. *Problems of History and Historiography of China,* 1968; see also 'The Ta Ching Lu Li Code of the Manchu Dynasty : Its Origin, etc'., paper (in English) at Orientalists' Conference, Canberra, 1971.
221. Contribution to *New History of China,* ed. Tikhvinski, 1972 ([500] below).

KHVOSTOV, V. M. :
222. 'The Entry "Chinese" on the Register, and the Historical Truth', in *International Life,* no. 10, 1964.

KOKOREV, N. A. :
223. *Socialist Transformation of Agriculture in the CPR,* 1958.

KOLOKOLOV, V. S. :
224. with Mamayev, I. *China, its Land, People and History,* 1924.
225. *Chinese Reader,* 1922.
226. *Concise Chinese–Russian Dictionary,* 1935.
227. *Chinese Grammar,* 1937.
228. Ed., *Chinese–Russian Dictionary of Scientific and Technical Terms,* 1959.
229. *Collected Works,* 1954.

KOLOSKOV, B. T. :
230. *The Struggle of the CPC for the Unity and Solidarity of the Revolutionary Forces,* 1967.
231. *The Soviet Union and China: Friendship or Alienation?* (in English), Moscow, 1971.
See also Borisov, O. B.

KONDRASHOVA, L. :
232. 'The Study of the Changes in the CPR's Theory and Practice of Industrialisation', in PSS 1973.

KONOVALOV, E. A. :
233. *The Socio-economic Consequences of the 'Great Leap' in the CPR*, 1968.
234. Article on the CPR's population problem, in PSS 1973.

KONRAD, N. I. :
235. *Japan, its People and State*, 1923.
236. *Japanese Literature in Examples and Outlines*, 1927.
237. *Syntax of the Japanese Literary Language*, 1937.
238. *Sun Tse, the Art of War*, 1950.
239. Trans., *Wu Tse*, 1958.
240. 'Short Outline of the History of Chinese Literature', in *Chinese Literature: A Reader*, 1959.
241. *West and East* (collection of articles), 1966.

KONSTANTINOV, N. N. :
242. Article on the political organisation of society in the CPR, in PSS 1973.

KORBASH, E. P. :
243. *The Economic 'Theories' of Maoism*, 1971.

KORKUNOV, I. N. :
244. with Kurbatov, V., Mugruzin, A. S., and Sukharchuk, G. D., *Socialist Transformation of Agriculture in the CPR*, 1960.

KOROTKOV, N. N. :
245. *Chinese–Russian Dictionary*, 1946.
246. *Textbook of the Chinese Language*, 1954.
247. *The Morphology of the Chinese Language*, 1968.
248. Contribution to *Concise Russo–Chinese Dictionary of Politico-Economic and Military Terminology*, ed. Sovetov, 1973 ([475] below).

KOTOV, K. F. :
249. *The New Sinkiang*, Alma Ata, 1955.
250. *Sinkiang on the Road to Socialism*, Alma Ata, 1957.
251. *Local National Autonomy in the CPR*, 1959.
252. 'The reality of Local Autonomy in China' (doctoral thesis), 1962.

KOVALEV, E. F. :
253. *Tenancy [arenda] and Tenant Relations in China*, 1947.
254. *Ideological-Theoretical Positions of the Contemporary Bourgeois Historiography of China*, 1964.

KOVALEV, F. L. :
255. 'With our Chinese Friends' (article), 1957 (deals with some industries; widely circulated in various reprints).

KRIVTSOV, V. A. :
  see Burov, V. G.
KROL', Yu. L. :
  256. *Ssu-ma Ch'ien, the Historian,* 1970.
KRUGLOV, A. M. :
  257. with Voyevodin, S. A., *The Socialist Reformation of Capitalist Industry and Trade in the CPR,* 1959.
KRYMOV, A. G. :
  258. 'Critique of the Philosophy of Lyan Shu-min' [Liang Shuming], in *Problems of Philosophy,* no. 1, 1957.
  259. 'Social thought and Ideological Struggle in China, 1917–27' (doctoral thesis), 1963.
KRYUKOV, M. V. :
  260. *The Ancient Chinese System of Kinship,* 1964.
  261. Paper (in English) at the 7th International Congress of Anthropological and Ethnological Sciences, Tokyo, 1966.
  262. *Forms of Social Organisation of the Ancient Chinese,* 1967.
  263. *Personal Names of the Peoples of the World,* 1970.
  264. *The Kinship System of the Chinese,* 1972.
KUKUSHKIN, K. V. :
  see Perevertailo, A. S.
KUMACHENKO, Ya, S. :
  265. *The Economic Structure of the CPR,* 1955.
KURTS, B. G. :
  266. *Russo–Chinese Relations in the Sixteenth, Seventeenth and Eighteenth Centuries,* Kharkov, 1929.
KYUNER, N. V. :
  267. *Geography of Japan,* Vladivostok, 1904; reprinted Moscow, 1927.
  268. *New History of the Countries of the Far East,* Vladivostok, 1908.
  269. *Description of Tibet,* Vladivostok, 1907–8.
  270. *Commercial Geography of China,* Vladivostok, 1909.
  271. *The European War and Chinese Industry,* Vladivostok, 1916.
  272. *Chinese Information on the Peoples of Siberia,* 1961.
KYUZADZHAN, L. S. :
  273. *Ideological Campaigns in the CPC, 1949–66,* 1970.
LAPINA, Z. G. :
  274. *The Political Struggle in Medieval China (1040–1080),* 1970.
  275. *Petty-Bourgeois Revolutionarism,* 1968.
LENIN ON CHINA :
  276. *Lenin and the Problems of Contemporary China,* 1971.

LENINGRAD STATE UNIVERSITY :
277. *Historiography of the Countries of the Orient* (collection of articles), 1969.
278. *Historiography and Source-Research on the Countries of Asia and Africa,* 2 vols, 1971–2; vol. III, 1974.

LISEVICH, I. S. :
279. *Ancient Chinese Poetry and Folksong [yüehfu], End of Third Century B.C. to Beginning of Third Century A.D.,* 1968.
280. *Literature of Ancient China* (collection of articles), 1969.
281. Ed., *Theoretical Problems of the Study of the Literature of the Far East* (collection of articles of Eidlin, L. Z., et al), 1970.
282. *Soviet Sinology in the Past Fifty Years (Literature)* (in English), Nauka, Moscow.

Literature textbook :
283. *Literature of the Orient in the Middle Ages* (Moscow State University textbook), 1970.

LIU DZUN-YUAN (LIU TSUNG-YÜAN) :
284. 'The Tale of a Carpenter' and 'I Accompany Hsueh Tsun-i', in *Chinese Classical Prose Translated by Academician V. M. Alexeyev,* 1959.

LUNYOV, A. E. :
285. *State Control in the CPR,* 1956.
286. *The Essence of the Constitution of the CPR,* 1958.
287. *Soviet Administrative Law,* 1960.
288. *Textbook of Administrative Law,* 1967.
289 *State Discipline and Socialist Legality,* 1972.
290. Ed., *Legal Aspects of the Economic Reform* (collection of articles), 1972.
291. *The Soviet State Apparatus,* 1972.
292. *Law and the Efficiency of Administration,* 1973.
293. *Fragen der wissenschaftlichen Organisation der staatlichen Leitung in der UdSSR* (in German), Potsdam-Babelsburg, 1970.

LYSKIN, O. :
294. 'Development of the Engineering Industry in the CPR' (article), 1954.

MAD'YAR, L. I. :
295. *Outlines of the Economy of China,* 1930.
296. *Economics of Agriculture in China,* 1931.

188   *Bibliography*

MAKALAKOV, A. A. :
297. 'Role of Heavy Metallurgy in Providing the Primary Base for the Industrialisation of the CPR' (master's thesis), 1956.

MANDALYAN, T. :
298. *The Proletariat of the Colonies in the Struggle against Imperialism*, 1927.
299. *The Workers' Movement in China*, 1927.

MANUKHIN, V. S. :
300. 'The Chin P'ing Mei (Seventeenth Century) : From Tradition to Innovation' (master's thesis), 1964.

MAO TSE-TUNG :
301. *Selected Works*, 4 vols., 1951–3.

Mao's anti-Marxist views (302–6 – Soviet critiques of Mao) :
302. *The anti-Marxist Essence of the Views and Policy of Mao Tse-tung*, 1969.
303. *The anti-Leninist Essence of the Views and Policy of Mao Tse-tung*, 1969.
304. *Critique of Mao Tse-tung's Theoretical Concepts*, 1970.

Mao's policy and the USA :
305. *The Nationalistic Policy of Mao Tse-tung and the USA*, 1968.

Mao's theories :
306. *Critique of Mao Tse-tung's Theoretical Concepts*, 1970.

MARTYNOV, A. S. :
307. Contribution in Stuzhina, P., *On Some Peculiarities of the Trade in Tea and Horses in the Ming Period*, n.d.

Marxism-Leninism :
308. *For the Purity of Marxism-Leninism*, 1964 (materials of a combined session of the CC CPSU's AON, its Institute of Marxism-Leninism, and its BPSh with the Humanities Institute of the Acad. Sci. of the USSR).

MASLENNIKOV, V. A. :
309. *China*, 1946.
310. *The Economic Structure of the CPR*, 1958.

Medieval history (Asia) :
311. *History of the Countries of Foreign Asia in the Middle Ages*, 1970 (textbook for higher educational institutions).

MELIKSETOV, A. V. :
312. 'Sun Yat-sen's views', in *Peoples of Asia and Africa*, no. 5, 1969.

MEN'SHIKOV, L. N. :
313. Article on Chinese written records, in PSS 1973.
Middle Ages :
314. *Reader on the History of the Middle Ages,* vol. 1 (incl. materials on peasant wars, 7th and 9th centuries), 1961; vol. 2, 1969.
MIKHAILOV, YA. :
315. with Zanegin, B. L., Sladkovski, M. I. (ed.), *et al., On the Events in China,* 1967. See Mironov, A., *Developments in China, Edited by Professor M. Sladkovski* (English translation), Progress Publishers, 1968.
316. *Military-Bureaucratic Dictatorship: An Arm of the Great-Power Policy of the Mao Group,* 1969.
317. *La Chine est-elle menacée de surpeuplement?* (in French), Novosti, 1971.
MINISTRY OF FOREIGN AFFAIRS, USSR :
318. Historical and Documentation Section, *Documents on Activities of V. K. Blyukher in China,* 1965–.
MINISTRY OF FOREIGN TRADE :
319. Ministry of Foreign Trade (MVT), *NIKI* (annual surveys of development of economies of the socialist countries); *BIKI Supplements,* no. 10 (for 1961), no. 4 (for 1962) and no. 5 (for 1963).
MIROVITSKAYA, R. A. :
320. Ed., PSS.
321. 'The Study, in the USSR in the 1960s, of Soviet–Chinese Relations', in PSS 1973.
322. 'The Establishment of Friendly Equal-Rights Relations between the USSR and China (1917–24) : On the History of the Conclusion of the Soviet–Chinese Agreement of 31 May 1924' (master's thesis), n.d.
323. *The Movement in China for the Recognition of Soviet Russia,* 1962.
MONASTYREV, N. :
324. *Notes on the Ch'un Ch'iu and Ancient Commentaries on it,* SPB 1876.
MUGRUZIN, A. S. :
325. *Agrarian Relations in China in the 1920s, 1930s and 1940s,* 1970.
MUNKUYEV, N. Ts. :
326. 'Some Chinese Sources on the History of Mongolia in the Twelfth Century' (master's thesis), 1965.

327. *A Chinese Source on the First Mongol Khans*, 1965.
328. 'Some Problems of the History of the Mongols in the Thirteenth Century' (doctoral thesis), 1970.

MUROMTSEVA (PANOVA), Z. A. :
329. *Problems of Industrialisation in the CPR* (monograph), 1971.

MYASNIKOV, V. S. :
330. Article on history of Russo–Chinese relations, in PSS 1973.

NADEYEV, I. M. :
331. *The 'Cultural Revolution' and the Fate of Chinese Literature*, 1969.

NAROCHNITSKI, A. L. :
332. *Colonial Policy of the Capitalist Powers in the Far East, 1860–95*, 1956.
333. *History of Diplomacy*, 1959.

NEPOMNIN, O. E. :
334. *The Genesis of Capitalism in the Agriculture of China*, 1966.

NETRUSOV, A. A. :
335. *Foreign Economic Links of the CPR*, 1958.
336. 'The Economic Co-operation of China with the Countries of the World[wide] Socialist System' (master's thesis), 1960.

NEVEL'SKOI, G. I. :
337. *Exploits of Russian Naval Officers in the Far East of Russia, 1849–55*, SPB 1878; republished 1947, 1950.

NIKIFOROV, S. :
338. 'Development of Light Industry in the CPR' (article), 1953.

NIKIFOROV, V. N. :
339. *The National-Liberation War of the Chinese People Against Japanese Imperialism, 1937–45*, 1950.
340. *The Kuomintang Reactionaries: The Betrayers of China, 1937–45*, 1953.
341. Ed., *Centuries of Unequal Struggle*, 1967.
342. *Soviet Historians on the Problems of China*, 1970.
343. Ed., *PSS* 1973.
344. 'Unsolved Problems in the Recent History of China', in PSS 1973. See also Perevertailo, A. S.

NIKOL'SKI, M. M. :
345. 'Formation and Development of the Economic Base of the CPR', in PSS 1973.

OBRAVTSOV, S. V. :
346. *My Profession* (the theatre), 1950; trans. (Foreign Publish-

ing House) into German (1952), English (1957) and French 1957).

347. *Five Hundred Years and Three Years: Travel Notes on the New China,* 1953.
348. *London* (a travelogue), 1955.
349. *The Theatre of the Chinese People,* 1957; trans. into German (Henschelverlag) as *Theater in China,* 1963.

OKLADNIKOV, A. P. (Academician Alexei Pavlovich):
350. *Ancient Cultures of the Far East* (i.e. the Maritime Provinces of Russia), 1963.
351. *History of Siberia,* 5 vols., 1965–8.
352. *History of the Yakut ASSR,* 1955.

OL'DENBURG, S. F.:
353. 'Memorials of Vassili Pavlovich Vasil'iev and his Works on Buddhism', in *Proceedings of the Russian Academy of Sciences,* SPB 1918.
354. Leading article in *The Orient [Vostok],* no. 1, 1922.

OREKHOV, V. L.:
See Akimov, V. I.

Oriental literature:
355. *Literature of the Orient in the Middle Ages,* pt 1, 1970 ([283] above).

OSHANIN, M. I.:
356. Ed., *Chinese–Russian Dictionary,* 1952; revised 1959.

PAMOR, A. P.:
357. with Yelin, I. M., 'On the Character of the "Changes" in the Economic Policy of the Maoists', in *Problems of the Far East,* IDV, no. 1, 1973.

PARNIKEL', B. B.:
358. *The Oral Discussion* [in 1965] *on Problems of Periodisation of the History of Literatures of the Peoples of the East,* 1968.

PASHKOVA, M. K.:
359. *In the Struggle for the Emancipation of the Chinese People,* 1939.
360. *The Youth of China,* 1940.

PAVLOVICH, M. P. (VEL'TMAN, M. L.):
361. *A Year of War, 1904–5, Iskra,* Geneva, 1905.
362. *Asia and its Role in the World War,* 1918.
363. *The Struggle for Asia and Africa,* 1923.
364. *Lenin and the Orient,* 1924.
365. *Imperialism and World Politics* (collected works), 1925.

PEKSHEV, YU. A. :
366. Contribution to Kapelinski, Yu. N. (ed.), *Development of the Economy and Foreign Economic Links of the CPR*, Foreign Trade Publishing House, 1956.

PENTKOVSKI, V. :
367. 'Conditions of Work and Problems of Labour Legislation in China under the Kuomintang (1927–49)' (master's thesis), 1954.

PERELOMOV, L. S. :
368. Article on ancient China, in PSS 1973.
369. *The Empire of Ch'in: The First Centralised State in China (221–202 B.C.)* (monograph), 1962.
370. Trans., *The Book of the Ruler of the Province of Shang*, 1968.

PEREVERTAILO, A. S. :
371. Chief ed., with Glunin, V. I., Kukushkin, K. V., and Nikiforov, V. N. (eds), *Outlines of the History of China in Recent Times*, 1959.

PERLOV, I. D. :
372. 'The CPR's Departure from Democratic Principles of Justice', in *Soviet State and Law*, no. 1, 1968.

PETROV, A. A. :
373. *Van Bi (from the History of Chinese Philosophy)* (monograph), 1936 (Wang Pi's tract on the *I Ching*).
374. 'Outline of Chinese Philosophy', in *China* (symposium), 1940.

PEVTSOV, M. V. :
375. *In the Wilds [v debryakh] of Asia: Outline of the Travels of Major-General Pevtsov*, SPB 1897.
376. *Travels in Kashgar and Tibet: A Preliminary Report*, 1891.
377. *Travels in Kashgar and the Kuen Lun*, 1949 (reprint of a book published in 1895).

POLIVANOV, E. D. :
378. *Introduction to the Uzbek Language*, Tashkent, 1925, 1927.
379. *For a Marxist Philology*, 1931.

POPOV, I. V. :
380. *[Industrial] Power in the Countries of People's Democracy*, 1961.

POPOV, K. M. :
381. *Problems of the Economies of Countries of the Orient*, 1958, 1960.
382. *Colonialism Yesterday and Today*, 1964.

PORSHNEVA, E. B. :
383. 'Popular Risings in China, 1796–1804, under the Leadership of the "White Lotus Sect" ' (master's thesis), 1963.
384. *A Study of the 'White Lotus' Rising, 1796–1804,* 1972.

POSPELOV, B. V. :
385. 'Japanese Sinology and Ideological Problems of the Chinese Revolution', in PSS 1973.

POTANIN, G. N. :
386. *Travels in Mongolia,* 1948 (travel diaries of 1881).
387. Bessonov, Ya. N., and Yakubovich, V. Ya., *In Inner Asia,* 1947, gives an account of Potanin's work.

POZDNEYEVA, L. D. :
388. *Lu Hsun, his Life and Works,* 1959.
389. Trans., *Chuang Tse,* 1960–4.
390. *Atheists, Materialists and Dialecticians of Ancient China,* 1967.
391. Compiler, *Literature of the Orient at the Mid-Century,* 1970.
392. Article on the idealisation of Confucianism, in PSS 1973.

PRZHEVALSKI, N. M. :
393. *Travels in the Ussuri Country, 1867–69,* SPB 1870.
394. *Mongolia, the Tangut Country and . . . Tibet* (in English), London, 1876; also in German.
395. *Mongolia,* 1876.
396. *Through Hami and Tibet,* 1883.
397. *How to Travel in Central Asia,* SPB 1888.
398. *Kuldja to Lop Nor,* 1947.

RADUL'-ZATULOVSKI, YA. B. :
399. *Confucianism and its Diffusion in Japan,* 1947.

RAKHIMOV, T. R. :
400. *Nationalism and Chauvinism as the Basis of the Policy of Mao Tse-tung's Group,* 1968.
401. Compiler, *Russo-Uighur Dictionary,* 1956.

RIFTIN, B. L. :
402. *Sung Stories,* 1957.
403. *Historical Epos and Folklore Tradition in China (Oral and Literary Versions of the Three Kingdoms),* 1969.
404. History, Epic and Folklore Tradition in China (doctoral thesis), 1969.
405. *Chinese Popular Stories,* 1957; republished 1972.
406. *A Tun-huang Manuscript, Panwen on the Retribution for Grace,* 1972.

ROZHDESTVENSKI, YU. V. :
407. Ed., *Problems of Language and Literature of the Countries of the Orient*, 1958.
408. *Forms of Words in the History of the Grammar of the Chinese Language*, 1958.
409. *Disputed Questions of the Structure of the Languages of South and South-East Asia*, 1964.
410. *Disputed Questions of the Structure of the Chinese Language*, 1965.
411. *Semiotics in Oriental Languages*, 1967.
412. 'Typology of Words' (doctoral thesis), 1970.
413. *Oriental Philology* (in memory of Professor B. K. Pashkov), 1971.

RUBIN, V. A. :
414. *Ideology and Culture of Ancient China*. n.d.
415. 'The *Tsao Chzuan* [*Tso Chuan*] as a Source of Social History of the Ch'un Ch'iu Period' (master's thesis), 1959.

RUDAKOV, A. V. :
416. *The Official Manchu Language*, Vladivostok, 1902.
417. *Chinese Conversations, Official and Commercial: A Guide to Translation from Russian into Chinese*, Vladivostok, 1910.
418. *Practical Chinese Dictionary*, Vladivostok, 1927.

RUMYANTSEV, A. M. :
419. 'Dialectics or Maoism?', in *Problems of the Contemporary Science of Society*, 1969.

RUMYANTSEV, M. K. :
420. *The Sentence-Subject in Modern Chinese*, 1957.
421. 'Tone and Intonation in Modern Chinese' (doctoral thesis), 1968; published by Moscow State University, 1972
Russian orientalism :
422. *Outlines of the History of Russian Oriental Studies* [*vostokovedeniya*], 1956.

Russo–Chinese relations (seventeenth century) :
423. *Russo–Chinese Relations in the Seventeenth Century: Materials and Documents*, vol. I (1608–1683), 1969; vol. II (1686–1691), 1972.

SAPOZHNIKOV, B. G. :
424. *The First Revolutionary Civil War in China, 1924–27*, 1954.
425. *The Struggle of the Peoples of Asia for Peace*, 1967.
426. *The Japan–China War and Japan's Colonial Policy in China (1937–41)*, 1970.
427. *The Chinese Front in the Second World War*, 1971.

Semanov, V. I. :
428. *Chinese Literature of the Nineteenth and Early Twentieth Centuries and Lu Hsun,* 1962.
429. *Lu Hsun and his Predecessors,* 1967.
430. *Evolution of the Chinese Novel, End of the Eighteenth and Beginning of the Nineteenth Century,* 1972.

Semyonov, N. N. (Academician) :
431. 'Science does not Tolerate Subjectivism', in *Science and Life,* no. 4, 1965.

Senin, N. G. :
432. 'The Study of Chinese Philosophy in the USSR', in PSS 1973.
433. *Socio-political and Philosophical Views of Sun Yat-sen,* 1956–7.
434. 'The Philosophy of China', in *History of Philosophy,* vols. i–v, 1957–61.
435. Ed., with Yan Khin-shun, *Selected Progressive Chinese Thinkers of Modern Times (1840–1898),* 1961.
436. 'Progressive Socio-political and Philosophical Thought of China in Modern Times (1840–1919)' (doctoral thesis), 1963.
437. 'Pseudo-dialectics is the Methodological Foundation of the Separatist Course of Mao Tse-tung and his Group', in *The anti-Marxist Essence of the views and Policy of Mao Tse-Tung,* 1969.
438. *Patriotism and Populism [narodnost'] of the Great Eighth Century Chinese Poet Tu Fu,* L 1954.

Sergeichuk, S. :
439. 'Lu Yü (1125–1210) : His Life and Works' (doctoral thesis), L 1973.
440. *The USA and China* (monograph), 1969.

Shabalin, V. I. :
441. *State Capitalism in the CPR* (master's thesis), 1960.

Shirayev, S. L. :
442. 'Development of Railway Transport in the CPR, 1949–65' (master's thesis), 1966.

Shmidt, P. P. :
443. *Chinese Classical Books,* Vladivostok, 1901.
444. *Chinese Reader for Beginners,* Vladivostok, 1902.
445. *The Study of China Abroad,* Vladivostok, 1909.
446. *The Language of the Samagirs* (in English), Riga, 1928.

196 *Bibliography*

SHMIGOL', N. N.
447. 'Revolutionary Agrarian Transformation in the CPR in 1950–52' (master's thesis), 1954.
448. *Materials on Taiwan*, 1955.
449. *On the Study of the Political Economy of Socialism (Facts and Figures on the Socialist Countries)*, 1970.

SHTEIN, V. M. :
450. with others, *The Kuan Tse* (trans. and commentary), 1959.

SHTUKIN, A. A. :
451. with Fedorenko, N. T. (trans.), *The Shih Ching*, 1960.

SHUTSKI, YU. K. :
452. *Trans., The Book of Changes*, 1960.

SIDIKHMENOV, V. YA. :
453. *Classes and the Class Struggle in a Distorting Mirror*, 1969.
454. 'Against the Distortion of Lenin's Philosophical Heritage', in *Lenin and the Problems of Contemporary China*, 1971.

SIMONOVSKAYA, L. V. :
455. 'Studies on Medieval China in the USSR' (posth.), in PSS 1973.

SLADKOVSKI, M. I. (Director, IVD) :
456. 'Present State and Tasks of Soviet Sinology', in PSS 1973.
457. *Outlines of the External Economic Relations of China*, 1953.
458. *Outline of the Economic Relations of the USSR with China*, 1957.
459. 'Foreign Relations and External Trade of China, 1842–1948' (master's thesis), 1952.
460. Ed., *The CPR: Economy, State and Law, Culture*, 1970.
461. Ed., *Recent History of China, 1917–1970*, 1972.
462. Ed., *Lenin and the Problems of Contemporary China*, 1971.
463. *China and Japan*, 1971.
464. *Leninism and Modern China's Problems* (in English), Progress Publishers, 1972.
See also Figurny, P. K.; IDV.

SMOLIN, G. YA. :
465. 'Medieval China', in PSS 1973.
466. *The Peasant Rebellion in Hunan and Hupei in 1130–1135*, 1961.
467. 'Demands on Farmers in China', in *Peoples of Asia and Africa*, no. 1, 1970.
468. 'Anti-feudal Risings in China, Second Half of Tenth Century to First Quarter of Twelfth Century' (doctoral thesis), L 1971.

Sokolova, I. I.:
469. 'The T'ang *syao sho* : The Chinese Novel, Seventh to Ninth Centuries (master's thesis), 1966.

Solntsev, V. M.:
470. 'Some Problems of Studying the Chinese Language in the USSR', in PSS 1973.

Sorokin, V. F. (Academician):
Ed., PSS.
471. 'Research on Contemporary Chinese Literature : Results and Problems', in PSS 1973.
472. *Chinese Literature: A Short Outline*, 1962.
473. 'Plays of the Tao Cycle (*T'ao Su*) : Genre Varieties of *tsatsui* of the Thirteenth and Fourteenth Centuries', in *Genres and Styles of the Literatures of China and Korea*, 1969.
474. 'Yuan Drama : Heroes and Conflicts', in *Theoretical Problems of Eastern Literatures*, 1969.

Sovetov, I. I.:
475. *Concise Russo–Chinese Dictionary of Politico-economic and Military Terminology*, 1973. See also [187] above.

Soviet–Chinese relations, (twentieth century) :
476. *Soviet–Chinese Relations, 1917–57* (collection of documents), 1959.

Spirin, V. S.:
477. *Some Methodological Problems of Studying Ancient Chinese Philosophy*, 1970.

Ssu-ma Ch'ien :
478. *The Historical Records (Shih Chi)*, vol. I, 1972 (trans. Vyatkin, R. V., and Taskin, V. S.).

State Political Publishing House (Gospolitizdat) :
479. *Our Friend China*, 1959.

Stepugina, T. V.:
480. 'China in the Fifth Century B.C. to the Second Century A.D.' (master's thesis), 1955.
481. Contribution to *World History* ([529] below).

Stuzhina, P.:
482. 'The Chinese Feudal Town in the 12th–13th Centuries', paper presented to International Congress of Anthropologists and Ethnographers, Moscow, 1964.
483. *Chinese Handicrafts [remeslo] in the Sixteenth to Eighteenth Centuries* 1971.

SUI SHO-PO :
484. 'Some Regional [Industrial] Power Problems of the CPR' (master's thesis), 1959.

SUKHARCHUK, G. D. :
485. Article on Pre-CPR economic history of China, in PSS 1973.

SUN YAT-SEN :
486. *Selected Works,* 1964.
487. *Sun Yat-sen, 1866–1966,* 1966 (centennial).

SVISTUNOVA, N. P. :
488. *Agrarian Policy of the Ming Dynasty,* 1966.

TASKIN, V. S. :
489. with Vyatkin, R. V., trans. of Ssu-ma Ch'ien ([478] above).

TIKHONOVA, E. A. :
490. *The National Question in the State Structure of the CPR* (in Ukrainian), Kiev, 1962.

TIKHVINSKI, S. L. :
491. *The Foreign Policy of Sun Yat-sen in the Light of West European Historiography,* 1963.
492. *Sun Yat-sen: [his] Views on Foreign Policy and [his] Practice,* 1964.
493. Trans., *The First Half of my Life: Memoirs of [Henry] P'u Yi,* 1968.
494. with Delyusin, L. P., 'Some Problems of Studying the History of China', in PSS 1973.
495. *The Reform Movement in China and K'ang Yu-wei,* 1958–9.
496. Ed., *Outlines of the Modern History of China,* n.d.
497. Ed., *Manchu Domination in China* (collection of articles), 1966.
498. *China and her Neighbours,* 1970.
499. *The Tartar Mongols in Asia and Europe,* 1970.
500. Ed., *New History of China,* 1972.
501. Ed., with Perelomov, L. S., *China and her Neighbours in Antiquity and the Middle Ages,* 1970.

TITARENKO, M. L. :
502. 'The Ancient Chinese School of Mo-ists and their Teaching' (master's thesis), 1965. See also article in *Philosophical Sciences,* no. 5, 1965.
503. 'Ancient and Medieval Philosophers', in *Anthology of World Philosophy,* vol. I, 1969.

TOPORNIN, B. N. :
See Gudoshnikov, L. M.
504. *The Political System of Socialism,* 1972.

TOROPTSEV, S. A. :
505. Article on the Chinese cinema, in PSS 1973.

TSIPEROVICH, I. E. :
506. *Wonderful Stories of our Time and Antiquity (from the Seventeenth Century Anthology 'Tsin ku tsiguan'),* M–L 1954.
507. 'Analects of the Chinese Writers of the Ninth to the Nineteenth Centuries' (master's thesis), L 1963; published 1969.

TURAYEV, S. V. :
508. Contribution to *Proceedings of the Higher Education Conference on the History of the Literatures of the Foreign Far East,* 1970.

TYAPKINA, N. I. :
509. 'Syntax in the Modern Chinese Language' (master's thesis), 1954.
510. 'On the Double Nominative in Chinese' (in English), paper presented to 28th Congress of Orientalists, Canberra, 1971.

TYURIN, A. YU. :
511. 'On the Social Organisation of the Rural Population in China', in *Society and State in China,* 2nd issue, n.d.
512. 'On the Forms of Exploitation of Farmers in China in the Third to Seventh Centuries', in *Bulletin of Moscow University,* Series XIV *(Vostokovedenie),* 1st issue, 1970.
513. 'Formation of Feudal-Dependent Peasantry in China in the Third to Eighth Centuries A.D. (doctoral thesis), 1973.

USTIN, P. M. :
514. with Faingar, A. A., new trans. of the wonder tales of Liao Chai.
515. 'The Stories of Pu Sun-lin' (master's thesis), 1965.

VASIL'IEV, K. V. :
516. *Aspects [plany] of the Warring States* (monograph), 1968.

VASIL'IEV, L. S.
517. *'Agrarian Relations and the Community in Ancient China (Eleventh to Seventh Centuries B.C.)'* (monograph), 1961.
518. Contribution to *Problems of the History of Pre-capitalist Societies,* 1968, pp. 455–515.
519. Ed., *The Common and the Particular in the Development of Countries of the Orient* (symposium), 1965.
520. *Cults, Religions and Traditions in China,* 1970.

VASIL'IEV, V. P. :
521. *Religions of the Orient: Confucianism, Buddhism and Taoism,* SPB 1873.

VINOGRADOVA, N. A. :
522. Works on pictorial arts in China (1950s).

VISHNYAKOVA-AKIMOVA, V. V. :
523. *Two Years in Insurgent China (1925–27)* (memoirs), 1965.

VOLKOVA, L. A. :
524. *Changes in the Socio-Economic Structure of the Chinese Village, 1949–70* (monograph), 1972.

VOYEVODIN, S. A. :
See Akimov, V. I., and Kruglov, A. M.

VYATKIN, R. V. :
525. with Zanegin, B. N., article on China studies in the USA, in **PSS 1973.**
526. with Tikhvinski, S. L., 'On Some Problems of Historical Science in the CPR', in *Problems of History,* no. 10, 1963.
527. 'The "New Left" in Western Countries', in *Problems of History,* no 2, 1971. See also Ssu-ma Ch'ien.
See also Taskin, V. S.

VYATSKI, V. I. :
528. with Dimin, K., *The Economic Adventurism of the Maoists,* 1970.

World history :
529. *World History [Vsemirnaya Istoria],* multivolume, 1955. See also [110] above.

YAKOVLEV, A. G. :
See Astaf'iev, G. V.

YAKOVLEVA, P. T. :
530. *'The First Russo–Chinese Treaty, 1689* (monograph), 1958
531. 'The Nerchinsk Treaty between Russia and the Ch'ing Empire', in *History of the USSR from the Most Ancient Times to the Present Day,* 1967.

YAN KHIN-SHUN (YANG HSING-SHUN) :
532. 'Critique of the Philosophy of Life', in *Problems of Philosophy,* 1948.
533. *Lao Tse and his Teaching,* 1950.
534. 'Materialist Thought in Ancient China' (doctoral thesis), 1967.

YAREMENKO, YU. V. :
535. *The 'Great Leap Forward' and the People's Communes in China,* 1968.

YEFIMOV, G. V. :
536. *Outlines of the Most Recent History of China,* 1949, 1951.
537. *The Foreign Policy of China, 1894–99.* n.d.
538. 'Western Sinology', in PSS 1973.

YERMACHENKO, I. E. :
539. 'The Markets of Ch'angan, Western Capital of the T'ang Empire', in *Summary Communications of the Institute for the Peoples of Asia,* no. 6, 1963.
540. 'The Character of the State Apparatus of the Ching Empire' (article), n.d.
541. *The Role of Tradition in the History of China.* n.d.

YEVGEN'IEV, A. G. :
542. 'The Beginning of the Spread of Marxism in China and the Struggle of the First Chinese Marxists with the Anarchists', in *The 4th May Movement* (symposium), 1971.

YEVGEN'IEV, M. :
543. 'Successes of China's Coal Industry' (article), 1955.

YUL'YANOVSKI, R. A. :
544. Ed., *The Comintern and the Orient: The Struggle for Leninist Strategy and Tactics in the National Liberation Movement* (symposium). n.d.

YUR'IEV, M. F. :
545. *The Revolution of 1925–27 in China.* n.d.

ZHELOKHOVTSEV, A. N. :
546. *The Hua pen (the Story-Teller's Prompt-Book): An Urban Tale of Medieval China. Some Problems of Origin and Genre.* n.d.
547. *The T'ang Novel 'The Saunterer and the Magician': T'ang Novels of the Seventh to Ninth Centuries,* 1970.

Index